D0916888

Bloom's Classic Critical Views

BENJAMIN FRANKLIN

Bloom's Classic Critical Views

Bloom's Classic Critical Views

BENJAMIN FRANKLIN

Edited and with an Introduction by
Harold Bloom
Sterling Professor of the Humanities
Yale University

BLOOM'S
LITERARY CRITICISM
An imprint of Infobase Publishing

Bloom's Classic Critical Views: Benjamin Franklin

Copyright © 2008 Infobase Publishing

Introduction © 2008 by Harold Bloom

Bloom's Literary Criticism
An imprint of Infobase Publishing
132 West 31st Street
New York NY 10001

Library of Congress Cataloging-in-Publication Data
Bloom, Harold.
 Benjamin Franklin / Harold Bloom.
  p. cm. — (Bloom's classic critical views)
 Includes bibliographical references and index.
 ISBN 978-1-60413-135-2 (hardcover)
 1. Franklin, Benjamin, 1706–1790—Criticism and interpretation. I. Title. II. Series.

 PS752.B58 2008
 818'.109—dc22

                              2008007063

Contributing editor: Kevin J. Hayes
Series design by Erika K. Arroyo
Cover design by Takeshi Takahashi
Printed in the United States of America
Bang EJB 10 9 8 7 6 5 4 3 2 1

Contents

‒‒‒‒‒‒ ‒‒‒‒‒‒ ‒‒‒‒‒‒

Series Introduction

Bloom's Classic Critical Views is a new series presenting a selection of the most important older literary criticism on the greatest authors commonly read in high school and college classes today. Unlike the Bloom's Modern Critical Views series, which for more than 20 years has provided the best contemporary criticism on great authors, Bloom's Classic Critical Views attempts to present the authors in the context of their time and to provide criticism that has proved over the years to be the most valuable to readers and writers. Selections range from contemporary reviews in popular magazines, which demonstrate how a work was received in its own era, to profound essays by some of the strongest critics in the British and American tradition, including Henry James, G.K. Chesterton, Matthew Arnold, and many more.

Some of the critical essays and extracts presented here have appeared previously in other titles edited by Harold Bloom, such as the New Moulton's Library of Literary Criticism. Other selections appear here for the first time in any book by this publisher. All were selected under Harold Bloom's guidance.

In addition, each volume in this series contains a series of essays by a contemporary expert, who comments on the most important critical selections, putting them in context and suggesting how they might be used by a student writer to influence his or her own writing. This series is intended above all for students, to help them think more deeply and write more powerfully about great writers and their works.

Introduction by Harold Bloom

Yale University continues to have its "Franklin Factory," perpetually at work editing and publishing the complete writings of Benjamin Franklin. Unlike the "Boswell Factory" and the "Walpole Factory," our local Franklin project rarely has interested me, even when the sly American cavorted with the ladies of Paris. The early political and diplomatic history of the United States frequently centers on Franklin, and our most distinguished living American historian, Edmund S. Morgan of Yale, has written memorably and sympathetically about the Philadelphia sage in a biography of 2002.

It is in a spirit of—I hope—*useful* mischief that I resort to the negative vision of Franklin in D.H. Lawrence's *Studies in Classic American Literature* (1923). The book is remarkable for its responses to Walt Whitman, Herman Melville, and Nathaniel Hawthorne, where Lawrence mingles praise and blame, frequently with enormous insight. The account of Franklin is not in itself as valuable, partly because Franklin's shrewd prudence and Lawrence's wild vitalism are irreconcilable. But if Lawrence, on Franklin, tells us more about the English novelist-poet than about the American sage, the violence of Lawrence's reaction becomes a highly original tribute-by-negation to Franklin.

Lawrence wrote a first version of *Studies in Classic American Literature* in 1918–19, where the treatment of Franklin is considerably more temperate than it became. If Lawrence had a flaw in his genius, it was the all but total absence of a sense of humor, a quality in which Franklin abounded. Though Lawrence was a profound student of changes in European culture, he seems unaware that he, a High Romantic, confronts in Franklin a luminary of the Enlightenment.

In the 1918–19 version, Franklin is at once the perfect human being of reason, nature, and society but also "a pure mechanism, an automaton." Lawrence admires Franklin while disliking him and is both impressed by and dismayed by his will-to-power, however enlightened. There is one poignant moment in Lawrence's first draft, when Lawrence observes: "He is like a child, so serious and earnest."

A kind of frenzy, almost incoherent, breaks into the final version of the Franklin essay:

> And now I, at least, know why I can't stand Benjamin. He tries to take away my wholeness and my dark forest, my freedom. For how can any man be free, without an illimitable background? And Benjamin tries to shove me into a barbed-wire paddock and make me grow potatoes or Chicagoes.
>
> And how can I be free, without gods that come and go? But Benjamin won't let anything exist, except my useful fellow-men, and I'm sick of them; as for his Godhead, his Providence, He is Head of nothing except a vast heavenly store that keeps every imaginable line of goods, from victrolas to cat-o-nine-tails.

Beneath the rancor, one hears the voice that is great within us, proclaiming the stance of High Romanticism. I find myself asking why does Franklin trouble Lawrence so intensely? Something in Franklin frightened Lawrence, and I think it was the inauguration of a specifically American sensibility. As early as 1917, Lawrence wanted to visit the United States but reached here only in 1922 to settle briefly in New Mexico. He returned there for a longer sojourn in 1924–25.

Ambivalence toward the United States became a perpetual fever in Lawrence's spirit. As a poet, he became a total if protesting disciple of Walt Whitman. I am grateful to Lawrence for his vision of America as an active opposition between Benjamin Franklin and Walt Whitman. That is as suggestive an American dialectic as any I know.

BIOGRAPHY

Benjamin Franklin
(1706–1790)

Born on January 17, 1706, Benjamin Franklin was the youngest son of Josiah Franklin, a tallow chandler, and Abiah Folger Franklin. He attended Boston Grammar School, a prestigious classical school, but his father withdrew him after one year and sent him to George Brownell's English school for another year. Benjamin then worked with his father making candles and soap but hated it. His father apprenticed Benjamin to his uncle James, a printer. At sixteen, Benjamin published his "Silence Dogood" essays in James Franklin's paper, the *New-England Courant*, the first essay series in colonial America and one of the finest. On September 25, 1723, Benjamin left Boston for New York. Finding no work there, he made his way to Philadelphia, where he arrived on October 6. Samuel Keimer, a local printer, hired him.

Governor William Keith, impressed with the young man's mind and industry, promised him letters of credit and introduction, which would allow him to visit London to obtain all the necessary equipment to establish his own printing business. On November 5, 1724, Franklin sailed for London, only to discover upon his arrival that the governor had never given him the letters he promised. Within a week, Franklin found work at Samuel Palmer's printing office, where he wrote *A Dissertation on Liberty and Necessity, Pleasure and Pain* (1725). The work helped introduce him to London's intellectual community. He left London on July 21, 1726, accompanied by Quaker merchant Thomas Denham, who hired him as both bookkeeper and shopkeeper when they returned to Philadelphia.

After Denham died unexpectedly, Franklin once again joined Samuel Keimer's shop. With several intelligent and ambitious Philadelphia friends, he formed the Junto, a society for the mutual improvement of its members. In 1728 Franklin quit Keimer's operation and formed a printing partnership with Hugh Meredith. He also kept writing, contributing the "Busy-Body" essays to Andrew Bradford's *American Weekly Mercury* and writing *A Modest Enquiry into the Nature and Necessity of a Paper Currency* (1729), a proposal to stimulate the economy by increasing the supply of currency. With his printing business thriving, Franklin bought the *Pennsylvania Gazette* from Keimer. Newspaper ownership and production tapped Franklin's talents as a printer and an author. With his editorial discrimination and his engaging wit, he transformed the *Gazette* into the greatest newspaper in colonial America.

By the early 1730s, Franklin's personal life achieved greater stability. Deborah Read's first husband had deserted her. Since his whereabouts remained unknown, she and Franklin could not formally marry. Consequently, they entered into a common-law union on September 1, 1730. The previous year Franklin's son William had been born out of wedlock to an unknown mother. Deborah agreed to raise him as her own. Sarah, the Franklins' first daughter, was born on August 31, 1743.

Franklin's intellectual activity and business interests expanded continually. In 1731 he and his friends formed the Library Company of Philadelphia, which provided a pattern for subscription libraries founded throughout colonial America. Transformed into a scholarly research library, the Library Company of Philadelphia thrives today. Also in 1731 Franklin formed a business partnership with Thomas Whitemarsh to establish a print shop in South Carolina, the first of several such financial partnerships he would enter into. *Poor Richard's Almanack*, which Franklin first published in 1732, provided a popular forum for his ideas and proved a lucrative business venture. *Poor Richard's Almanack* quickly became the most highly esteemed almanac in colonial America. Franklin continued it annually until 1757, when he published *Poor Richard's Almanack for 1758*, which contained "Father Abraham's Speech," a playful recap of Poor Richard's most memorable sayings. Published separately as *The Way to Wealth*, the work would become enormously popular and would shape Franklin's public image more than any other of his writings published in his lifetime.

During the 1730s Franklin developed a sharpened sense of civic responsibility. In 1735 he proposed a fire protection society and a system of paid night watchmen for Philadelphia. He became clerk of the Pennsylvania Assembly in 1736 and postmaster of Philadelphia the following year. His efforts to establish institutions for public benefit continued as well. In 1751 he founded the Pennsylvania Hospital, the first hospital in America. It, too, thrives today, one of the finest hospitals in the United States. Franklin's intellectual abilities and his penchant for forming groups and societies prompted him to draft *A Proposal for Promoting Useful Knowledge* (1743). This work led to the formation of the American Philosophical Society, which also thrives today, still the most prestigious scientific body in America. Similarly, Franklin's *Proposals Relating to the Education of Youth in Pensilvania* (1749) established the Philadelphia Academy, which would become the University of Pennsylvania.

In 1748 Franklin retired as a printer to devote himself to civic and scientific affairs. The scientific realm had increasingly captured his attention since 1745, when he began experimenting with electricity. Two years later, he would send his first account of electrical experiments to Peter Collinson, who presented it to the

Royal Society of London. *Experiments and Observations on Electricity*, a collection of Franklin's scientific letters, appeared in 1751. The following year, he conducted his famous kite experiment, proving that lightning is electrical in nature. Understanding how this scientific discovery could benefit the public, he began to design lightning rods to protect homes and public buildings. *Supplemental Experiments and Observations*, his second set of electrical experiments, appeared in 1753. *New Experiments and Observations on Electricity* appeared the following year. Combined editions of *Experiments and Observations* would appear through the 1760s. Franklin's contributions to the field of electrical research prompted his unanimous election to the Royal Society of London in 1756. Other honors followed. In 1758 he received an honorary doctorate from the University of St. Andrews in Scotland and became known as Dr. Franklin. He received an honorary degree in civil law from Oxford University in 1762.

Political activity would dominate the second half of Franklin's life. Nominated by the Pennsylvania Assembly to serve as an agent to England in 1757, he traveled with his son to England, where he continued his literary and scientific activities as well. In 1760 he published *The Interest of Great Britain Considered*, a pamphlet emphasizing the importance of Canada to Great Britain. During his time in England, Franklin became a prominent member of London's intellectual community, socializing with many of the city's leading scientists and authors. He also traveled through Great Britain and the Netherlands, returning to Philadelphia the first week of November 1762.

In 1764 Franklin was elected speaker of the Pennsylvania Assembly, but the assembly soon chose him to serve as its London agent again. He returned to England by the end of that year. When Parliament passed the Stamp Act the following year, Franklin was on the scene to work toward its repeal. Most importantly he spoke before the House of Commons on February 13, 1766. His eloquent defense of American rights contributed significantly to the repeal of the act and established him as the leading spokesman of the American colonies. Other colonies—Georgia, Massachusetts, and New Jersey—chose Franklin to represent their interests in London too. He published *Causes of the American Discontents before 1768* (1768), an eloquent historical overview of the subject. His most prominent satirical writings of the period—"Rules by Which a Great Empire May Be Reduced to a Small One," "Edict by the King of Prussia"—slyly reinforce the importance of American rights and the injustice of British control. What may be the most dramatic moment of Franklin's lengthy stay in London came when Solicitor General Alexander Wedderburn unfairly denounced him before the Privy Council. To avoid war, Franklin attempted to settle differences between Great Britain and America diplomatically but to no avail.

He left London in 1775, reaching Philadelphia the first week of May. The Pennsylvania Assembly quickly elected him as a delegate to the Continental Congress. He served on several congressional committees and drafted the Articles of

Confederation. In 1776 he was appointed by Congress to the committee to draft the Declaration of Independence. Later that year, Congress elected him commissioner to France. Seventy years old at the time, Franklin left Philadelphia in October accompanied by two of his grandsons, William Temple Franklin and Benjamin Franklin Bache. The most famous American in the world, Franklin kept busy in social, intellectual, and political circles throughout his time in Paris.

He signed a definitive treaty of peace between Great Britain and the United States in September 1783. Two years later, Franklin left France for the last time, reaching Philadelphia on September 14, 1785. The following month, he was elected to the presidency of the Supreme Executive Council of Pennsylvania. He was also named president of the Pennsylvania Society for Promoting the Abolition of Slavery and devoted much effort toward abolition in his final years. He died on April 17, 1790.

PERSONAL

Benjamin Franklin was a great storyteller. The personal anecdotes he included in his writings represent only a small percentage of the stories he told orally over the course of his long and gregarious life. Many of his other anecdotes appear in the writings of his friends, who felt compelled to set them down on paper. They recorded these remembrances in their letters, diaries, and published writings. Samuel Johnson had James Boswell to record his wit and wisdom: Franklin made every man a Boswell. Though none of Franklin's contemporaries compiled his various anecdotes, those that survive individually or in small clusters in the writings of others, constitute a major contribution to the history of American humor.

After his death in 1790, numerous Franklin anecdotes appeared in the periodical press and in collections of joke books. The challenge is separating the genuine from the spurious. In an anecdote that appeared in the *American Museum* in June 1790, one contributor told a story about the time Franklin crated a collection of live rattlesnakes and sent them to Robert Walpole because Great Britain was sending its convicts to America. This anecdote does have a precedent in Franklin's literary life. In "Rattlesnakes for Felons," he facetiously suggested that rattlesnakes be sent to Great Britain, but he never actually sent them.

This example shows how Franklin's writings could, through repeated retellings, take on the ring of truth and be transformed into anecdotes. Franklin himself became such a popular figure that he often made his way into traditional stories that had been circulating in the oral culture and in humorous books for centuries. Many of the Franklin anecdotes recorded by travelers, friends, and relatives do have a basis in fact, however.

The contents of this section provides a series of personal stories related by those who knew Franklin. They are organized chronologically according to the date they were published or, in the case of diaries and letters, when they were written. The first selection comes from Joseph Priestley, a prolific writer, brilliant scientist, and founder of the Unitarian Church. Priestley was also a good friend of Franklin's, and the American provided him with an account of the kite experiment, which Priestley included in his *History of Electricity*, the source of the first document in this collection. Priestley's account provides virtually all that is known about Franklin's experiment. How has this story been elaborated in subsequent retellings? There is a topic ripe for research: the cultural history of Franklin's kite.

Travelers' accounts provide good sources of information about Franklin. Swedish botanist Peter Kalm published, in English in 1770, an account of his North American travels, but he had visited several years earlier, when he met Franklin. Since Kalm was curious about asbestos, Franklin told him about the first time he went to London, met Sir Hans Sloane, and offered him a fireproof asbestos purse for his vast collection of curiosities. Sloane paid Franklin handsomely for the purse. As Kalm recorded the story, however, Franklin *presented* the purse to Sloane. Did Kalm misunderstand Franklin? Or did Franklin reshape the experience as he retold it, transforming himself from a needy youth into a patron of science? This particular example suggests another topic for research: how well do Franklin's anecdotes hold up in light of biographical fact?

Andrew Burnaby, whose travels form another important account of life in colonial America, recorded a great story about Franklin traveling through New England and the hospitable, if inquisitive, people he met. Burnaby does not mention Franklin by name, identifying him solely as "B.F.," but eighteenth-century readers knew who Burnaby was talking about, and the anecdote was widely reprinted in the newspaper and periodical press. Search the early American periodicals to find variations of this anecdote. How do they compare?

Many personal stories about Franklin survive from the 1785–1790 period, that is, between the time Franklin returned to Philadelphia from his final mission to France, where he became the most famous American in the world, until his death in 1790. Franklin's home in Philadelphia became an important destination for distinguished visitors. Andrew Ellicott, whose diary provides the source for the third selection, found Franklin dispensing some characteristic wisdom. In other words, Franklin conformed to Ellicott's expectations of him. Is Ellicott's experience typical? To what extent did the famous Franklin meet the expectations of people he met?

Dr. Benjamin Rush frequently dined with Franklin and recorded their time together in his diary, the source of the next selection. Rush, an Edinburgh-trained physician, had known Franklin since medical school and even dedicated his dissertation to him. They served together in the Continental Congress: both were signers of the Declaration of Independence. Despite his own distinguished career, Rush realized he could still learn much from Franklin and attentively listened to what the great man had to say, as these diary entries show.

Rush was right. Franklin did have much to teach in his final years. The comparison he made one day between walking through a fair and reading the advertisements in a newspaper is a poignant one. To what extent can the printed word serve as a surrogate for real-life experience? The diversity of modern media has prompted people to ask this question repeatedly in recent years. Franklin's comparison shows that the question became relevant as the printed word began providing consumers with an alternative experience to attending fairs.

Most often, contemporary biographical accounts record what people said in indirect discourse. In other words, their accounts are commonly phrased or structured as: "He said that . . ." Rush, to the advantage of historians and future Franklin fans alike, sometimes recorded what Franklin said in direct discourse, providing snippets of conversation in his diary entries. A recorded conversation is the biographer's holy grail: it can help animate a story in a way mere facts cannot.

The journal of Manessah Cutler, another man who visited Franklin in Philadelphia in the late 1780s, provides the single best description of his house from this period. Cutler's account also presents the most detailed description of the library at Franklin Court. He describes the layout of the library, the location of the books, and the gadgets Franklin invented to make the library more convenient. His account also shows the pride Franklin took in his library. Cutler had a good eye for detail. He helps us better understand the material culture of Franklin's day and provides a starting point for further thought. How does Franklin's attitude toward the material world compare with that of his contemporaries, such as John Adams or Thomas Jefferson?

Published in the year of his death, the next selection records a humorous remark Franklin purportedly said as a boy, that it would be better to say grace over a whole cask of salted, preserved foods instead of having to say grace before every meal. This characteristic anecdote shows Franklin's efficiency, his practicality, and his reluctance to accept standard religious practices without question. Even as a boy, he exemplified new ways of thinking and new approaches to the ways of God and man.

Isaiah Thomas, a leading antiquarian, sought to chronicle the history of printing in early America, releasing his results in 1810 with *The History of Printing*. Franklin naturally plays an important part in the story. Thomas relates an anecdote demonstrating Franklin's sense of responsibility as an editor, his powers of discrimination, and his willingness to sacrifice personal comforts to maintain his professional integrity.

William Temple Franklin included a selection of anecdotes in his three-volume edition of his grandfather's writings. Perhaps there was no aspect of the edition that was more disappointing. No one had a better chance to be Franklin's Boswell than his grandson. Temple went with his grandfather to Paris in 1776, stayed with him his entire time there serving as his personal secretary, returned with him to Philadelphia, and continued living with him until his death. He must have heard hundreds of his grandfather's anecdotes, but when it can time to prepare his edition of Franklin's writings, he included only seven anecdotes. Seven! And two of the seven—the one about traveling through New England and the one about saying grace over the cask—were already well known. The other five are reprinted here.

Writing a biography of Franklin in the early nineteenth century, Robert Walsh approached Thomas Jefferson to see if he had any stories about him. Jefferson's 1818 letter to Walsh is an absolute delight. Unlike Temple Franklin, Jefferson fully developed his stories about Franklin. Jefferson told stories about Franklin more readily than he told stories about himself. He expanded the anecdotes into tales, capturing their cultural contexts and Franklin's definitive sense of humor. Jefferson's stories about Franklin form an important contribution to Franklin's biography—and to Jefferson's.

Joseph Priestley
"Dr. Franklin on Lightning" (1769)

The Doctor, after having published his method of verifying his hypothesis concerning the sameness of electricity with the matter of lightning, was waiting for the erection of a spire in Philadelphia to carry his views into execution, not imagining that a pointed rod of a moderate height could answer the purpose; when it occurred to him, that by means of a common kite, he could have a readier and better access to the regions of thunder than by any spire whatever. Preparing, therefore, a large silk handkerchief, and two cross sticks, of a proper length, on which to extend it, he took the opportunity of the first approaching thunder storm to take a walk into the field, in which there was a shed convenient for his purpose. But dreading the ridicule which too commonly attends unsuccessful attempts in science, he communicated his intended experiment to nobody but his son, who assisted him in raising the kite.

The kite being raised, a considerable time elapsed before there was any appearance of its being electrified. One very promising cloud had passed over it without any effect; when, at length, just as he was beginning to despair of his contrivance, he observed some loose threads of the hempen string to stand erect, and to avoid one another, just as if they had been suspended on a common conductor. Struck with this favourable appearance, he immediately presented his knuckle to the key,—and let the reader judge of the exquisite pleasure he must have felt at that moment,—the discovery was complete. He perceived a very evident electric spark. Others succeeded even before the string was wet, so as to put the matter past all dispute: and when the rain had wet the string, he collected electric fire very copiously. This happened in June, 1752, a month after the electricians in France had verified the same theory, but before he had heard of any thing they had done.

Peter Kalm "A Visit with Franklin" (1770)

Mr. *Franklin* told me, that, twenty and some odd years ago, when he made a voyage to *England*, he had a little purse with him, made of the mountain flax of this country, which he presented to Sir *Hans Sloane*. I have likewise seen paper made of this stone: and I have likewise received some small pieces of it, which I keep in my cabinet. Mr. *Franklin* had been told by others that on exposing this mountain flax to the open air in winter, and leaving it in the cold and wet, it would grow together, and more fit for spinning. But he did not venture to determine how far this opinion was grounded. On this occasion he related a very pleasant accident which happened to him with this mountain flax: he had, several years ago, got a piece of it, which he gave to one of his journeymen printers, in order to get it made into a sheet at the paper mill. As soon as the fellow brought the paper, Mr. *Franklin* rolled it up, and threw it into the fire, telling the journeyman he would see a miracle, a sheet of paper which did not burn: the ignorant fellow asserted the contrary, but was greatly astonished upon seeing himself convinced. Mr. *Franklin* then explained to him, though not very clearly, the peculiar qualities of the paper. As soon as he was gone, some of his acquaintance came in, who immediately knew the paper. The journeyman thought he would shew them a great curiosity and astonish them. He accordingly told them, that he had curiously made a sheet of paper which would not burn, though it was thrown into the fire. They pretended to think it impossible, and he as strenuously maintained his assertion. At last they laid a wager about it; but whilst he was busy with stirring up the fire, the others slyly besmeared the paper with fat: the journeyman, who was not aware of it, threw it into the fire, and that moment it was all in flames: this astonished him so much, that he was almost speechless; upon which they could not help laughing, and so discovered the whole artifice.

In several houses of the town, a number of little *Ants* run about, living under ground, and in holes in the wall. The length of their bodies is one geometrical line. Their colour is either black or dark red: they have the custom of carrying off sweet things, if they can come at them, in common with the ants of other countries. Mr. *Franklin* was much inclined to believe that these little insects could by some means communicate their thoughts or desires to each other, and he confirmed his opinion by some examples. When an ant finds some sugar, it runs immediately under ground to its hole, where, having stayed a little while, a whole army comes out, unites and marches to the place where the sugar is, and carries it off by pieces; or if an ant meets with a dead fly, which it cannot carry alone, it immediately hastens home, and soon after some more come out, creep to the fly, and carry it away. Some time ago Mr. *Franklin* put a little earthen pot with treacle into a closet. A number of ants got into the pot, and devoured the treacle very quickly. But as he observed it, he shook them out, and tied the pot with a thin string to a nail which he had fastened in the ceiling; so that the pot hung down by the string. A single ant by chance remained in the pot: this ant ate till it was satisfied; but when it wanted to get off, it was under great concern to find its way out: it ran about the bottom of the pot, but in vain: at last it found after many attempts the way to get to the ceiling by the string. After it was come there, it ran to the wall, and from thence to the ground. It had hardly been away for half an hour, when a great swarm of ants came out, got up to the ceiling, and crept along the string into the pot, and began to eat again: this they continued till the treacle was all eaten: in the mean time one swarm running down the string, and the other up.

Andrew Burnaby
"Anecdote of a Traveler" (1775)

I was told of a gentleman of Philadelphia, who, in travelling through the provinces of New England, having met with many impertinencies, from this extraordinary turn of character, at length fell upon an expedient almost as extraordinary, to get rid of them. He had observed, when he went into an ordinary[1], that every individual of the family had a question or two to propose to him, relative to his history; and that, till each was satisfied; and they had conferred and compared: together their information, there was no possibility of procuring any refreshment. He, therefore, the moment he went into any of these places, inquired for the matter, the mistress, the sons, the daughters, the men-servants and the maid-servants; and having assembled them all together, he began in this manner. "Worthy people, I am B. F. of Philadelphia, by trade a —, and a bachelor; I have some relations at Boston, to whom I am going to make a visit: my stay will be short, and I shall then return and follow my business, as a prudent man ought to do. This is all I know of myself, and all I can possibly inform you of; I beg therefore that you will have pity upon me and my horse, and give us both some refreshment."

Note
1. Inns are so called in America.

Andrew Ellicott
"Diary Entry for 4 December" (1785)

Immediately after brakefast I went by perticular Invitation to spend the Day with Doctr. Franklin— I found him in his little Room Among his Papers— he received me very politely and immediately entered into conversation about the Western Country—his Room makes a Singular Appearance, being filled with old philosophical Instruments, Papers, Boxes, Tables, and Stools— About 10 O Clock he sat some water on the fire and not being expert through his great age I desired him to give me the pleasure of assisting him, he thanked me and replied that he ever made it a point to wait upon himself and although he began to find himself infirm he was determined not to encrease his Infirmities by giving way to them— After his water was hot I observed his Object was to shave himself which Operation he performed without a Glass and with great expedition— I Asked him if he never employed a Barber he answered, "no" and continued nearly in the following words "I think happiness does not consist so much in perticular pieces of good fortune that perhaps accidentally fall to a Mans Lot as to be able in his old age to do those little things which was he unable to perform himself would be done by others with a sparing hand—" Several Foreigners of Distinction dined with us— About 9 O Clock in the Evening I took my leave of this Venerable Nestor of America—

Benjamin Rush "Conversations with Dr. Franklin" (1785–1789)

1785.—Dined with the Dr. with Dr. Ramsay, Mr. Rittinhouse, Mr. Littlepage, 'Littlepage's Salutation,' &c. He said the foundation of the American revolution was laid in 1733, by a clause in a bill to subject the Colonies to being gov'd by Royal instructions which was rejected. He said in 1766, when he went to England, he had a long conversation with Mr. Pratt (afterwards Lord Camden) who told him that Britain would drive the colonies to independance. This he said first led him to realise its occurring shortly.

1786 Augt.—I waited on the Dr. with a Dr. Minto. He said he believed that Tobacco would in a few years go out of use. That, about 80 years ago, when he went to England, Smoaking was universal in taverns, coffe-houses, & private families, but that it was now generally laid aside, that the use of Snuff, from being universal in France, was become unfashionable among genteel people, no person of fashion under 30 years of age now snuffed in France. He added that, Sir John Pringle & he had observed that tremors of the hands were more frequent in France than elsewhere, & probably from the excessive use of Snuff. They once saw in a company of 16 but two persons who had not these tremors at a table in France. He said Sir John was cured of a tremor by leaving off Snuff. He concluded that there was no great advantage in using Tobacco in any way, for that he had kept company with persons who used it all his life, & no one had ever advised him to use it. The Dr. in the 81st year of his age declared he had never snuffed, chewed, or smoked.

Septem'r 23rd.—Three persons who don't care how little they get for their money, waited upon the Dr. with Mr Bee. He said he believed the Accts. of the plague in Turkey were exaggerated. He once conversed with a Dr. MacKensie who had resided 38 years at Constantinople, who told him there were *five* plagues in that town. The plague of the drugger-men or interpreters, who spread false stories of the prevalence of the plague in Order to drive foreign ministers into the country, in order that they might enjoy a little leisure. 2. The plague of debtors, who when dunned, looked out of their windows, and told their creditors, not to come in for the plague is in their houses. 3. The plague of the Doctors, for as they are never paid for their Attendance on such patients as die, Unless it be with the plague, they make most of *fatal* diseases the plague. The Dr. forgot the other two. He added that Dr. MacKensie upon hearing that 660 dead with the plague, were carried out of one of the gates daily, had the curiosity to stand by that gate for one whole day, & counted only 66.

1786 Sepr.—Waited upon the Dr. with Mr. R. Stockton, he told us that in 1728, people went to market with cut silver, those who had it not, procured provisions by taking the country people to two Stalls in the market, & giving them goods for them, which goods were charged to their Acct's. & paid for once or twice a year. He added that, it would be an advantage to our country for the Europeans to be the carriers of our produce for many years, for as they could not afford to lye long in our ports, they must always sell 10 per cent lower & buy 10 per cent higher than our own merchants product of German Industry.

Octobr 1.—Dined with the Dr., with Mr. Bee, Dr. Minto, Dr. Kuhn, &c. He said interest was 8 per cent per month, for 10 months in China, or 80 per cent per anm., which promoted industry, kept down the price of land, & made freeholds more common. Upon another occasion he said that *Credit* produced Idleness & vice, & he wished that all debts should like debts of honor or game Debts be irrecoverable by law. He added this day that in the last 80 years of his life, he had never enjoyed better health, than at present.

Octobr 12.—Waited on him with Dr. Nisbet. He observed that by raising the ear with his hand, he heard better than without it, & still better if he formed a concave with his hand round his ear. He spoke in high terms of the game of Chess.

1787 May 3rd.—Drank tea with Dr. F., he spoke in high terms ag'st. negro Slavery, & said he printed a book 40 years ago written by Ben. Lay ag'st. it, w'ch. tho' confused, contained just tho'ts & good sense, but in bad order.

April.—Dined with Dr. He spoke of the talkativeness of the French nation, & told a story of the Abbé Raynal, who was a great talker, who came into a company where a French man talked so long & so incessantly that, he could not get in a word. At last he cried out "il e pendu, si il crache" "He is lost, if he spits." His grandson told another story of a Frenchman, who was dining, complaining to his companions that their noise kept him from tasting his Victuals.

1788 April 19th.—Spent half an hour with Dr. F. in his library. "He observed that a man lost 10 per cent on the *value*, by lending his books; that he once knew a man who never returned a borrowed book, because no one ever returned books borrowed from him." He condemned the *foreign* commerce of the United States, and observed that the greatest part of the trade of the World, was carried on for Luxuries most of which were really injurious to health or Society, such as *tea, tobacco, Rum, Sugar,* and *negro Slaves.* He added, "when I read the advertisements in our papers of imported goods for sale, I think of the Speech of a philosopher upon walking thro' a fair, "how happy am I that I want none of these things."

Sepr 22.—Waited upon Dr. Franklin with Doctor Thibou, of Antigua. The Dr. said few but quacks ever made money by physic, & that no bill drawn upon the credulity of the people of London by quacks, was ever protested. He ascribed the success of quacks partly to patients extolling the efficacy of the remedies they took from them, rather than confess their ignorance & credulity, hence it was justly said, "quacks were the greatest lyers in the world, except their patients." He told two stories, the one of a Jew who had peculated in the French army, being told when under confinement that he would be hanged, to wch. the Jew answered, "who ever heard of a man being hanged worth 200,000 livres," & he accordingly escaped. The Judges in Mexico being ordered to prosecute a man for peculation, found him innocent, for wch. they said, "they were sorry both for his own, & their sakes."

British Commissary. Story of ears more faithful than eyes(?) He added further, that in riding thro' New Eng'd. he overtook a poet Rider that was once a shoemaker, & fell into consumption, but upon riding two years as a post in all weathers, between New York, & Connecticut river (140 miles), he recovered perfectly, upon which he returned to his old business, but upon finding a return of his consumption, he rode post again, in which business he continued in good health 30 years. He said that he could have *purchased* the independance of America at 1/10 of the money expended in defending it; such was the venality of the British Court. (?)

Novr.—Spend half an hour with Dr. in company with the Revd. Mr. Bisset & Mr. Goldeborough. He said Sir Jno Pringle once told him 92 fevers out of 100 cured themselves, 4 were cured by Art, & 4 proved fatal.

About the end of this month, I saw him alone. He talked of Climates; I borrowed some hints from this Conversation for the essay on Climates.

1789. June 12th.—Had a long conversation with him on the Latin and Greek languages. He called them the "quackery of literature". He spent only abt. a year at a Latin School, when between 8 & 9 years of Age. At 33, he learned French, after this Italian & Spanish wch. led him to learn Latin wch. he acquired with great ease. He highly approved of learning Geography in early life, & said that he had taught himself it, when a boy, while his father was at prayers, by looking over four large maps which hung in his father's parlour.

MANASSEH CUTLER
"A VISIT TO FRANKLIN COURT" (1787)

Dr. Franklin lives in Market Street, between Second and Third Streets, but his house stands up a court-yard at some distance from the street. We found him in his Garden, sitting upon a grass plat under a very large Mulberry, with several other gentlemen and two or three ladies. There was no curiosity in Philadelphia which I felt so anxious to see as this great man, who has been the wonder of Europe as well as the glory of America. But a man who stood first in the literary world, and had spent so many years in the Courts of Kings, particularly in the refined Court of France, I conceived would not be of very easy access, and must certainly have much of the air of grandeur and majesty about him. Common folks must expect only to gaze at him at a distance, and answer such questions as he might please to ask. In short, when I entered his house, I felt as if I was going to be introduced to the presence of an European Monarch. But how were my ideas changed, when I saw a short, fat, trunched old man, in a plain Quaker dress, bald pate, and short white locks, sitting without his hat under the tree, and, as Mr. Gerry introduced me, rose from his chair, took me by the hand, expressed his joy to see me, welcomed me to the city, and begged me to seat myself close to him. His voice was low, but his countenance open, frank, and pleasing. He instantly reminded me of old Captain Cummings, for he is nearly of his pitch, and no more of the air of superiority about him. I delivered him my letters. After he had read them, he took me again by the hand, and, with the usual compliments, introduced me to the other gentlemen of the company, who were most of them members of the Convention. Here we entered into a free conversation, and spent our time most agreeably until it was dark. The tea-table was spread under the tree, and Mrs. Bache, a very gross and rather homely lady, who is the only daughter of the Doctor and lives with him, served it out to the company. She had three of her children about her, over whom she seemed to have no kind of command, but who appeared to be excessively fond of their Grandpapa. The Doctor showed me a curiosity he had just received, and with which he was much pleased. It was a snake with two heads, preserved in a large vial. It was taken near the confluence of the Schuylkill with the Delaware, about four miles from this city. It was about ten inches long, well proportioned, the heads perfect, and united to the body about one-fourth of an inch below the extremities of the jaws. The snake was of a dark brown, approaching to black, and the back beautifully speckled (if beauty can be applied to a snake) with white; the belly was rather checkered with a reddish color and white. The Doctor supposed it to be full grown, which I think appears probable, and thinks it must be a *sui generis* of that class of animals. He grounds his opinion of its not being an extraordinary production, but a distinct genus, on the perfect form of the snake, the probability of its being of some age, and there having been found a snake entirely similar (of which the Doctor has a drawing, which he showed us) near Lake Champlain, in the time of the late war. The Doctor mentioned the situation of this snake, if it was traveling among bushes, and one head should choose to go on one side of the stem of a bush and the other head should prefer the other side, and that neither of the heads would consent to come back or give way to the other. He was then going to mention a humorous matter that had that day taken place in Convention, in consequence of his comparing the snake to America, for he seemed to forget that every thing in Convention was to be kept a profound secret; but the secrecy of Convention matters was suggested to him, which stopped him, and deprived me of the story he was going to tell. After it was dark, we went into the house, and the Doctor invited me into his library, which is likewise his study. It is a very large chamber, and high studded. The walls were covered with book-shelves filled with books; besides, there are four large alcoves, extending two-thirds of the length of the Chamber, filled in the same manner. I presume this is the largest, and by far the best, private library in America. He showed us a glass machine for exhibiting the circulation of the blood in the arteries and veins of the human body. The circulation is exhibited by the passing of a red fluid from a reservoir into numerous capillary tubes of glass, ramified in every direction, and then returning in similar tubes to the reservoir, which was done with great velocity, without any power to act visibly on the fluid, and had the appearance of perpetual motion. Another great curiosity was a rolling press, for taking the copies of letters or any other writing. A sheet of paper is completely copied in less than two minutes, the copy as fair as the original, and without effacing it in the smallest degree. It is an invention of his own, and extremely useful in many situations in life. He also showed us his long artificial arm and band, for taking down and putting books up on high shelves which are out of reach; and his great armed chair, with rockers, and a large fan placed over it, with which he fans himself, keeps off flies, etc., while he sits reading, with only a small motion of his foot; and many other curiosities and inventions, all his own, but of lesser note. Over his mantel-tree, he has a prodigious number of medals, busts, and casts in wax or plaster of Paris, which are the effigies of the most noted characters in Europe. But what the Doctor wished principally to show to me was a huge volume on Botany, and which, indeed, afforded me the greatest pleasure of any one thing in his library. It was a single volume, but so large that it was with great difficulty that the Doctor was able to raise it from a low shelf and lift it on to the table; but with that senile ambition common to old people, he insisted on doing it himself, and would permit no person to assist him, merely to show us how much strength he had remaining. It contained the whole of Linnaeus Systima Vegetabilia, with large cuts of every plant, and colored from nature. It was a feast to me, and the Doctor seemed to enjoy it as well as myself. We spent a couple of hours in examining this volume, while the other gentlemen amused themselves with other matters. The Doctor is not a Botanist, but lamented that he did not in early life attend to this science. He delights in natural history, and expressed an earnest wish that I would pursue the plan I had begun, and hoped this science, so much neglected in America, would be pursued with as much ardor here as it is now in every part of Europe. I wanted for three months at least to have devoted myself entirely to this one volume. But fearing I should be tedious to the Doctor, I shut up the volume, though he urged me to examine it longer. The Doctor seemed extremely fond, through the course of the visit, of dwelling on Philosophical subjects, and particularly that of natural History, while the other Gentlemen were swallowed up with politics. This was a favorable circumstance to me, for almost the whole of his conversation was addressed to me; and I was highly delighted with the extensive knowledge he appeared to have of every subject, the brightness of his memory, and clearness and vivacity of all his mental faculties. Notwithstanding his age (eighty-four), his manners are perfectly easy, and every thing about him seems to diffuse an unrestrained freedom and happiness. He has an incessant vein of humor, accompanied with an uncommon vivacity, which seems as natural and involuntary as his breathing. He urged me to call on him again, but my short tarry would not admit. We took our leave at ten, and I retired to my lodgings.

Anonymous "Franklin as a Child" (1790)

Dr. Franklin, when a child, found the long graces used by his father before and after meals very tedious. One day after the winter's provisions had been salted, "I think, Father," says Benjamin, "if you said *grace* over the whole *cask—*once for all—it would be a vast *saving of time.*"

Isaiah Thomas "Franklin as Editor" (1810)

Soon after the establishment of his paper, a person brought him a piece, which he requested him to publish in the *Pennsylvania Gazette.* Franklin desired that the piece might be left for his consideration until next day, when he would give an answer. The person returned at the time appointed, and received from Franklin this communication: "I have perused your piece, and find it to be scurrilous And defamatory. To determine whether I should publish it or not, I went home in the evening, purchased a two penny loaf at the baker's, and with water from the pump made my supper; I then wrapped myself up in my great coat, and laid down on the floor and slept till morning, when, on another loaf and a mug of water, I made my breakfast. From this regimen I feel no inconvenience whatever. Finding I can live in this manner, I have formed a determination never to prostitute my press to the purposes of corruption, and abuse of this kind, for the sake of gaining a more comfortable subsistence."

William Temple Franklin "Anecdotes Relative to Dr. Franklin" (1818)

When Franklin came to England previous to the breaking out of the American war, he went to Mr. Hett's Printing Office in Wild Court, Wild Street, Lincoln's Inn Fields, and entering the press-room, he went up to a particular press, and thus addressed the two men who were working: "Come, my friends, we will drink together; it is now forty years since I worked like you at this press as journeyman printer:" on this he sent for a gallon of porter, and they drank "success to printing."

In one of the assemblies in America, wherein there was a majority of Presbyterians, a law was proposed to forbid the praying for the King by the Episcopalians; who, however, could not conveniently omit that prayer, it being prescribed in their Liturgy. Dr. Franklin, one of the members, seeing that such a law would occasion more disturbance than it was worth, said, that he thought it quite *unnecessary*, for, added he, "those people have, to my certain knowledge, been praying constantly these twenty years past, that *"God would give to the King and his counsel wisdom,"* and we all know that not the least notice has ever been taken of that prayer; so that it is plain they have no interest in the court of Heaven." The house smiled, and the motion was dropt.

In Philadelphia, where there are no *Noblesse*, but the inhabitants are all either merchants or mechanics, the merchants, many years since, set up an assembly for dancing, and desiring to make a distinction, and to assume a rank above the mechanics, they at first proposed this among the rules for regulating the assembly, "that *no mechanic or mechanic's wife or daughter should be admitted on any terms."* These rules being shown by a manager to Dr. Franklin for his opinion, he remarked, that one of them excluded GOD ALMIGHTY: "How so?" said the manager. *"Because,"* replied the Doctor, *"he is notoriously the greatest mechanic in the universe*; having, as the Scripture testifies, made all things, and that by weight and measure." The intended new gentlemen became ashamed of their rule, and struck it out.

About the year 1752, Dr. Franklin having entered into a correspondence with Samuel Johnson, doctor of divinity in the University of Oxford, and afterwards president of King's College, in New York, and having endeavored to induce the latter to accept the presidency of the College at Philadelphia, and as an additional motive to his doing so, having offered to procure the erection of a new Episcopal church for him in that city; and Doctor Johnson having expressed some doubts respecting the propriety of such a measure, Dr. Franklin wrote a letter for the purpose of removing his scruples, of which the following extract has been preserved, viz. "Your tenderness of the church's peace is truly laudable; but, methinks, to build a new church in a growing place, is not properly dividing, but *multiplying*, and will really be a means of increasing the number of those who worship God in that way. Many who cannot now be accommodated in the church, go to other places, or stay at home; and if we had another church, many who go to other places, or stay at home, would go to church. I had for several years nailed against the wall of my house a pigeon-box that would hold six pair; and though they bred as fast as my neighbor's pigeons, I never had more than six pair, the old and strong driving out the young and weak, and obliging them to seek new habitations. At length I put up an additional box, with apartments for entertaining twelve pair more, and it was soon filled with inhabitants, by the overflowing of my first box, and of others in the neighborhood. This I take to be a parallel case with the building a new *church* here."

Dr. Franklin was so immoderately fond of chess, that one evening at Passy, he sat at that amusement from six in the afternoon till sun-rise. On the point of losing one of his games, his king being attacked, by what is called a check, but an opportunity offering at the same time of giving a fatal blow to his adversary, provided he might neglect the defence of his king, he chose to do so, though contrary to the rules, and made his move. "Sir," said the French gentleman, his antagonist, "you cannot do that, and leave your king in *check*." "I see he is in check," said the Doctor, "but I shall not defend him. If he was a good king like yours, he would deserve the protection of his subjects; but he is a tyrant, and has cost them already more than he is worth:—Take him, if you please; I can do without him, and will fight out the rest of the battle, *en Républicain*—as a Commonwealth's man."

THOMAS JEFFERSON
"ANECDOTES OF DOCTOR FRANKLIN" (1818)

When the Declaration of Independence was under the consideration of Congress, there were two or three unlucky expressions in it which gave offence to some members. The words "Scotch and other foreign auxiliaries" excited the ire of a gentleman or two of that country. Severe strictures on the conduct of the British king, in negotiating our repeated repeals of the law which permitted the importation of slaves, were disapproved by some Southern gentlemen, whose reflections were not yet matured to the full abhorrence of that traffic. Although the offensive expressions were immediately yielded, these gentlemen continued their depredations on other parts of the instrument. I was sitting by Dr. Franklin, who perceived that I was not insensible to these mutilations. "I have made it a rule," said he, "whenever in my power, to avoid becoming the draughtsman of papers to be reviewed by a public body. I took my lesson from an incident which I will relate to you. When I was a journeyman printer, one of my companions, an apprentice hatter, having served out his time, was about to open shop for himself. His first concern was to have a handsome sign-board, with a proper inscription. He composed it in these words, 'John Thompson, *Hatter, makes and sells hats* for ready money,' with a figure of a hat subjoined; but he thought he would submit it to his friends for their amendments. The first he showed it to thought the word '*Hatter*' tautologous, because followed by the words 'makes hats,' which show he was a hatter. It was struck out. The next observed that the word 'makes' might as well be omitted, because his customers would not care who made the hats. If good and to their mind, they would buy, by whomsoever made. He struck it out. A third said he thought the words '*for ready money*' were useless, as it was not the custom of the place to sell on credit. Every one who purchased expected to pay. They were parted with, and the inscription now stood, 'John Thompson sells hats.' '*Sells hats*' says his next friend! Why nobody will expect you to give them away, what then is the use of that word? It was stricken out, and '*hats*' followed it, the rather as there was one painted on the board. So the inscription was reduced ultimately to 'John Thompson' with the figure of a hat subjoined."

The Doctor told me at Paris the two following anecdotes of the Abbé Raynal. He had a party to dine with him one day at Passy, of whom one half were Americans, the other half French, and among the last was the Abbé. During the dinner he got on his favorite theory of the degeneracy of animals, and even of man, in America, and urged it with his usual eloquence. The Doctor at length noticing the accidental stature and position of his guests, at table, "Come," says he, "M. l'Abbé, let us try this question by the fact before us. We are here one half Americans, and one half French, and it happens that the Americans have placed themselves on one side of the table, and our French friends are on the other. Let both parties rise, and we will see on which side nature has degenerated." It happened that his American guests were Carmichael, Harmer, Humphreys, and others of the finest stature and form; while those of the other side were remarkably diminutive, and the Abbé himself particularly, was a mere shrimp. He parried the appeal, however, by a complimentary admission of exceptions, among which the Doctor himself was a conspicuous one.

The Doctor and Silas Deane were in conversation one day at Passy, on the numerous errors in the Abbé's "*Histoire des deux Indes*," when he happened to step in. After the usual salutations, Silas Deane said to him, "The Doctor and myself, Abbé, were just speaking of the errors of fact into which you have been ed in your history." "Oh, no, Sir," said the Abbé, "that is impossible. I took the greatest care not to insert a single fact, for which I had not the most unquestionable authority." "Why," says Deane, "there is the story of Polly Baker, and the eloquent apology you have put into her mouth, when brought before a court of Massachusetts to suffer punishment under a law which you cite, for having had a bastard. I know there never was such a law in Massachusetts." "Be assured," said the Abbé, "you are mistaken, and that that is a true story. I do not immediately recollect indeed the particular information on which I quote it; but I am certain that I had for it unquestionable authority." Doctor Franklin, who had been for some time shaking with unrestrained laughter at the Abbé's confidence in his authority for that tale, said, "I will tell you, Abbé, the origin of that story. When I was a printer and editor of a newspaper, we were sometimes slack of news, and, to amuse our customers, I used to fill up our vacant columns with anecdotes and fables, and fancies of my own; and this of Polly Baker is a story of my making, on one of these occasions." The Abbé, without the least disconcert, exclaimed with a laugh, "Oh, very well, Doctor, I had rather relate your stories than other men's truths."

GENERAL

In both Great Britain and America, Benjamin Franklin's popularity and esteem were greater than ever at the time of his death in 1790. Though the Revolutionary War naturally created much animosity between the two nations, many British readers were able to separate Franklin's contributions to literature and the sciences from his politics and to recognize his extraordinary accomplishments. Through the nineteenth and into the early twentieth centuries, Americans retained a high opinion of Franklin's life and accomplishments. In terms of national greatness, he was considered second only to George Washington. British attitudes toward Franklin changed somewhat during the nineteenth century. Some prominent British men of letters grew skeptical of the way of life Franklin represented.

The first document in this section comes from an article in a British literary journal published three years after Franklin's death. Written in the form of a personal letter of advice, this article shows the ongoing respect for Franklin among British readers. The author applauds Franklin's writings for both the instruction and inspiration that they could provide. Do they still work this way? To what extent can Franklin's writings serve as conduct literature, that is, works that offer readers prescriptions of how to live their lives?

The next selection presents part of a lengthy essay that appeared anonymously in the *Southern Literary Messenger* in 1841. This appreciative essay from the leading literary magazine of the South shows that sectional differences did little to lessen American attitudes toward Franklin, who continued to be lauded in the North and the South. The author notes that there were a few who questioned what Franklin represented. Some Christian readers wondered about his belief in God. And there were others who would "sneer at his personal and systematic efforts to school himself in the Art of Virtue."

Leigh Hunt belongs with those who sneered. To understand Hunt's belligerence toward Franklin, much less to understand the history of Franklin's critical reception, it is crucial to know about *The Way to Wealth*, the pamphlet that significantly shaped Franklin's public perception. Hunt, a British essayist and bon vivant, does not mention *The Way to Wealth* in his autobiography, the source of the next item in this section, but his willingness to equate Franklin with Poor Richard shows the pamphlet's influence. Hunt conveniently ignores Franklin's numerous civic and scientific accomplishments. Hunt also critiques Franklin for virtually disowning his son William, who came out as a royalist during the American Revolution. (Hunt conveniently ignores the fact that Benjamin Franklin took William's son, William Temple Franklin, born out of wedlock, into his home and raised him.) Hunt's problem with Benjamin Franklin comes down to a matter of class. His defense of William Franklin is a defense of family connections over personal merit. Hunt resented Benjamin Franklin's humble origins and disliked the idea that Franklin represented, that a man could make his way in the world without the help of family.

Herman Melville's *Israel Potter*, a historical novel set during the Revolutionary War, is the source of the next selection. During the course of his adventures, Potter goes on a secret mission to France, where he meets Franklin. His meeting with Franklin is a delight. In the chapter after they meet, reprinted here, Melville takes the opportunity to reflect on Franklin's character. He compares Franklin with the biblical Jacob and then with Thomas Hobbes. The first comparison is fanciful, but the next may be worth exploring further. Melville had the ability to make off-the-cuff judgments that cut to the heart of the matter. His discussion of Franklin's personal character exemplifies this ability. Overall, Melville emphasizes Franklin's personal charm, his tranquility, and his waggishness.

Many of the long essays published in the nineteenth century devote much space to retelling the story of Franklin's life or quoting liberally from his writings. Henry T. Tuckerman's essay is different. He provides an insightful overview of Franklin's accomplishments. Tuckerman may not have Melville's style (who does?), but what he lacks in style he makes up for in thoroughness. He emphasizes the practical nature of Franklin's writings. Franklin wrote for the moment, to accomplish a specific purpose. In this capacity, he resembles Jonathan Swift. Tuckerman's comparison is worth developing further. Compare Swift's "Modest Proposal" to

Franklin's "Rattlesnakes for Felons." Or, alternatively, compare Swift's "Meditation on a Broomstick" to Franklin's "Meditation on a Quart Mugg." Tuckerman's essay provides other ideas worth exploring. He recognizes Franklin's electrical experiments not only as important in themselves but also important metaphorically. To explain electrical polarity, Franklin coined the terms *positive* and *negative,* words that have had a long afterlife in terms of their figurative meanings.

Matthew Arnold's comment on Franklin from *Culture and Anarchy*, though brief, shows his understanding of Franklin's common-sense philosophy, but also reveals that Arnold underwent an epiphany in his thinking about Franklin. He ultimately recognized Franklin's humanity. Besides being a poet, Arnold was one of the most important thinkers in Victorian England. Precisely how did Franklin influence Arnold's thought?

Mark Twain, the author of the next selection, obviously had great fun writing about Benjamin Franklin. He provides a picture of Franklin from the nineteenth-century child's perspective. Whenever children engaged in frivolous, unproductive behavior, their parents would throw the figure of Franklin in their faces. Parents set Franklin up as a model of behavior and children had little recourse when this paragon of conduct was cited. Though Twain was being facetious, his essay makes a crucial point. But is this true? Search nineteenth-century children's literature that mentions Franklin. How is he portrayed there? The nineteenth century saw a growing body of pedagogical literature too. How is Franklin represented in nineteenth-century educational writings?

E.P. Powell concentrates on Franklin's diplomatic life in the next essay. Powell mentions the famous meeting between Franklin and Voltaire, which was seen as the coming together of America's and France's greatest minds, respectively. Situating Franklin's diplomatic efforts within his biography, Powell emphasizes the importance of his New England heritage, an idea Tuckerman had stressed earlier. Franklin's diplomacy marked the second half of his life. Powell offers a good comparison between Benjamin Franklin and Thomas Jefferson. These two could be compared not only as diplomats, but also as authors, inventors, politicians, and scientists.

Moses Coit Tyler is a major figure in the study of American literature. Tyler's *Literary History of the American Revolution, 1763–1783*, still the standard work on the subject, provides the source of the next selection. Tyler scrutinizes several of Franklin's important writings of the period, including *The Examination of Doctor Benjamin Franklin*, the work that established his reputation as a spokesman for America. Tyler also compares Franklin to Swift in terms of both technique and the use of realistic detail. Tyler appreciates Franklin as a satirist and a purveyor of hoaxes too. Furthermore, he identifies Franklin as the greatest letter writer of the Revolutionary period: high praise considering such other great letter writers of the period as John Adams, Abigail Adams, and Thomas Jefferson.

This section closes with a reprint of the Franklin chapter from D.H. Lawrence's *Studies in Classic American Literature.* Lawrence's work, in itself a classic of American literary historiography, recalls Leigh Hunt's belligerence toward Franklin. Like Hunt, Lawrence does not mention *The Way to Wealth*, but his general attitude has also been shaped by the Poor Richard sayings the pamphlet popularized. Lawrence's primary focus is Franklin's autobiography. He takes Franklin to task for his plan for attaining moral perfection. A "barbed wire moral enclosure," Lawrence calls it.

Lawrence resents Franklin's creed and his list of virtues but ends up emulating Franklin by writing his own creed and devising his own list of virtues. How do the two lists differ? Which list do you prefer? Does one seem more appropriate today than the other? If you were to devise your own list of virtues, which would you choose? Are there important virtues omitted from either list that you would include? Though brash and opinionated, Lawrence often wins us over through the brilliance of his writing style. To that extent, perhaps he and Franklin are not so different as Lawrence wants to believe.

Anonymous "Critical Remarks on Benjamin Franklin" (1793)

Of all the literary men in my time, Benjamin Franklin occupied the first rank in respect to elegance, conjoined with philosophical accuracy, and depth of observation. Every subject he treated, assumed, under his hand, a new and more inviting appearance than any other person could ever give it. His magical touch converted the science of electricity into one of the most interesting amusements that was ever laid open to the minds of men. Politics, religion, science, in all its branches, which used to be dry and unamiable studies, he taught by apologues, fables, and tales, calculated not less to inform, than to amuse; and these are always constructed with an elegance of taste that is highly delightful. The miscellaneous philosophical works of Franklin, I consider as one of the most valuable presents that can be put into the hands of youth. Read them my dear,—with care. If you can lay them aside with indifference, you have not those dispositions of mind I have flattered myself you possess. In perusing them, you will find more amusement than in reading a romance, and be more improved than even in listening to some sermons. I know no book from which you can derive so much improvement and amusement.

Anonymous "Benjamin Franklin" (1841)

A distinguishing feature in the character of Franklin, is its Individuality. He did not amalgamate himself with the mass. Modes and customs were not laws to him. He had his own way for doing everything. His philosophy was not ashamed to dress in homespun, and was with him in all his occupations, from the trundling of his wheelbarrow to the study of the heavens. He had a habit of constant observation. He looked upon every thing as a means of knowledge. He reduced to practice those time-hallowed maxims that had been retarded as simply ingenious theories. He tried proverbs in the crucible of experience. What was another's wit, he made his own wisdom. He was strictly conscientious, even in the minor moralities. He was a gentleman by principle. Philanthropy was a semi-circle of his religion. He worshipped the Supreme Ruler of the Universe, as a Being who delights in the happiness of his creatures; and looked upon the promotion of that happiness as his own most acceptable service. If he was not a constant attendant upon the preaching of his times, it was because that preaching was so unlike the Sermon on the Mount. He could not depart from his own vineyard, to glean the tythes of mint, annise and cumin in the fields of his neighbors. We make no controversy with those who sneer at his personal and systematic efforts to school himself in the Art of Virtue. It was his own way of subduing his own propensities—of fulfilling the great purposes of his moral being; and his tree asks no judgment except by its fruits. If there was humanity in the execution, there was divinity in the attempt. If he cut himself off from particular creeds, he did not divide himself from the church universal. He claimed fellowship with all, of whatever name, who worshipped God in sincerity. Unbending in principle, but pliant in charity, he was like the rock-rooted oak that shelters the lambkin but defies the tempest. Yet he was not a child, to tamper with the cockatrice. He looked upon Infidelity as a tiger—upon Atheism as a fool's mask—but upon man, as his brother.

Another peculiarity of Franklin's character, was its Practicalness. He did not exercise himself in beating the air. He had ever before him some useful end, and his whole philosophy was a well of useful means. He thought no more of throwing himself upon abstractions, than of building his house upon the sand. In every important pursuit he took men as they might happen to be. He was not afraid to trust himself to the common mind. He made himself a glass to every man, in which each could see his own reflection. He had an infinite perception of the strong points of a subject. These he would elucidate, and leave the rest to their own sequence. If eloquence be the art of persuading, then was Franklin eloquent. In public bodies, his influence was commanding. His purity of character—his firmness—his modesty—his openness to conviction—all conspired to disarm suspicion and provoke compliance. He was a stranger to dogmatism. For more than a half century, he was not heard to utter a single tone of dictation. In his diplomacy, he never confounded the sign and the thing signified. Intent upon securing solid advantages to his country, he seldom chaffered about the shin-plasters of empty etiquette, when solid bullion was offered for their redemption. Above all, he was eminently practical in his benevolence, so much so, that when desirous to benefit some young man, he considered the showing him how to manage his own razor, to be as fruitful a favor as he could confer.

These and the other praiseworthy traits of his character, were the results of severe mental and moral discipline. If they constituted him a *made* man, let it be remembered that he was a *self*-made man. Was he temperate, prudent, wise, excellent in all the virtues? These qualities were the fruits of a settled purpose. Was he distinguished by the faithful discharge of his public trusts? Of those qualities, public trusts were the reward. Was he favored by circumstances? Let it be forever remembered that he and his compatriots by their firmness and daring, created the circumstances that rendered their names illustrious. It should be graven on our hearts as with the point of a diamond, that the Immortals of Mortality are not splendid exceptions in point of natural gifts. As by a wise grafting, the unlikeliest vine yields the choicest fruit, so our fallen nature, by a skilful training, becomes a praise and a glory.

But there is a certain class of persons with whom we apprehend we shall find little favor. These are the hero-worshippers of our age. They love the terrible—the stormy—the convulsive of human nature. They forget that the precipice is a barren rock—the whirlwind, a besom of wrath—the earthquake, a living grave. They "like to be despised;" and only let the damps of disappointment, gloom and misanthropy breed a glaring meteor in the upper sky—though it be "a pathless comet and a curse"—still, they all conspire to do it homage. Such, we imagine, will poorly appreciate the steady, placid beacon which Franklin has left burning above the quicksands of life. But those who, with humble hearts and warm desires, endeavor to exalt the dignity of their immortal natures, will love his counsels, and cherish his memory. Surely, no uninspired man has left a richer store of wisdom to posterity. He has bequeathed a lofty example, to the high and to the low. He has lived, to vindicate the dignity of labor—to make "I, too, am a printer!" as proud a boast, as, "I, too, am a painter!" He has lived, to proclaim universally, that the humblest occupation has advantages with the most exalted—that even the smallest duties of Life, are subordinate to its chief end. Lesser than Bacon, and greater; not so happy, yet much happier: Scarcely inferior in his powers, yet more fortunate in his virtues—he must forever share with his illustrious antitype, the reverence, but not the pity of mankind.

LEIGH HUNT "CHARACTER OF FRANKLIN" (1850)

I acquired a dislike for my grandfather's friend Dr. Franklin, author of *Poor Richard's Almanack*: a heap, as it appeared to me, of "Scoundrel maxims." I think I now appreciate Dr. Franklin as I ought; but although I can see the utility of such publications an his Almanack for a rising commercial state, and hold it useful as a memorandum to uncalculating persons like myself, who happen to live in an old one, I think it has no business either in commercial nations long established, or in others who do not found their happiness in that sort of power. Franklin, with all his abilities, is but at the head of those who think that man lives "by bread alone." He will commit none of the follies, none of the intolerances, the absence of which is necessary to the perfection of his system; and in setting his face against these, he discountenances a great number of things very inimical to higher speculations. But he was no more a fit representative of what human nature largely requires, and may reasonably hope to attain to, than negative represents positive, or the clearing away a ground in the back-settlements, and setting to work upon it, represents the work in its completion. Something of the pettiness and materiality of his first occupation always stuck to him. He took nothing for a truth or a matter-of-fact that he could not handle, as it were, like his types: and yet, like all men of this kind, he was liable, when put out of the ordinary pale of his calculations, to fall into the greatest errors, and substitute the integrity of his reputation for that of whatsoever he chose to do. From never doing wrong in little things, he conceived that he could do no wrong in great; and, in the most deliberate act of his life, he showed he had grievously mistaken himself. He was, I allow, one of the *cardinal* great men of his time. He was Prudence. But he was not what he took himself for—all the other Virtues besides; and, inasmuch as he was deficient in those, he was deficient even in his favorite one. He was not Temperance; for, in the teeth of his capital recommendations of that virtue, he did not scruple to get burly and big with the enjoyments that he cared for. He was not Justice; for he knew not how to see fair play between his own wisdom and that of a thousand wants and aspirations, of which he knew nothing: and he cut off his son with a shilling, for differing with him in politics. Lastly, he was not Fortitude; for having few passions and no imagination, he knew not what it was to be severely tried; and if he had been there is every reason to conclude, from the way in which he treated his son, that his self-love would have been the part in which he felt the torture; that as his Justice was only arithmetic, so his Fortitude would have been nothing but stubbornness.

If Franklin had been the only great man of his time, he would merely have contributed to make the best of a bad system, and so hurt the world by prolonging it; but, luckily, there were the French and English philosophers besides, who saw farther than he did, and provided for higher wants. I feel grateful to him, for one, inasmuch as he extended the sphere of liberty, and helped to clear the earth of the weeds of sloth and ignorance, and the wild beasts of superstition; but when he comes to build final homes for us, I rejoice that wiser hands interfere. His line and rule are not every thing; they are not even a tenth part of it. Cocker's numbers are good; but those of Plato and Pythagoras have their merits too, or we should have been made of dry bones and tangents, and not had the fancies in our heads, and the hearts beating in our bosoms, that make us what we are. We should not even have known that Cocker's numbers were worth any thing; nor would, Dr. Franklin himself have played on the harmonica, albeit he must have done it in a style very different from that of Milton or Cimarosa. Finally, the writer of this passage on the Doctor would not have ventured to give his opinion of so great a span in so explicit a manner. I should not have ventured to give it, had I not been backed by so many powerful interests of humanity, and had I not suffered in common, and more than in common, with the rest of the world, from a system which, under the guise of economy and social advantage, tends to double the love of wealth and the hostility of competition, to force the best things down to a level with the worst, and to reduce mankind to the simplest and most mechanical law of their nature, divested of its heart and soul—the law of being in motion. Most of the advantages of the present system of money-making, which may be called the great *lay* superstition of modern times, might be obtained by a fifth part of the labor, if more equally distributed. Yet all the advantages could not be so obtained; and the system is necessary as a portion of the movement of time and progress, and as the ultimate means of dispensing with its very self.

HERMAN MELVILLE "DOCTOR FRANKLIN AND THE LATIN QUARTER" (1855)

The first, both in point of time and merit, of American envoys was famous not less for the pastoral simplicity of his manners than for the politic grace of his mind. Viewed from a certain point, there was a touch of primeval orientalness in Benjamin Franklin. Neither is there wanting something like his Scriptural parallel. The history of the patriarch Jacob is interesting not less from the unselfish devotion which we are bound to ascribe to him, than from the deep worldly wisdom and polished Italian tact, gleaming under an air of Arcadian unaffectedness. The diplomatist and the shepherd are blended—a union not without warrant; the apostolic serpent and dove; a tanned Machiavelli in tents.

Doubtless, too, notwithstanding his eminence as lord of the moving manor, Jacob's raiment was of homespun; the economic envoy's plain coat and hose, who has not heard of?

Franklin all over is of a piece. He dressed his person as his periods; neat, trim, nothing superfluous, nothing deficient. In some of his works his style is only surpassed by the unimprovable sentences of Hobbes of Malmsbury, the paragon of perspicuity. The mental habits of Hobbes and Franklin in several points, especially in one of some moment, assimilated. Indeed, making due allowance for soil and era, history presents few trios more akin, upon the whole, than Jacob, Hobbes, and Franklin; three labyrinth-minded, but plain-spoken Broadbrims, at once politicians and philosophers; keen observers of the main chance; prudent courtiers; practical magians in linsey-woolsey.

In keeping with his general habitudes, Doctor Franklin while at the French Court did not reside in the aristocratical faubourgs. He deemed his worsted hose and scientific tastes more adapted in a domestic way to the other side of the Seine, where the Latin Quarter, at once the haunt of erudition and economy seemed peculiarly to invite the philosophical Poor Richard to its venerable retreats. Here, of gray, chilly, drizzly November mornings, in the dark-stoned quadrangle of the time-honoured Sorbonne, walked the lean and slippered metaphysician,—oblivious for the moment that his sublime thoughts and tattered wardrobe were famous throughout Europe,—meditating on the theme of his next lecture; at the same time, in the well-worn chambers overhead, some clayey-visaged chemist in ragged robe-de-chambre, and with a soiled green flap over his left eye, was hard at work stooping over retorts and crucibles, discovering new antipathies in acids, again risking strange explosions similar to that whereby he had already lost the use of one optic; while in the lofty lodging-houses of the neighbouring streets, indigent young students from all parts of France were ironing their shabby cocked hats, or inking the whity seams of their small-clothes, prior to a promenade with their pink-ribboned little grisettes in the garden of the Luxembourg.

Long ago the haunt of rank, the Latin Quarter still retains many old buildings whose imposing architecture singularly contrasts with the unassuming habits of their present occupants. In some parts its general air is dreary and dim; monastic and theurgic. In those lonely narrow ways—long-drawn prospectives of desertion—lined with huge piles of silent, vaulted, old iron-grated buildings of dark gray stone, one almost expects to encounter Paracelsus or Friar Bacon turning the next corner, with some awful vial of Black-Art elixir in his hand.

But all the lodging-houses are not so grim. Not to speak of many of comparatively modern erection, the others of the better class, however stern in exterior, evince a feminine gaiety of taste, more or less, in their furnishings within. The embellishing, or softening, or screening hand of woman is to be seen all over the interiors of this metropolis. Like Augustus Caesar with respect to Rome, the Frenchwoman leaves her obvious mark on Paris. Like the hand in nature, you know it can be none else but hers. Yet sometimes she overdoes it, as nature in the peony; or underdoes it, as nature in the bramble; or—what is still more frequent—is a little slatternly about it, as nature in the pig-weed.

In this congenial vicinity of the Latin Quarter, and in as ancient building something like those alluded to, at a point midway between the Palais des Beaux Arts and the College of the Sorbonne, the venerable American envoy pitched his tent when not passing his time at his country retreat at Passy. The frugality of his manner of life did not lose him the good opinion even of the voluptuaries of the showiest of capitals, whose very iron railings are not free from gilt. Franklin was not less a lady's man, than a man's man a wise man, and an old man. Not only did he enjoy the homage of the choicest Parisian literati, but at the age of seventy-two he was the caressed favourite of the highest born beauties of the court; who through blind fashion having been originally attracted to him as a famous *savan*, were permanently retained as his admirers by his Plato-like graciousness of good humour. Having carefully weighed the world, Franklin could act any part in it. By nature turned to knowledge, his mind was often grave, but never serious. At times he had seriousness—extreme seriousness—for others, but never for himself. Tranquillity was to him instead of it. This philosophical levity of tranquillity, so to speak, is shown in his easy variety of pursuits. Printer, postmaster, almanac maker, essayist, chemist, orator, tinker, statesman, humourist, philosopher, parlour man, political economist, professor of housewifery, ambassador, projector, maxim-monger, herb-doctor, wit:—Jack of all trades, master of each and mastered by none,—the type and genius of his land. Franklin was everything but a poet. But since a soul with many qualities, forming of itself a sort of handy index and pocket congress of all humanity, needs the contact of just as many different men, or subjects in order to the exhibition of its totality; hence very little indeed of the sage's multifariousness will be portrayed in a simple narrative like the present. This casual private intercourse with Israel, but served to manifest him in his far lesser lights; thrifty, domestic, dietarian, and, it may be, didactically waggish. There was much benevolent irony, innocent mischievousness, in the wise man. Seeking here to depict him in his lees exalted habitudes, the narrator feels more as if he were playing with one of the sage's worsted hose, than reverentially handling the honoured hat which once oracularly sat upon his brow.

So, then in the Latin Quarter lived Doctor Franklin. And accordingly in the Latin Quarter tarried Israel for the time. And it was into a room of a house in this same Latin Quarter that Israel had been directed when the sage had requested privacy for a while.

Henry T. Tuckerman
"The Character of Franklin" (1856)

Sixty-six years have elapsed since the mortal remains of Benjamin Franklin were placed beneath a tablet in the Friends' Cemetery in Philadelphia; the granite obelisk which marks the last resting-place of his parents is a familiar object to all who walk the streets of his native city; but these graves, thus humbly designated, were, until a few days since, the only visible monuments of a name as illustrious as it is endeared. Its fame, however, had become so thoroughly identified with American institutions and life, that an artistic memorial is far more important as a tribute of gratitude and reverence, than as a method of keeping his example before our minds or his image in our hearts. Yet it is, on all accounts, a subject of congratulation, that at length we have, in the city of Franklin's birth, and from the hands of one of her own sons, a statue of the patriot and philosopher worthy of the man and the place. We embrace the moment when his story is revived to the popular mind, and his services to humanity are recognized anew,—and when the admirable collection of his writings, for which we are indebted to Mr. Sparks, has just appeared in a fresh and improved edition,—to recall some of his prominent characteristics and his permanent claims to love and honor.

The pervading trait of Franklin's character was allegiance to the Practical. Few devotees of knowledge have so consistently manifested this instinct, the more remarkable because united to speculative tendencies which quickened his intelligence and occupied his leisure to the very close of his existence. For the intangible aims of the metaphysician, the vagaries of the imaginative, the "airy bubble—reputation," he exhibited no concern; but the application of truth to the facts of nature and of life,—the discovery of material laws and their conversion to human welfare,—the actual influence of morals, economy, politics, and education upon civil society and individual deportment,—were problems upon which he never failed to think, read, talk, write, and experiment. A striking evidence of this was his youthful disdain of the Muses (although he wrote quite a respectable ballad at the age of twelve), because "verse-makers generally make beggars"; as also his preference in maturity for that circle abroad where the "understanding" found such exclusive recognition and utterance. "I believe Scotland," he wrote to Lord Kames, "would be the country I should choose to spend my days in." The history of the man is, therefore, that of some of the most pregnant of great external interests; and his entire devotion to them, to the exclusion of more ideal, vague, and purely intellectual subjects, arose chiefly from his peculiar mental organization, and also, in no small degree, from the transition period in government, society, and popular intelligence during which he lived. Accordingly, he was so indifferent to literary fame, that the indefatigable editor of his works informs us that some of his most characteristic writings were never intended for the press, very few were published under his own supervision, and nearly all came forth anonymously. His object, like Swift's, was immediate effect. In youth he studied the art of perspicuous expression in order to act with facility upon the minds of others; but it was in order to disseminate useful knowledge, to enlarge the boundaries of science, to advocate political reform, and to direct into expedient channels the enterprise, speculation, and party zeal of his day, rather than to build for himself a monument in the library or a shrine in household lore. What he achieved as a writer was incidental, not premeditated; for he valued the pen as he did time, money, and experience, for its direct tendency to diffuse knowledge, comfort, utility, and settled principles of inference and action. The most deliberate of his writings, that is, the one which seems inspired least by a definite purpose and most by the anticipated pleasure of the undertaking, is his famous autobiography, and even in this it is evident that the luxury of reminiscence was in abeyance to the desire of imparting, especially to the young, the benefit of his own experience. For many years, indeed, the pen of Franklin was too variously employed, and dedicated too constantly to the advancement of immediate national interests, to admit of any well-considered, elaborate, and finished work. What his written and spoken word, however, thus lost in permanent value, it gained in vigor and in direct utility. If we glance at the subjects and occasions of his tracts, letters, reports, paragraphs, and essays, we shall find that they embrace the whole circle of questions important to his country and his age,—morals, the economy of life, commerce, finance, history, and politics. We find in them the germs of ideas now triumphant, of principles— through his advocacy in no small degree—since embodied in action and brought to grand practical results. A parable wins men to toleration; a maxim guides them to frugality; a comprehensive argument initiates the plan of that federal union which has proved the key-stone of our national prosperity; the farmer or the mariner, consulting *Poor Richard's Almanac* to learn the fluctuation of weather or tide, finds, besides mere chronicles of nature's mysteries, advice which puts him unconsciously on the track of provident habits, temperance, and contentment; the patriot in the field is cheered by the wisdom of the sage in counsel; the shipwright, the Horticulturist, the printer, the lowly aspirant for self-improvement, as well as the statesman and the philosopher, draw wisdom and encouragement from his "words spoken in season"; in the prudent household his name is associated with the invaluable heating-apparatus that saves the fuel and increases the genial warmth of the evening fireside; in the disconsolate council of war his foreign diplomacy and judicious hints warm the heart of valor with the prescience of success; in the land of his country's enemies his clear statement of grievances and his intrepid reproof of injustice conciliate the nobler spirits there, and vindicate the leaders at home; the encroachments of savage tribes are checked, the policy of colonial rule softened, the comforts of domestic life enhanced, the resources of the mind elicited, and, in a word, the basis of national prosperity laid on the eternal foundation of popular enlightenment, self-reliance, and foresight, by the oracles of the American philosopher thus casually uttered and incidentally promulgated.

But while official duty and patriotism gave Franklin occasion to propagate and actualize so many useful and requisite principles,—to become the thinker and advocate,—the incarnated common-sense of his country and his time,—there was another sphere of mental activity, another range of sagacious enterprise, in which he expatiated with kindred success. This was the domain of science. When he was not required to apply reflection to conduct, and to deal with great crises in the political world, he turned with alacrity to that of natural philosophy. This was his congenial element. "I have got my niche," he writes exultingly, "after having been kept out of it for twenty-four years by foreign appointments." He was, by instinct, a philosopher,—one whom Bacon would have hailed as a disciple, and to whom Sir Kenelm Digby would have delighted to unfold the merits of the "sympathetic powder," Sir Thomas Browne to lament "vulgar errors," and Bishop Berkeley to explain the laws of optics and the merits of tar-water. Lord Brougham expresses the conviction, that he would have promulgated the inductive philosophy had not Bacon anticipated him.

At the commencement of the seventeenth century the provincial town built upon three hills on the coast of Massachusetts was an excellent place for the education of circumstances. Among its inhabitants were the most enlightened of the English emigrants, who brought with them the industrious habits, the domestic discipline, the taste for reading, and the love of thrift and enterprise, which induce and sustain commercial prosperity and municipal order. Questions of church and state, the conservatism of an old and the innovations of a new country,—the meeting-house, the newspaper, the fireside, and the school-room,—were their elements of civilization. The arts of luxury, the venerable in architecture, and the beautiful in decoration, had not yet superseded more stringent provisions for utility and comfort.

The back settlements of the continent were exposed to savage invasion. The mother country, with her rich historical associations, her time-hallowed precedents, her glorious trophies of literature, her royal prerogatives, and her ancestral graves, was to the colonists the grand and mellow perspective of life, to which their New England dwellings on those bleak hillsides and beside that rock-bound bay were the rude foreground, where they were to realize great principles of religion and government, achieve individual prosperity, and eventually battle manfully for freedom and truth. Meanwhile honest subsistence, religious zeal, and the cause of education, employed their energies. Months of dreary winter, when roofs were white with snow and the harbor a sheet of ice, alternated with a brief season of heat, more than tempered by a keen breeze from the east; so that only their hardy maize and tough grass yielded reliable crops. Orchards were their only vineyards, a good sermon their most available entertainment, and fast and thanksgiving days their festivals. The great event of the month was an arrival from England,— usually a weather-beaten craft, often ten weeks on the voyage; and her epitome of London news, the colonial agent she brought, the original copies of Pope's verses, Addison's essay or De Foe's novel, the new fashion for the "gude dame" and her daughters, and the watch or shoe-buckles for her husband, made themes for the street and the hearthstone for many days. The isolation of such a community, the fact that non-conformity had driven their fathers thither, the Providence and frugality incident to the climate, the demand for foresight and self-denial, the force of public opinion, the distinction yielded to character, the comparative dearth of temptation, and the rigorous observance of family, church, and municipal discipline, though unfavorable to the more graceful and tender, moulded the sterner elements of humanity into an unusual rectitude of purpose. For the expanded intellect and free aspirations of youth there might be too much of the Puritan inflexibility and narrowness in such an environment; but as a means of acquiring the habit of self-dependence and self-control—the vestibule of more enlarged and spontaneous development—we cannot but recognize its inestimable value.

The early circumstances, physical and moral, of men who leave distinct and permanent influences behind them, are more significant than we imagine. It was no accidental coincidence that reared the most fervent of false prophets in the and vales of Arabia, the greatest of religious reformers among the cold heights of Germany, or the most fanatical of usurpers beside the monotonous fens of Huntingdon. How intimate was the connection of the civil strife in Tuscany with the shadowy and sharp features of Dante's Muse, of the sunny lassitude of Southern Italy and France with the amorous melody of Petrarch's numbers, of the fiery passions and stern hardihood of Corsican life with the indomitable will of Napoleon! And who that knows New England, even as modified by a foreign population, by the facilities of modern intercourse and the liberality of an advanced civilization, does not recognize in the sagacity, prudence, hardihood, love of knowledge, industry, and practical consistency and wisdom of Franklin, the vigorous training of that Spartan mother,—the self-reliant discipline of that hard soil and rigid climate?

If the prime of Franklin's life was the critical era of our national fortunes, it was no less a period of literary and political transition in Great Britain. It was the epoch when History assumed a more philosophical development under the thoughtful pen of Hume, when sentiment and humor grew bold and vagrant in expression through Sterne, when the greatest orator of the age recorded its events in the Annual Register, when humane letters rose in public esteem by virtue of Goldsmith's graceful style, when Garrick made the stage illustrious, when Methodism began its work, when the seer of Stockholm proclaimed spiritual science, and the bard of Olney sang the pleasures of rural and domestic life. Yet how diverse from them all was the renown their American contemporary won, and the method of its acquisition! It is the clear vista to a humble origin and the gradual rise from the condition of a poor mechanic to that of a statesman and philosopher, opened by Franklin in his artless memoir of himself, which gives at once individuality and universality to his fame. Who can estimate the vast encouragement derived by the lowliest seeker for knowledge and social elevation from such a minute chart of life, frankly revealing every stage of poverty, scepticism, obscure toil, dissipation, on the one side, and, on the other, of manly resolution, indefatigable industry, frugal self-denial, patient study, honest and intelligent conviction, by means of which the fugitive printer's boy, with no library but an odd volume of the Spectator, an Essay of De Foe's, translations of Plutarch and Xenophon, the treatises of Shaftesbury and Locke, an English Grammar, and the "Pilgrim's Progress," trained himself to observe, to write, and to think, while earning often a precarious subsistence in Philadelphia and London by type-setting and pen-work? The play-house alternating with the club made up of vagabonds and steady fellows, equally "lovers of reading," a swimming-match and experiments in diet, conversation with "ingenious acquaintances," hard work, constant observation, and the habit of "improving by experience," exhibit the youth as he develops into the man, who, with remorse for the "errata" in his life, goes on to reveal the process— available to all with self-control and understanding—whereby from a printer he became a shop-keeper, then a journalist, and subsequently launched upon an unprecedented career of public usefulness and honor.

The example of Franklin is invaluable as a triumph of self-culture. His name was not only an honorable passport among the learned, but an endeared watchword to the humble. The lowliest laborer of the undistinguished multitude claims a part in his fame, as well as the great discoverer or the regal patron. Never dawned a self-reliant character more opportunely on the world; at home, illustrating to a new country what perseverance, honesty, observation, and wisdom can effect with the most limited resources; abroad, proving to an ancient regime how independent a genuine man may be of courts, academics, and luxury;" both the most requisite lessons for which humanity thirsted, and both enforced with an attractive candor, a gracious consistency, a modest resolution, which no argument could attain and no rhetoric enhance.

Let us glance at the variety of subjects identified with human welfare and apart from political interests, which, from first to last, employed his mind, and elicited either sagacious conjectures or positive suggestions;—the causes of earthquakes and the art of printing, the circulation of the blood and the cultivation of grasses, theories of light and the treatment of fevers, the manufacture of salt by evaporation and the arrangement of musical glasses, a remedy for smoky chimneys and the tendency of rivers to the sea, husbandry and fireplaces, magnetism and water-spouts, the effect of oil on water, meteorology, the aurora borealis, toads, balloons, thermometers, and ventilation. He searches out the mossy inscriptions on the gravestones of his ancestors in Northamptonshire, and acquires proficiency in a foreign language after sixty. He is one of a commission to examine the claims of Mesmer's theory in France, and to protect St. Paul's from lightning in London. He could not watch a shooting star, glance at a metallic crystal, behold the flush of sunset clouds or the hectic on an invalid's cheek, feel the impulse of the tide or the greeting of the wind, examine a proposed law of state or a vegetable product of the earth, hear a beetle hum or feel a quivering pulse, gaze on a petrifaction or a type, converse with a stranger or meet a committee, draft a plan or look at a machine, without feeling the plea of causality, striving to trace the origin of effects, and to infer a law applicable to the wants of his race, or the elucidation of truth. No experiment was too insignificant for his philosophy, no task too humble for his patriotism. Open his correspondence at random: here you find precautionary hints for a voyage, there a sketch of an English school; now observations on maize, and again remarks on paper currency; to-day he draws up a plan of union for the Colonies, to-morrow a dialogue with the Gout; at one time he invents a letter from China, and at another counsels the settler beyond the Alleghanies.

Commerce one moment and a *jeu d'esprit* the next, advice to a Yankee tradesman and a bagatelle for a Parisian lady, seem equally congenial themes; a state paper and a proverb, allegory and statistics, the way to save money and the way to form a government, an article for the "Busy Body," a fable for the Almanac, and an epitaph for himself,—health, finance, natural history, the story of "The Whistle,"—a theory of water-spouts, and "Cool Thoughts on Public Affairs,"—alternately occupy his pen; and to determine how many valuable precedents were established, what useful principles were realized, and what impulse was given to individual minds and to social progress by his enlightened activity, were as hopeless a task as to define the respective influence of the elements in fructification. He benignly and opportunely scattered the seeds of popular knowledge and of experimental science; they took root in the virgin soil of a new civilization; and the tiller of the earth, the reader of the newspaper, the frugal housewife, the public-spirited citizen, the aspiring mechanic, the honest tradesman, the legislator, the man of science, the worker, thinker, companion, writer, the baffled and the novice, the adventurous and the truth-seeking of America, caught gleams of wisdom, warnings of prudence, perceptions of law, moral and physical, from Franklin, which gave them a clew to prosperity and a motive to culture.

As with all resolute intelligences thus spontaneously breasting the vast ocean of truth, vigilant for discovery and intent upon deduction, his earnest confidence and patient search were rewarded by a signal triumph. Philosophy, thus loyally wooed, smiled upon her votary; and Nature, ever indulgent to the heart that loves her, whether with scientific insight or poetic enthusiasm, opened her arcana to his vision. The history of Franklin's electrical experiments and discoveries is one of the most attractive, beautiful, and pregnant episodes in modern science. The grand simplicity of his theory, the familiar apparatus by which it was tested, the accuracy of his foresight, and the unpretending spirit with which he received the fame incident to so great a result, form together one of those memorable instances of the conquest of mind over matter, of human intelligence over the secret facts of nature, which add the cognizance of new laws to the domain of knowledge, and brighter names to the catalogue of her immortal disciples. However temporary in *their prestige*, or limited in their absolute use, may be the other fruits of his studies, Electricity is identified with Franklin. It is the common destiny of scientific discoverers to be forgotten in the very progress they initiate; the pioneer is superseded in his march by the advanced guard, and what is a brilliant novelty to-day becomes a familiar truth to-morrow. The modern chemist forgets the alchemist who, amid his illusive researches, brought to light some of the very principles that subserve later and more useful inquiries. The astronomer, as he sees through a telescope undreamed of by the Chaldeans a new planet wheel into the field of vision, bestows no thought upon the isolated and self-denying astrologer, who, in the fanciful task of casting nativities, systematized the first rude alphabet of the stars, which modern science has elaborated into that "poetry of heaven" whereby genius keeps vigil, and the trackless sea is navigated without perplexity. But it is otherwise with the initiation of an absolutely new branch of knowledge. When Franklin drew down the lightning and identified it with electricity, he for ever allied his name to a subtile element, whose every subsequent revelation is associated with the kite and key, the thunder and the conductor, the benign image and endeared name of the Boston printer, the Philadelphia sage, and the American patriot. The vista his experiments opened has never ceased to lead farther and deeper into the undiscovered mysteries of the universe; and at this moment the element of natural science most prophetic of new wonders and subtile uses is electricity. The phenomena of consciousness and nervous sympathy point more and more to an intimate relation between the electric fluid and the vital principle. The most inscrutable of material forces, it appears to be the direct medium of sensation, emotion, and all the modes of interaction between material existences and the embodied human soul. As the most intense agent for decomposing the latent affinities of matter, and generating forces of locomotion and intercourse, its wonders are but foreshadowed in the electric telegraph, the application of magnetism as a motive power, and its use as a curative agent and a disintegrating element. And it is worthy of remark, that the magnetic expression of the human countenance, especially of the eye, and the affinities of the individual temperament, are graduated by the moral as well as the physical condition, and are capable of apparent extinction through grossly material habits and perverted natural instincts,—facts which seem to confirm the near relation of the electric principle with life, emotion, and spiritual development as exhibited in organic forms. The prevalence of this unseen but ever-vital principle in nature, in the amber of the torrent's bed and the fur of the domestic animal, in the circumambient air, in our own consciousness of attraction and repulsion, of cheerfulness and depression, in the healthy and the morbid experiences of humanity, would seem clearly to indicate that the sphere whose latent significance was first revealed by Franklin is limitless in its resources of power, use, and beauty.

Franklin's varied aptitudes, offices, inquiries, and discoveries secured for him a sphere of acquaintance and friendship embracing the widest range of human character, vocation, and renown. Among his early intimates were three colonial Governors; Godfrey, the inventor of the quadrant; and Ralph, a writer of history and verse. He took counsel on national affairs with Washington, the revolutionary leaders, and the framers of the Constitution; confronted the inimical scrutiny of the British ministry and Parliament; was the messenger to Lord Howe, after a foreign army had encamped on our shores; conferred with Gates, Schuyler, Adams, Hancock, Jay, Hopkinson, Morris, Jefferson, Livingston, and Quincy; corresponded or conversed with Colden and Bartram on natural history, with Priestley and Sir Joseph Banks on scientific questions, with Hume on mental philosophy, on a large diversity of subjects with Paine and Cobbet; was in intimate intercourse with Lafayette and the Count de Vergennes, Foy and Mazzel; Whitefield and the Duke of Orleans, Lord Kames, the Abbé Morellet, and Dr. Stiles, Madame Brillon and Dr. Robertson, Voltaire and Houdon, Darwin, Lord Chatham, Dr. Fothergill, D'Alembert, David Hartley, Diderot, and Madame Helvetius. From republican America to aristocratic France, at Philadelphia, London, and Versailles, in the court and the congress, the laboratory and the saloon, he enjoyed the best facilities and the most intimate associations. It is because of his readiness and versatility, his self-possession and independence, that in his life and letters we seem to behold, although ever conscious of his identity, at one time a grave philosopher, and at another a genial companion, a patriarch here and a man of pleasure there, the wary statesman to-day and the playful humorist to-morrow,—ever active, cognizant, alert, content, inventive, useful, wise, cheerful, self-sustained, provident, far-sighted,—the type of good sense and urbanity, of thoroughness and insight, of tact and aptness. Nor was he insensible to that social privilege and consideration, which, in the retrospect of eminent lives, always seem the most desirable of their felicities. "The regard and friendship I meet with," he writes to his wife from London, "from persons of word, and the conversation of ingenious men, give me no small pleasure"; and he adds, with that superiority to circumstances and tenacity of purpose so characteristic: "I am for doing effectually what I came about, and I find it requires both time and patience." He elsewhere speaks of society as being his "dearest happiness." He tells us of his youthful zest for improving association when a printer's boy. His image, costume, manner, sayings and doings, as a man of society, are among the traditions of the old French court. One of the last-written descriptions of him, dated in his lifetime, is that of a benign and cheerful octogenarian, seated in pleasant discourse under a mulberry-tree, beside his dwelling, exhibiting to his attached grandchild a two-headed snake. In a letter to Washington, written the same year, he says:—

"For my own personal ease, I should have died two years ago; but, though those years have been spent in excruciating pain, yet I am pleased that I have lived them, since they have brought me to see our present situation. I am now finishing my eighty-fourth year, and probably with it my career in this life; but whatever state of existence I am placed in hereafter, if I retain any memory of what has passed here, I shall with it retain the esteem, respect, and affection, with which I have long been, my dear friend, yours most sincerely," &e.

Parallel with his devotion to scientific inquiry was a ceaseless activity for the public good,—wherein his career is eminently distinguished from that of the majority of modern philosophers. One of the earliest projectors of the conquest of Canada, he was also an efficient agent in raising troops for the unfortunate Braddock. We find him vigorously at work throughout the scale of official duty and volunteer patriotism, at home and abroad, through the press and in society; speaker of the Pennsylvania Assembly, a postmaster, on committees, promoting the culture of silk in America, enlightening the British public on colonial affairs, bringing from Europe the latest facts in science and polity for the benefit of his own countrymen, casting type at Passy for a Philadelphia journal, interceding for prisoners of war, planning maritime expeditions with Paul Jones, befriending Captain Cook, exciting French sympathy for the American cause and baffling English prejudice, a signer of the Declaration of Independence, framing treaties of alliance for his native land, the counsellor of the exile, the adviser of the official, a commissioner to Versailles, a delegate to the Convention which framed the Constitution of the United States,—a versatile and responsible series of occupations, enough to furnish alone the materials of a noble and distinguished life, and yet constituting but a single phase of the illustrious career of Franklin.

The silent dignity with which he was content, amid the inevitable attacks, and even insults, misrepresentations, and sneers, which attend success in every path and superiority of whatever kind; is one of the most admirable traits of Franklin's character, and one that was generously acknowledged by his opponents when the tide of prejudice and animosity ebbed. He met the caprices of delegated authority, the jealousy of his colleagues, the injustice of his political antagonists, the tirade of the Solicitor-General of the Crown, the attempts at bribery and intimidation, with a serene and un demonstrative resolution. "My rule is," he said, "to go straight forward in doing what appears to me right at the time, leaving the consequences to Providence. I wish every kind of prosperity to my friends, and forgive my enemies."

If there were no blemishes in this picture, it would scarcely be human; but the blemishes are casual, and like flitting shadows, of vague import, while through and above them the bland and sagacious, the honest and wise lineaments tranquilly beam. The spirit of calculation, the narrowness of prudence, the limits of a matter-of-fact vision, the gallantries tolerated by the social standard of the times, the absence of that impulse and *abandon*, that generous and ardent mood which seems inseparable from the noblest and most aspiring natures, sometimes render Franklin too exclusively a provident utilitarian and a creature of the immediate, to satisfy our loftiest ideal of character or our sympathies with genius as spontaneously and unconsciously manifest. Gossip has bequeathed hints of amours that derogate somewhat from the gravity of the sage; partisan spite has whispered of a too selfish estimate of the chances of expediency; and there are those who find in the doctrine and practice of the American philosopher an undue estimate of thrift, and an illustration of the creed that man "lives by bread alone," which chills enthusiasm and subdues praise; but when we contemplate the amount of enduring good he achieved, the value of his scientific discoveries, the uprightness, self-devotion, and consistency of the man, the loyal activity of the patriot, and the interests he promoted, the habits he exemplified, the truths he made vital, and the prosperity he initiated, our sense of obligation, our admiration of his practical wisdom, and our love of his genial usefulness, merge critical objection in honor and gratitude. What is the flippant sarcasm of the queer Madame du Barry, that he ate asparagus like a savage, to intellectual Hume's assertion, "America has sent us many good things, gold, silver, sugar, tobacco, indigo, &c.,—but you are the first philosopher"? If, on the one hand, his having embraced Voltaire in the presence of the French Academy be cited as proof of *persiflage*, on the other, his frank expression of religious convictions to Dr. Stiles evidences a deliberate faith in things unseen and eternal. If the graphic pen of Mrs. Grant, in depicting the candid graces of colonial life in America, attributes the subsequent devotion to gain to the economical maxims of Franklin, the sacred opinion of Washington affords a more just view of the legitimate rank their author held in the affections of his countrymen. "If to be venerated for benevolence, if to be admired for talents, if to be esteemed for patriotism, if to be beloved for philanthropy, can gratify the human mind, you must have the pleasing consolation to know that you have not lived in vain."

It must be confessed that the spiritual was not developed in Franklin's nature in proportion to the scientific element, and, as an inevitable consequence, religion was a grand social interest, or at most a private conviction, rather than a matter of profession or of sentiment; It is probable that an early, and not auspicious, familiarity with the conflicts of sects, confirmed his aversion to a merely doctrinal faith. He was conversant, in his native town and in his adopted home, respectively with the two extremes of prescriptive belief and strongly marked individualism, as displayed by the Puritans and the Quakers, and found enough of vital piety and moral worth in both to emancipate him from superstitious reliance on a positive creed. But there is ample evidence that he recognized those broad and eternal truths which lie at the basis of all religion. He seems to have profoundly felt his responsibleness to a higher than earthly power; everywhere he beheld a wise and beneficent Creator, in the operation of material and moral laws; always he sought the traces of Divine wisdom in the universe and in events. We find him advising his daughter to rely more upon prayer than sermons; recognizing the hand of Providence in the destinies of his country; moving a resolution for devotional services in the Convention that framed the Constitution; preparing an abridgment of the ritual; and, in his last days, enjoying those devotional poems which have so long endeared the name of Watts. It is not so much the comparative silence of Franklin on religious, or rather sectarian questions, which has given rise to a vague notion of his scepticism and indifference, as the fact that he acknowledged deistical opinions in youth, subsequently worked almost exclusively in the sphere of material interests, and was intimately associated with the infidel philosophers of France. Other affinities than those of speculative opinions, however, allied him to a class of men whose names have become watchwords of unbelief; literature and science, government and philosophy, were themes of mutual investigation common to them and him; and if, in order to attest their sense of his intelligence and republicanism, they placed his bust upon the altar of the Jacobin Club with those of Brutus, Helvetius, Mirabeau, and Rousseau, it was chiefly because, like those friends of popular freedom and social reform, he had proved himself an independent thinker and a noble devotee of human progress, and because, to the vague though eloquent sentiment of social amelioration kindled by Jean Jacques, his practical sagacity had given actual embodiment. Few men, indeed, have lived, whose time, mind, and resources were more wisely and conscientiously directed to the elevation of society, the enlightenment of the mass, and the improvement of human condition. He was indisputably one of the greatest benefactors of mankind.

Except in a scientific direction, however, it must be acknowledged that the spirit of Franklin's precepts and theories is not adapted to beguile us "along the line of infinite desires"; his wisdom was applicable to the immediate and the essential in daily and common life; he dealt chiefly with details; he advocated habits, ideas, and methods based on positive utility,—success as derived from patient and gradual but determined action, minute observation, careful practice, rather than from broad generalization, daring achievement, or the imagination and enthusiasm which so often prove intuitive means of triumph, which are indispensable in art, and constitute the difference between the process of genius and that of talent. There is nothing certain, he used to say, but death and taxes; happiness he believed the aggregate of small satisfactions, rather than the instant realization of a great hope; and fortune he regarded as the reward of assiduity and prudence, rather than of prosperous adventure or of daring enterprise. Compared with the ephemeral impulses, the obscure theories, the visionary and uncertain principles in vogue elsewhere, and before and since his day, there was incalculable value in his maxims and example. But it would be gross injustice to the versatile and comprehensive nature of man, to the aspirations of exalted minds, to the facts of spiritual philosophy, to the needs of immortal instincts, to the faith of the soul, the annals of genius, and the possible elevation of society, to admit that he supplied more than the material basis of human progress or the external conditions of individual development. What the ballast is to the ship, the trellis to the vine, health of body to activity of mind, that was Franklin's social philosophy to human welfare,—all-important as a means, inadequate as a final provision,—a method of insuring the co-operation of natural aids, and fostering intrinsic resources, whereby the higher elements may freely do their work, and man, sustained by favorable circumstances, and unhampered by want, neglect, and improvidence, may the more certainly enjoy, aspire, love, conceive, expand, and labor according to the noblest inspiration and the grandest scope of his nature and his destiny.

If we compare the life of Franklin, as a whole, with that of other renowned philosophers, we find that the isolated self-devotion, the egotism and vanity, which too often derogate from the interest and dignity of their characters as men, do not mar the unity of the tranquil, honest, and benign disposition which lends a gracious charm to the American philosopher. Archimedes invented warlike machines to overthrow the invaders of his country; but his heart did not warm like Franklin's, nor did his brain work to devise the means of elevating his poor and ignorant fellow-citizens in the scale of knowledge and self-government. Newton proclaimed vast and universal laws; but there was in his temper a morbid tenacity of personal fame, beside which the disinterested zeal of Franklin is beautiful. The scope of Franklin's research was limited in comparison with that of Humboldt; but, unsustained, like that noble savant, by royal patronage, he sacrificed his love of science for half his lifetime to the cause of his country. Arago excelled him in the power of rhetorical eulogy of the votaries of their common pursuits; but while the French philosopher spoke eloquently to a learned Academy, the American had a people for his audience, and disseminated among them truths vital to their progress and happiness, in a diction so clear, direct, and convincing, that it won them simultaneously to the love of science and the practice of wisdom.

When he was released from official care, his mental activity, though unremitted, was singularly genial; and to this characteristic of the philosophical temperament we attribute his self-possession, rational enjoyment, and consequent longevity; for, of all pursuits, that which has for its aim general knowledge and the discovery and application of truth, while it raises the mind above casual disturbance, supplies it with an object at once unimpassioned and attractive, serene yet absorbing, a motive in social intercourse and a resource in seclusion. Just before Thierry's recent death, although he was long a martyr to disease, he remarked to a friend: "Had I to begin my life again, I would again set out in the path which has led me to where I am. Blind and suffering, without hope and without intermission, I may say, without giving testimony which can be suspected, there is something in this world better than material pleasure, better than fortune, better than health itself,—and this is attachment to science." Of this good Franklin was a large partaker, and we cannot but imagine the delight and sympathy with which he would have followed the miraculous progress of the modern sciences and of those ideas of which he beheld but the dawn. "I have sometimes almost wished," he writes, "it had been my destiny to be born two or three centuries hence; for inventions and improvements are prolific, and beget more of their kind." Had he lived a little more than another fifty years, he would have seen the mode of popular education initiated by the Spectator, expanded into the elaborate Review, the brilliant Magazine, the Household Words, and Scientific Journals of the present day; the rude hand-press upon which he arranged the miniature "form" of the New England Courant, transformed into electrotyped cylinders worked by steam and throwing off thirty thousand printed sheets an hour; the thin almanac, with its proverbs and calendar, grown to a plethoric volume, rich in astronomical lore and the statistics of a continent; the vessel dependent on the caprice of the winds and an imperfect science of navigation, self-impelled with a pre-calculated rate of speed and by the most authentic charts; and the subtile fluid that his prescience caught up and directed safely by a metallic rod, sent along leagues of wire, the silent and instant messenger of the world. With what keen interest would he have followed Davy, with his safety-lamp, into the treacherous mine; accompanied Fulton in his first steam voyage up the Hudson; watched Daguerre as he made his sun-pictures; seen the vineyards along the Ohio attest his prophetic advocacy of the Rhenish grape-culture; heard Miller discourse of the "Old Red Sandstone," Morse explain the Telegraph, or Maury the tidal laws! Chemistry—almost born since his day—would open a new and wonderful realm to his consciousness; the Cosmos of Humboldt, draw his entranced gaze down every vista of natural science, as if to reveal at a glance a programme of all the great and beautiful secrets of the universe; and the reckless enterprise and mad extravagance of his prosperous country, elicit more emphatic warnings than Poor Richard breathed of old.

There have been many writers who, in simple and forcible English, by arguments drawn from pure common-sense and enlivened by wit or eloquence, interpreted political truth, and vastly aided the education of the people. But in the case of Franklin, this practical service of authorship was immeasurably extended and enforced by the *prestige* of his electrical discoveries, by the dawning greatness and original principles of the country of which he was so prominent a representative, and by the extraordinary circumstances of his times, when great social and political questions were brought to new and popular tests, and made the homely scientific republican an oracle in the most luxurious and artificial of despotic courts. When the intricate tactics of rival armies have been exhausted, the able general has recourse to a *coup de main*, and effects by simple bravery what stratagem failed to win. When a question has been discussed until its primary significance is most forgotten in a multitude of side-issues, the true orator suddenly brings to a focus the scattered elements of the theme, and, by a clear and emphatic statement, reproduces its normal features, and, through a bold analysis, places it in the open light of day, and heralds the bewildered council to a final decision. In like manner, when vital principles of government and society have been complicated by interest, speculation, and misfortune, when men have grown impatient of formulas and ceremonies and aspire to realities, he who in his speech, dress, habits, writings, manners, and achievements—or in the exponent of all these, his character—represents most truly the normal instincts, average common sense, and practicable good of his race, is welcomed as an exemplar, an authority, and a representative. Such was the American philosopher at once in the eyes of a newly organized and self-dependent nation, and in those of an ancient people, in its transition from an outgrown to an experimental *régime*.

He took his degree in the school of humanity, before the technical honor was awarded by Oxford, Edinburgh, and the Royal Society. It was this pre-eminent distinction which led Sydney Smith to playfully threaten his daughter, "I will disinherit you if you do not admire everything written by Franklin"; and which enshrines his memory in the popular heart, makes him still the annual hero of the printer's festival, associates his name with townships and counties, inns and ships, societies and periodicals,—with all the arrangements and objects of civilization that aim to promote the enlightenment and convenience of man. The press and the lightning-rod, the almanac, the postage-stamp, and the free-school medal, attest his usefulness and renown; maxims of practical wisdom more numerous than Don Quixote's garrulous squire cited, gave birth under his hand to a current proverbial philosophy; and his effigy is, therefore, the familiar symbol of independence, of popular education, and self-culture. Those shrewd and kindly features, and that patriarchal head, are as precious to the humble as to the learned; and in every land and every language, Franklin, through the prestige of a brilliant discovery in science and the fame of a wise patriot, typifies the "greatest good of the greatest number." Mignot rightly defines him as "gifted with the spirit of observation and discovery"; Davy calls his inductive power felicitous; Paul Jones augured success in his desperate sea-fight from the "Bon Homme Richard"; and the memorable epigraph of Turgot is the acknowledged motto of his escutcheon:—

"Eripuit coelo fulmen, sceptrumque tyrannis."

MATTHEW ARNOLD
"FRANKLIN'S HUMANITY" (1869)

Culture directs our attention to the current in human affairs, and to its continual working, and will not let us rivet our faith upon any one man and his doings. It makes us see, not only his good side, but also how much in him was of necessity limited and transient; nay, it even feels a pleasure, a sense of an increased freedom and of an ampler future, in so doing. I remember, when I was under the influence of a mind to which I feel the greatest obligations; the mind of a man who was the very incarnation of sanity and clear sense, a man the most considerable, it seems to me, whom

America has yet produced,—Benjamin Franklin,—I remember the relief with which, after long feeling the sway of Franklin's imperturbable common-sense, I came upon a project of his for a new version of the Book of Job, to replace the old version; the style of which, says Franklin, has become obsolete, and thence less agreeable. "I give," he continues, "a few verses, which may serve as a sample of the kind of version I would recommend." We all recollect the famous verse in our translation: "Then Satan answered the Lord and said: 'Doth Job fear God for nought?'" Franklin makes this: "Does Your Majesty imagine that Job's good conduct is the effect of mere personal attachment and affection?" I well remember how when first I read that, I drew a deep breath of relief, and said to myself: "After all, there is a stretch of humanity beyond Franklin's victorious good sense!"

MARK TWAIN
"THE LATE BENJAMIN FRANKLIN" (1870)

["Never put off till to-morrow what you can do day after to-morrow just
    as well."—B. F.]

This party was one of those persons whom they call Philosophers. He was twins, being born simultaneously in two different houses in the city of Boston. These houses remain unto this day, and have signs upon them worded in accordance with the facts. The signs are considered well enough to have, though not necessary, because the inhabitants point out the two birth-places to the stranger anyhow, and sometimes as often as several times in the same day. The subject of this memoir was of a vicious disposition, and early prostituted his talents to the invention of maxims and aphorisms calculated to inflict suffering upon the rising generation of all subsequent ages. His simplest acts, also, were contrived with a view to their being held up for the emulation of boys for ever—boys who might otherwise have been happy. It was in this spirit that he became the son of a soap-boiler, and probably for no other reason than that the efforts of all future boys who tried to be anything might be looked upon with suspicion unless they were the sons of soap-boilers. With a malevolence which is without parallel in history, he would work all day, and then sit up nights, and let on to be studying algebra by the light of a smouldering fire, so that all other boys might have to do that also or else have Benjamin Franklin thrown up to them. Not satisfied with these proceedings, he had a fashion of living wholly on bread and water, and studying astronomy at meal time—a thing which has brought affliction to millions of boys since, whose fathers had read Franklin's pernicious biography.

His maxims were full of animosity toward boys. Nowadays a boy cannot follow out a single natural instinct without tumbling over some of those everlasting aphorisms and hearing from Franklin on the spot. If he buys two cents' worth of peanuts, his father says, "Remember what Franklin has said, my son—'A groat a day's a penny a year;'" and the comfort is all gone out of those peanuts. If he wants to spin his top when he has done work, his father quotes, "Procrastination is the thief of time." If he does a virtuous action, he never gets any thing for it, because "Virtue is its own reward." And that boy is hounded to death and robbed of his natural rest, because Franklin said once, in one of his inspired flights of malignity—

"Early to bed and early to rise
Makes a man healthy and wealthy and wise."

As if it were any object to a boy to be healthy and wealthy and wise on such terms. The sorrow that that maxim has cost me through my parents' experimenting on me with it, tongue cannot tell. The legitimate result is my present state of general debility, indigence, and mental aberration. My parents used to have me up before nine o'clock in the morning, sometimes, when I was a boy. If they had let me take my natural rest, where would I have been now? Keeping store, no doubt, and respected by all.

And what an adroit old adventurer the subject of this memoir was! In order to get a chance to fly his kite on Sunday he used to hang a key on the string and let on to be fishing for lightning. And a guileless public would go home chirping about the "wisdom" and the "genius" of the hoary Sabbath-breaker. If anybody caught him playing "mumble-peg" by himself, after the age of sixty, he would immediately appear to be ciphering out how the grass grew—as if it was any of his business. My grandfather knew him well, and he says Franklin was always fixed—always ready. If a body, during his old age, happened on him unexpectedly when he was catching flies, or making mud pies, or sliding on a cellar-door, he would immediately look wise, and rip out a maxim, and walk off with his nose in the air and his cap turned wrong side before, trying to appear absent-minded and eccentric. He was a hard lot.

He invented a stove that would smoke your head off in four hours by the clock. One can see the almost devilish satisfaction he took in it by his giving it his name.

He was always proud of telling how he entered Philadelphia for the first time, with nothing in the world but two shillings in his pocket and four rolls of bread under his arm. But really, when you come to examine it critically, it was nothing. Anybody could have done it.

To the subject of this memoir belongs the honor of recommending the army to go back to bows and arrows in place of bayonets and muskets. He observed, with his customary force, that the bayonet was very well under some circumstances, but that he doubted whether it could be used with accuracy at a long range.

Benjamin Franklin did a great many notable things for his country, and made her young name to be honored in many lands as the mother of such a son. It is not the idea of this memoir to ignore that or cover it up. No; the simple idea of it is to snub those pretentious maxims of his, which he worked up with a great show of originality out of truisms that had become wearisome platitudes as early as the dispersion from Babel; and also to snub his stove, and his military inspirations, his unseemly endeavor to make himself conspicuous when he entered Philadelphia, and his flying his kite and fooling away his time in all sorts of such ways when he ought to have been foraging for soap-fat, or constructing candles. I merely desired to do away with somewhat of the prevalent calamitous idea among heads of families that Franklin acquired his great genius by working for nothing, studying by moonlight, and getting up in the night instead of waiting till morning like a Christian; and that this programme, rigidly inflicted, will make a Franklin of every father's fool. It is time these gentlemen were finding out that these execrable eccentricities of instinct and conduct are only the *evidences* of genius, not the *creators* of it. I wish I had been the father of my parents long enough to make them comprehend this truth, and thus prepare them to let their son have an easier time of it. When I was a child I had to boil soap, notwithstanding my father was wealthy, and I had to get up early and study geometry at breakfast, and peddle my own poetry, and do everything just as Franklin did, in the solemn hope that I would be a Franklin some day. And here I am.

E.P. Powell
"A Study of Benjamin Franklin" (1893)

Two men stand pre-eminent in history in the middle of the eighteenth century as intellectual forces shaping events preliminary to the establishment of our republic. These were Benjamin Franklin and Thomas Paine. Colonial familiarity has handed down one of these as Ben, the other as Tom, as the older Adams was also Sam. It is not easy to habilitate Ben, in the language of Bancroft, as the greatest diplomatist of the eighteenth century, or Tom as the man who precipitated the Declaration of Independence, and carried the armies through the crisis of almost total despair. Yet it is true that during our Revolution, if never at any other period, the pen was mightier than the sword. The creation of the republic was not a possibility by any force of arms that we possessed, or, indeed, possible at all by any other power than that of reason and diplomacy.

The difficulty of a study of Franklin is intensified by the fact that he was the most-sided man that ever appeared in our history, if not, indeed, in history at all. To be comprehended we must know him, not only as diplomatist, but as the foremost scientist in the world; a most remarkable financier and business manager; an author whose work has a fixed place among the higher classics; a philosopher who found rank with Voltaire and Leibnitz; as Kant expressed it, "the Prometheus of modern days." John Adams, whose jealousy was irrepressible, wrote from Paris that Franklin's reputation was "more universal than that of Newton." Nor do we find our task minified by the fact that Franklin was a man as simple as he was great, as childlike as he was philosophic. Like Lincoln, he loved a joke, but, unlike Lincoln, he put his jokes into state papers. It has been hinted that for this reason no great historic document, of the period was intrusted to his pen. His economy was not only political, it was domestic; and in "Poor Richard" popular estimation cannot easily recognize the controlling mind of the world's affairs and the builder of democracy. He wrote almanacs instead of constitutions. He was as marked for his toleration in theology as for his democracy in statecraft. In both he was clearsighted and even prophetic, far beyond his age.

The famous scene in the Academy of Sciences, when he and Voltaire were brought forward dramatically before the most eminent scholars of Europe, and embraced, as emblematic of the wedding of two worlds in the cause of freedom, was far from being the embrace of men of similar aim and spirit. The little, weazened, bright-eyed poet of Verney hated the old; the rotund and serene American loved the new. Voltaire flourished in the dust of destroyed opinions; Franklin sought to build a system of morals that might be universal for enlightened peoples. His favorite scheme, projected in early life, worked at in his prime, and never quite given over till age enfeebled him, was to write "The Art of Virtue," a system of morals; a plan which seems only now about to be worked out and engrafted on our scheme of both secular and religious education. Shrewd and masterly as a business man, he saw also that underneath all human progress must lie the power of society to construct character.

But it is my present purpose to study Franklin only as a diplomatist—the man whose pen and tongue matched the sword of Washington. Prerequisite to such a study it is necessary to comprehend his heredity, both in family and in commonwealth. The not over-generous soil of New England had set the religious refugees of Europe upon new lines of evolution. The Puritans, who had developed the most marvellous other-worldliness, were compelled by nature to develop as absorbing worldliness. Equally good at praying and at bargaining, they learned to make virtues of necessities and piety of economics. They moralized over corn-huskings, and said ten minutes' grace over a salted mackerel with pumpkin pie. Thanksgiving was a happy commingling of stomach and "heart," wherein chicken pie was made to harmonize with two-hour sermons and serious reflections about a day of judgment. Yet their digestion was good. This was the sort of heredity that Franklin received—wise, penny-wise, and pious after the excellent manner of the Mayflower. Being a New Englander, whatever else he did, he never failed to preach. He could not escape the controlling conviction that the chief end of life is salvation; but in his creed, salvation pertained less to the soul than to the pocket. He married righteousness to political economy. His position as a diplomat was always shaded by his character as a philosopher. His home-spun suit and simplicity were invaluable adjuncts to his winning logic.

We must also ascribe to heredity the extremely constructive ability of Franklin. It was an era of "off-clearings" in general. Mediaevalism, since Erasmus and Luther, had been gaping open in great seams. Feudalism had yielded to monarchy, and monarchy was on trial. Voltaire had gone a rifle's range further than Calvin, and Roger Williams' soul was in the ascendant with William Pitt. Vague ideas of democracy and human equality were abroad. Largely the period was destructive, but Anglo-Saxon sturdiness has always preferred construction. Franklin was from first to last a builder. He planned a "Union of the Colonies" and anticipated a new ecclesiasticism, with equal facility. He invented the first American stove, and set up the first lightning rod. He founded a philosophical society, and the University of Pennsylvania. He was equally successful as printer, editor, and author, making the press to be the foremost power in America. He was brilliant as a conversationalist; and as a letter writer, he was one of the most renowned in as age devoted to wit and philosophy in correspondence. He was no greater as a writer than as a diplomatist, and in neither of these ways surpassed his achievements in science. His early life was full of force, badly or unequally directed; and for a time he seemed about to become a social pest, dissolute and wasted. But out of the chaos of contending influences he emerged, in due time, with power still to lead the age in every department of thought, and to anticipate a future age in matters both of public and private importance—in education, in research, in toleration, and in constructive institutions of government.

To comprehend Franklin as a patriot and diplomatist, we must also understand the exact stage of the contention for popular rights. The Magna Charta of 1200 had rested till 1700, before being followed by the Bill of Rights. But ecclesiastical reformation on the continent had exercised a vital reaction on the state. Democracy was in the air, but England and all Europe sincerely believed in the divine right of kings and of the aristocracy. Events only led or compelled the American colonies to reject the idea of *Dei gratia* and stand for the principle *vox populi, vox Dei.* At the opening of the contention between the colonies and the parent country, there was no thought of rebelling against monarchy. Curiously the grievance of the Americans was wholly with the representative body of government, the Parliament.

"You are not our representatives," said Sam Adams. "We have no representation anywhere in government," said Otis. Lord Mansfield answered: "No one is represented in special, but only in general. You are virtually represented by every member of Parliament." "The Americans are right," said Pitt and Camden; but when it came to vote, there were but five with Pitt. The English doctrine remains to this day "virtual representation." The American doctrine soon became "actual representation," and without that no power to levy taxes. And this doctrine of actual representation is still leavening society, and is at the bottom of the demand for female suffrage. Those who dance—must pay for the fiddler, and those who pay may dance.

Franklin, while on his first mission to England, was for a long time very warm in his good-will for George III. "The sovereignty of the crown," he said, "I understand. The sovereignty of the British legislature out of Britain I do not understand. We are free subjects of the king; and fellow-subjects of his dominions are not sovereigns over fellow-subjects in any other part."

The American people were slow to become disloyal; they were hot for a principle of government before they were able to become anti-royalists. To the last a large minority remained monarchists, and over one hundred thousand left the country rather than forsake the king. Even the establishment of a republic did not create a universal conviction of democracy. Fisher Ames wrote: "A democracy cannot last. Its nature ordains that it shall change into a military despotism, as of all governments the most prone to shift its head and the slowest to mend its vices." "Hamilton believed," says Morris, "that our administration would be enfeebled progressively at each new election, and become at last contemptible." Who shall wonder? Who shall blame? The problem of popular government was novel beyond precedent, and it involved the vastest evolution since society was organized. To trust the people, or not to trust the people—that was what must be settled. Franklin, when at last he saw that the royal power was involved in the contest with Britain, took his position with the people, and so preceded the party which Jefferson soon headed against the aristocrats, and succeeded in placing in permanent control of the country.

The great Saxon race at this point divided asunder in their contest against prerogative. Led by circumstances unforeseen, the Americans developed a system of popular government resting entirely on the good faith of the people. Out of the seething sprang, as by inspiration, the principle enunciated in the Declaration of Independence—that all men are born with equal rights. The war closed with English people still strong in the idea of inequality of rights by birth; while the United States has based its prosperity on the opposite doctrine. Carlyle summed up British sentiment when he wrote, "Democracy will prevail when men believe the vote of Judas as good as that of Jesus Christ." But Wendell Phillips answered, "The right to choose your governor rests on precisely the same foundation as the right to choose your own religion."

Franklin believed in diplomacy as stronger than the sword. His own history gave him much warrant for this. He was first sent abroad by the state of Pennsylvania, in the popular struggle to compel the successors of William Penn, the proprietaries of the colony, to pay their share of the taxes. These dignitaries lived in England, and drew their annual revenue of two hundred thousand dollars from the vast American estate granted to Penn, but refused to pay taxes on their private lands. They appointed the governor, and the people selected their assemblymen; but the governor could get his salary only by vote of the Assembly. It became a fair field for contention, and not seldom a deadlock.

In 1757 Franklin was selected to cross the ocean, in order to seek redress from Parliament, also to induce the king to resume the province of Pennsylvania as his own. So it happened that the very nature of this errand started out the colonial diplomatist as a royalist. This visit of Franklin to the old country was exceedingly exasperating, for he stood almost alone, representing an insignificant colony which was looked upon purely as British property. He had no prestige, no powerful nation to back him, no friends to assist. Looked at from this standpoint, the result was the most remarkable achievement of his career as a representative; for after vexatious delays and gross insults, he succeeded in bringing about very nearly what Pennsylvania desired. The king and Parliament emphatically sided with the proprietaries, bluntly suggesting that the real aim of the colonists was "to establish a democracy in place of his majesty's government." But at the very last Lord Mansfield took Franklin aside, and entered into a personal agreement with him that the demand of the colonists should be granted, on certain conditions, to which Franklin readily agreed.

The result was so remarkable that it is not surprising that Franklin became a still more devout devotee of diplomacy. It was a work of three years; but then it was worth three years' time that the people should triumph. When be reached home the citizens of Philadelphia met him with a warm welcome; the Assembly voted him fifteen thousand dollars, to cover his expenses; and England appointed his son governor of New Jersey.

Franklin's second mission to England was by appointment of the same colony, and on a like errand. He was commissioned to urge a total change of government from a proprietary to a royal. This time three hundred mounted citizens escorted him down the river to his ship. He reached England at the close of 1764. It was the very time when the British Parliament began to crowd colonial taxation, in order to aid in covering its expenses during the war with France. The culmination was the Stamp Act. Whatever excuse the English people had for their course toward the colonies, the latter saw none; and the majority of the people would consider none. Otis, Sam Adams, and Patrick Henry raised a storm that seemed to Franklin to be a tempest in a teapot. He was too cool-headed to sympathize with rash action. He believed with all his nature in diplomacy, and this he undertook at first by uniting in compromise propositions.

But the Philadelphians soon gave him to understand that diplomacy must be turned in another direction. They mobbed his family, and burned him in effigy. He at once shifted his position. The mission on which he was sent was so insignificant that it was lost sight of. He became, by general consent, representative of all the American colonies. The people of the provinces were in dead earnest; that was clear. They ceased to eat lamb, so that more wool might be grown, and home-spun clothes be made and worn. They would retaliate on English trade. The great question was now shaping itself, "No taxation without representation." But you are represented, answered Parliament; we all represent you. Pitt sided with the colonies, saying: "The Americans are not the bastards of England, but the sons." "Virtual representation is a contemptible idea."

In February, 1766, Franklin was summoned by Parliament to give testimony as to the state and temper of the colonies, and what measures of pacification would be adopted. He had now developed into an uncompromising leader of the patriots, but he had no thought of independence or of war. His examination was one of the most able and brilliant in history. One passage only will suffice to give the logic and spirit of his position: "The Parliament of Great Britain has not, never had, and of right never can have, without consent given, either before or after, power to make laws of sufficient force to bind the subjects of America in any case whatever, and particularly in taxation. We are free subjects of the king, and fellow-subjects of his dominions are not sovereigns over fellow-subjects in any other part." Still he remained royalist.

In 1769 he wrote, "I hope nothing that has happened or that may happen will diminish in the least our loyalty to our sovereign, or affection for his nation in general." In 1770 he counselled the colonies to be true to the excellent king. "I can scarce conceive a king of better disposition." So far he is a true diplomatist, believing the tongue more powerful than the sword. But soon he writes, "Between you and me, the late measures have been, I suspect, very much the king's." Meanwhile the Stamp Act was abolished, mainly by the influence of Franklin. The citizens of Philadelphia had a large barge built, forty feet long, which they named Franklin, and carried it in a great procession, firing salutes from it as they marched. By 1770 Franklin was agent, by formal appointment, of not only Pennsylvania, but Massachusetts, Georgia, and New Jersey.

The Stamp Act out of the way, it looked for a time as if the ferment would end, and harmony be restored. Franklin stood steadily as peacemaker, calmly advising both parties. He complained that he suffered on both sides—in England being suspected of being too much an American, in America of being too much an Englishman. A grand triumph came to encourage him. Earl Hillsborough was secretary of state for the colonies, under Lord North. He insulted our agent from the outset, and did it grossly. Franklin presented a plan to the Parliament for the creation of a great frontier to the west of the colonies, which should consist of twenty-three millions of acres, these to be granted by England to America. Hillsborough opposed the measure hotly; but he was worsted in his plans, and, flying into a rage, resigned. This raised Franklin considerably in popular estimation; and he was called on to nominate the earl's successor, which he did.

In 1775 began the quarrel in Massachusetts with Governor Hutchinson. The colonial assemblies were growing quite independent. Franklin advised Parliament not to hear too much; that in reality America was loyal. "It is words only," he said. He had constantly urged that, in his opinion, "If the colonies were restored to the state they were in before the Stamp Act, they would be satisfied." As late as 1774 he was still diplomatically arguing that the war was only a ministerial one, and could be stopped by wise parliamentary and cabinet action; but he began to confess that, if he were an Englishman, he could not see what step might be taken to diminish the mischief. He was evidently in his mind convinced the day was passed for healing the bitterness. He was ready for bloodshed, if it must come—a man of terrible decision and undying hate, when hope for honorable treatment was past. As far back as 1766, when the question of the Stamp Act was still open, he had said: "I have some little property in America. I will freely spend nineteen shillings in the pound to defend my right of giving or refusing the other shilling. And after all, if I cannot defend that right, I can retire cheerfully with my family into the boundless woods of America, which are sure to afford freedom and subsistence to any man who can bait a hook or pull a trigger." David Crockett was hardly the model after which Franklin would have chosen to conform his life; but that he had Crockett's stuff in him for all emergencies, is beyond question. But his plan was still of the Seward, Union-preserving sort. He would have the colonies refuse to buy a pound of tea, or whatever else involved payment of odious taxes. "If we continue firm, and persist in the non-consumption agreement, this adverse ministry cannot possibly last another year." He thought a cup of tea, the cost of which helped to pay the salaries of tyrants, would choke any decent American."

It was well we had exactly this man at that time in that place. The colonies did not need precipitating before due time into war. They were steadily being consolidated and unified. A national spirit was taking the place of the colonial. But the day of action was close at hand. Troops had been sent over to Boston. Franklin bitterly complained of this. "Americans advised it," replied an official. "It cannot be," said Franklin. "I will prove it," was the reply; and in a few days a bundle of letters from Governor Hutchinson and Lieutenant-Governor Oliver was handed to Franklin. These he sent to America for examination but not for publication, as he asserted; but the recipient did publish them. This incensed the British government beyond measure.

In January, 1774, Franklin was cited to appear before the Lords of the Committee for Plantation Affairs. I suppose a more cowardly assault on a man unable to defend himself was never made by a government; more detestable abuse was never poured over a man who deserved none of it. Dr. Priestley, who was present, said, "The real object of the court was to insult Dr. Franklin." Franklin showed not a sign of rage or even indignation, but he stood calmly unmoved and let them bark on. Only when he went home, he put away the coat he had on, and never wore it again until he sat as commissioner to sign the treaty that confessed the independence of the United States.

The king now tumbled him out of his office of postmaster-general of the United States, and there was a growl of treason raised throughout England. He was warned that if a blow should be struck in New England he would be doubtless seized. Lord Chatham stood firmly by him, as did Sir Thomas Walpole. Evidently affairs had passed all limits of peace, although war was not yet formally declared.

From this hour the diplomat became as bitter a foe as England ever had, and the most dangerous. Had the British ministers been large enough to be both honest and honorable, and made fast friendship with Franklin, the war of the Revolution would have been a failure. They did undertake to bribe him, as they had undertaken before; but they mistook the man. In March, 1775, he started for home, having first handed to Mr. Walpole a document in which, as agent of the colonies, he demanded for them, of the British government, reparation for injuries done by the blockade of Boston, and closing thus: "I give notice that satisfaction will probably one day be demanded for all the injuries that may be done and suffered in the execution of the fisheries act; depriving the colonies of just rights; and that the injustice of the proceeding is likely to give such umbrage to all the colonies that in no future war, either a man or a shilling will be obtained from any of them till full satisfaction be made as aforesaid." This was as good as a declaration of war. Walpole hustled him out of England as quickly as possible, to prevent his arrest.

Franklin was drilled well by the English people, not only to hate them, but to act as the most skilful of diplomatists against them in case of war. Lexington and Concord were fought while he was on mid-ocean. He landed, to find the two countries locked in a struggle of blood. Washington was in command, and the Provincial Congress was assembled. Franklin was at once elected a delegate. A nation was to be born. Everything was to be done *de novo*. The air was full, not only of independence, but of revolution. Democracy was a problem. There was not even a cradle for the government, whenever born; neither money nor financial system. Many hung back from absolute independence. Pennsylvania formed a separate government. New England threatened a league by herself. The confederacy that followed was loose at every joint; not strong enough to have endured a year of peace; barely held together by war. But everything was redeemed by that magnificent document, the Declaration of Independence—a glorious inheritance for a free people; a standard about which the sentiment of sixty-five millions of Americans still rally; the proclamation of philosophers defying brute force. It was at this point that Franklin and Jefferson first became cooperators and friends.

Lord Howe arrived in July. He wished to renew diplomatic discussion. He was a friend of Franklin in England, and a conciliator. Franklin was allowed to reply. He closed by saying: "I know your great motive, in coming hither, was the hope of being instrumental in a reconciliation; and I believe that when you find that impossible, on any terms given you to propose, you will relinquish so odious a command, and return to a more honorable private station."

Now followed as fine a bit of negotiation as any Franklin was ever engaged in, and it called for all his wit and versatility. It was concluded by Congress to send delegates to meet Lord Howe and his brother, who claimed plenipotentiary powers for treaty. At the conference Howe was conciliatory and polite as he was generous. He wished, however, to treat "back of the step of independency." Franklin answered: "Forces have been sent out, and towns have been burnt. We cannot expect happiness under the domination of Great Britain. All former attachments are obliterated."

It was critical that Lord Howe should be met in some manner by Congress, for the land was full of Tories. All the patriots had not yet signed, even in spirit, a declaration of independence. It was equally important that no yielding of one jot of ground should be apparent. The conference was held; it was over with. There was no more diplomatic danger from smooth tongues and honeyed pens. Bayonets and bullets at last became a necessity.

France and England were natural enemies; it followed that France and America became artificial friends. In September of 1776, Franklin, then seventy years of age, was despatched as ambassador to the Court at Versailles. The English raged and threatened war if he was received; but the French welcomed him with a frenzy of enthusiasm. They praised him from top to toe. They admired even his weaknesses. His pictures were everywhere. The situation was one of extraordinary delicacy. One injudicious word or mistaken step, and he would have spoiled all. But he never made a mistake. He was neither too fast nor too slow. He was cool, cautious, and yet frank and prompt. I believe the very secret of his success as a diplomatist, however, was honesty. His versatility enabled him to read men and adapt himself to circumstances; but he was felt to be, above all, adherent to principles. His power of generalization had been shown in science; it was equally remarkable in politics. He foresaw the far-reaching consequences of events. He wrote that America was sure of receiving an enormous access of families as soon as independence should be established. "Our cause is the cause of all mankind. It is a glorious task assigned to us by Providence."

Precisely what Franklin did not do in his French embassage would be more easily stated than what he did do. A treaty of alliance was of course the object, in brief, of his commission. But it was the policy of the French government to aid by comfort instead of open effort and direct treaty offensive.

In 1777 Burgoyne was captured. Austin was despatched from America to tell Franklin. Now followed the strangest episode of the Revolution. Franklin forwarded this same messenger over the channel, and he was actually received by men high in rank. He was domesticated with the Earl of Shelburne; introduced to the Prince of Wales, and dined by a large Parliamentary "opposition." He did excellent service. January, 1778, Mr. Gerard informed Franklin that the government had concluded to form a treaty of friendship and commercial alliance with the colonies. Exactly as the news of the surrender of Burgoyne broke upon England, came also intimations of the French treaty.

Then followed one of the most astounding periods of diplomacy ever recorded. Lord North sent word to Franklin that if he would come over to England, he could obtain a treaty on satisfactory terms. Parliament voted it had no intention of taxing the colonies without representation; it also passed a bill to send commissioners to treat with Congress or with Washington, to order a truce, to suspend laws, to grant pardons and rewards. Fox screamed out, "You are ten days too late." The French had already formed a treaty with America. Franklin was victor. He was, in fact, at that moment the most important man in Europe. France hurried off a frigate to carry the news of a treaty; England despatched another, close after, with all speed, hoping to get ahead with news of its conciliatory temper. Franklin laughed. The king of France sent for him; and when presented to Louis, the latter said: "I wish Congress to be assured of my friendship. I beg leave also to say that I am exceedingly pleased, in particular, with your own conduct during your residence in my kingdom."

Franklin went to the royal reception without any formal dress, with a white hat under his arm instead of a sword; and his white hair flowed freely without a wig. The French people went wild with enthusiasm over his republican simplicity. The government was nobly generous to the young republic, and took no mean advantage of the predominance of France in the league; Franklin took occasion of his prestige to secure the passage of a great international law allowing free ships to carry goods freely and passengers also—soldiers of the enemy only excepted. He urged Congress not hereafter to molest foreign ships, but to accord prompt adhesion to Russia's proposition of "an armed neutrality for the protection of the liberty of commerce." Thus began the establishment, not only of an American republic but a republic of the high seas. To-day the waters of the earth are a great commonwealth of the peoples, covering two thirds of the globe.

But Franklin's work was not done; it was only now that it could be done. Fate was against England, and France came out ahead. Franklin had no disposition to lighten the blow for our mother country. He despatched John Paul Jones, in hopes of burning Liverpool or Glasgow,—and "save blood elsewhere." Meanwhile financial burdens were necessarily greater, the needs of Congress increasing. The great diplomatist was exactly equal to the occasion. He succeeded, in the face of difficulties apparently insurmountable, in borrowing large sums, and in meeting all the drafts made on him by Congress. He had to fit out his own cruisers, and, indeed, carry the expenses of all other American representatives in Europe. France was poor. Her treasury was almost always overdrawn. Yet every time Franklin, protesting and sometimes sharply reprimanding, managed to meet all needful calls. Every week the bills ranged from two hundred thousand dollars down to small affairs of daily expense. Jay was in Spain to secure a loan, but he had to appeal to Franklin to pay his current expenses for him. So the work of this mighty man culminated. He stood for a nation not yet created—for a Congress without power. Himself an ambassador without a country, he made a treaty with France; he blockaded the ports of England; he sent money to sustain the army of Washington, he supported the American representatives at other courts; he created international treaties. At that moment Washington was the great man of the new world; Franklin of the old world—and both were Americans.

He is said to have been vain. It was impossible for men like Lee and Deane and Izard, or even John Adams, to measure such a man. They are therefore not blamable for false estimates. He was fond of friends, and of the high esteem of the world; but he endured without perturbation the assaults of the great and the stings of the small; nor is there on record an instance where his vanity or his resentment led him to lose his prudence as an ambassador or his skill as a negotiator.

The war was now over. The man who in 1776 signed the Declaration of Independence with the remark, "We must hang together or we shall all hang separate," now signed, not only the Treaty of Peace with England, but treaty after treaty between the United States and foreign governments. In 1784 Jefferson reached Paris, and Franklin was allowed to return home. "Come you," they said to Jefferson, "to replace Doctor Franklin?" He replied, "No one can replace him; I am only his successor." The greatest American statesman thus followed as minister to France the greatest American diplomatist. They were a well-mated pair. Each approached the rights of man on a different road, but they stood on a common platform. Franklin felt the wrongs of his fellow-men; Jefferson had faith in great human principles. They were both eminently democratic in manners, and popular in their sentiments. Besides Washington, no other man so eminently won the hearts of the people. With admirable grace Mr. Lodge says of Franklin, "He moved with an easy and assured step, with a poise and balance which nothing could shake, among the great men of the world; he stood before kings and princes and courtiers unmoved and unawed. He was strongly averse to breaking with England; but when the war came, he was the one man who could go forth and represent to Europe the new nationality without a touch of the colonist about him. He met them all, great ministers and great sovereigns, on a common ground, as if the colonies of yesterday had been an independent nation for generations."

In the summer of 1785 Franklin returned to America. He left France with the best regard of her people and her king. He met at home a welcome beyond measure enthusiastic. He was elected governor of Pennsylvania, and in 1787 a member of the Constitutional Convention. He was thus at the laying of the cornerstone of the new nation in July, 1776; and he assisted in the completion of the grand idea of a federated, democratic republic eleven years later—"All of which he saw; and a very large part of which he was."

MOSES COIT TYLER "FRANKLIN IN THE LITERATURE OF THE REVOLUTION" (1897)

Rising above the throng of his writings upon the American question in all its varying issues and aspects, from the beginning to the end, are some eight or ten productions which stand out as most worthy of mention in this place.

The first of these is the celebrated pamphlet entitled "The Examination of Doctor Benjamin Franklin, in the British House of Commons, relative to the Repeal of the American Stamp Act, in 1766."[1] Though a mere report of a certain memorable transaction in parliament, this pamphlet is, in reality, the result of a most consummate piece of political and editorial craftsmanship on the part of Franklin himself—a master without a master in the art of touching the springs of popular conviction and sympathy. First published in London in 1767, it had in England "a great run," as even Franklin permitted himself to acknowledge.[2] Being promptly translated into French, it was also widely circulated upon the continent, and for its pithy, dramatic, and amusing way of putting the American case, it was read by multitudes of people in many countries who thus got their first distinct impression as to the nature of the trouble then brewing in America, and as to the American people themselves—their number, character, resources, dispositions, opinions, purposes. Moreover, if the pamphlet thus gave a great impulse to the American cause in Europe—an impulse which was at once transmitted with tremendous effect to America, also—not less did it contribute to the reputation and standing of Franklin himself on both sides of the Atlantic; for, by its incidental and modest exhibition of his marvelous presence of mind, under the shower of questions that were rained upon him in the House of Commons, of his unfailing resources both in knowledge and in argument, of his frankness, reasonableness, shrewdness, wit, temper, tact, good humor, it simply extended to the public outside the house the impression he had produced inside it, namely, that thenceforward, upon the American question, this elderly and quiet philosopher was to be reckoned with as a statesman and a diplomatist of the first order. "From this examination of Doctor Franklin," said the "Gentleman's Magazine" for July, 1767, "the reader may form a clearer and more comprehensive idea of the state and disposition of America, and of the expediency or inexpediency of the measure in question, and of the character and conduct of the minister who proposed it, than from all that has been written upon the subject in newspapers and pamphlets, under the titles of essays, letters, speeches, and considerations, from the first moment of its becoming the object of public attention till now."[3]

Early in the year 1768, under the guise of an Englishman having unusual acquaintance with the colonies, he published in the "London Chronicle" a long and sprightly article on the "Causes of American Discontents before 1768."[4] Though greatly mutilated and weakened by the editor of the journal in which it first appeared,—so that, as Franklin complained, with its teeth drawn and its nails pared, it could "neither scratch nor bite," and could only "paw and mumble,"[5]—there was enough left of it to shew Franklin's great skill in winning favor for his side of the question by a novel and a half-grumbling presentation of its claims, and even by an ironical disparagement of them.

So, too, in 1974, over the signature of "A Londoner," be contributed to the "Public Advertiser" a series of short articles "On the Rise and Progress of the Differences between Great Britain and her American Colonies,"[6] in which, with the frankness of a discontented Englishman, he caustically exposes the dunce-like methods of the ministry in dealing with the American problem, and the stupid pertinacity of those writers for the English press who seemed to think that they were solving that problem by calling the Americans hard names and by propagating all sorts of calumnies against them. "Surely," exclaims the

"Londoner" at the close of his last article, "the great commerce of this nation with the Americans is of too much importance to be risked in a quarrel which has no foundation but ministerial pique and obstinacy! . . . Will our reviling them as cheats, hypocrites, scoundrels, traitors, cowards, tyrants, etc., etc., according to the present mode in all our papers, make them more our friends, more fond of our merchandize? Did ever any tradesman succeed, who attempted to drub customers into his shop? And will honest John Bull, the farmer, be long satisfied with servants that before his face attempt to kill his plough-horses?"[7]

Probably no writer ever understood better than he how to make dull subjects lively, and how, by consequence, to attract readers to the consideration of matters in themselves unattractive. As he well knew, the European public, whether upon the continent or in Great Britain, were not likely to give their days and nights to the perusal of long and solemn dissertations on the rights and wrongs of his countrymen in the other hemisphere. Accordingly, such dissertations he never gave them, but, upon occasion, brief and pithy and apparently casual statements of the American case; exposing, also, the weak points of the case against his own, by means of anecdotes, epigrams, jeux-d'esprit; especially contriving to throw the whole argument into some sort of dramatic form,—as in "A Dialogue between Britain, France, Spain, Holland, Saxony, and America,"[8] or as in "A Catechism relative to the English Debt "[9]; or, again, setting forth in pictorial form some stirring aspect of the dispute, as, in 1774, his famous emblematic drawing to illustrate "the result of England's persistence in her policy towards the colonies,"[10] wherein Britannia is represented as a huge desolate female-figure occupying a conspicuous place on the globe, but with all her limbs—that is, her colonies—cut off and lying scattered about—these dismembered limbs being severally labelled Virginia, New England, Pennsylvania, and New York. In this sorry plight, as Franklin says in the "Explanation" accompanying the picture, Britannia lifts "her eyes and mangled stumps to Heaven; her shield, which she is unable to wield, lies useless by her side; her lance has pierced New England; the laurel branch has fallen from the hand of Pennsylvania; the English oak has lost its head, and stands a bare trunk, with a few withered branches; briers and thorns are on the ground beneath it; the British ships have brooms at their topmast heads, denoting their being on sale; and Britannia herself is seen sliding off the world,—no longer able to hold its balance,—her fragments overspread with the label, 'Date obolum Belisario.'"[11]

It remains to be mentioned that Franklin's favorite weapon in political controversy—a weapon which, perhaps, no other writer in English since

Dean Swift has handled with so much cleverness and effect—was that of satire in the form of ludicrous analogue, thereby burlesquing the acts and pretensions of his adversary, and simply overwhelming him with ridicule. His very first dash into the Revolutionary controversy after his arrival in England in 1764, furnishes a case in point; when, in a letter to a newspaper, over the signature of "A Traveler," he chaffs the English public about their habit of swallowing preposterous stories concerning the colonies, as then commonly told them in their journals,—himself, however, ironically maintaining the truth of these very stories, and even capping them by others just as true: as the one about the tails of the American sheep being "so laden with wool, that each has a little car or wagon on four little wheels to support and keep it from trailing on the ground"; or, as the one about the inhabitants of Canada "making preparations for a cod and whale fishery this summer in the upper lakes. Ignorant people may object that the upper lakes are fresh, and that cod and whales are salt-water fish; but let them know, sir, that cod, like other fish, when attacked by their enemies, fly into any water where they can be safest; that whales, when they have a mind to eat cod, pursue them wherever they fly, and that the grand leap of the whale in the chase up the Falls of Niagara is esteemed, by all who have seen it, as one of the finest spectacles in nature."[12]

Moreover, with Franklin, as had been the case with Dean Swift before him, this species of satire took a form at once so realistic and so comically apt, as to result in several examples of brilliant literary hoaxing—a result which, in the controversy then going on, was likely to be beneficial to the solemn and self-satisfied British Philistine of the period, since it compelled him for once to do a little thinking, and also to stand off and view his own portrait as it then appeared to other people, and even in spite of himself to laugh at his own portentous and costly stupidity in the management of an empire that seemed already grown too big for him to take proper care of. Of Franklin's work in the vein of literary burlesque, three pieces claim mention for their preeminent wit and point:—first, "Rules for Reducing a Great Empire to a Small One,"[13] secondly, "An Edict by the King of Prussia,"[14] both printed in the English newspapers in the early autumn of 1773; and, thirdly, a pretended letter of instructions "From the Count de Schaumbergh to the Baron Hohendorf commanding the Hessian Troops in America,"[15] this being dated at Rome, 18 February, 1777.

Referring to the first two of these pieces, soon after their publication, Franklin told his son that his object in writing them was to expose the conduct of England toward the colonies, "in a short, comprehensive, and striking view, and stated, therefore, in out-of-the-way forms, as most likely to take the general attention." "In my own mind," he adds, "I preferred the first, as a composition, for the quantity and variety of the matter contained, and a kind of spirited ending of each paragraph. But I find that others here generally prefer the second."[16] Probably, the chief reason for the greater attention paid in England to the second piece is to be found in the more direct and palpable character of its satire, dealing as it did with ideas and even phrases then uncommonly familiar to the English public. It made its appearance in the midst of the busy preparations then in progress for sending out the guileful tea-ships; when, of course, the very air was vibrant with allusions to the almost limitless claims of the mother country upon her American children, to the propriety and beauty of the English laws for controlling the commerce and manufactures of the colonies, and, above all, to the base ingratitude of England's American children in objecting to being taxed at will by their affectionate national parent. Under these circumstances it occurred to Franklin to set forth in some lively way the absurdity of all this; especially, that it was an argument which proved much more than its inventors would care to be responsible for. If, indeed, England had such limitless claims upon the American colonies because she was their mother country, why had not Germany, the mother country of England, the same claims upon her? This. idea, accordingly, Franklin worked out in a manner thoroughly Franklinian,— causing to be published, first, is the "Public Advertiser," what purported to be a solemn edict of Frederick the Great,—"Given at Potsdam, this twenty-fifth day of the month of August, one thousand seven hundred and seventy-three, and in the thirty-third year of our reign,"[17]—wherein that monarch, in a tone of command very natural to him, uses the characteristic words of the English acts of parliament regulating the commerce and manufactures of the American colonies, and then proclaims on behalf of Prussia the same regulations over "the island of Great Britain": "And all persons in the said island are hereby cautioned not to oppose in any wise the execution of this our edict, or any part thereof, such opposition being high treason; of which all who are suspected shall be transported in fetters from Britain to Prussia, there to be tried and executed according to the Prussian law."[18]

In England this travesty made a great hit;—all the more so for the reason, as Franklin explained to his son, "that people in reading it were, as the phrase is, 'taken in,' till they had got half through it, and imagined it a real edict, to which mistake, I suppose, the king of Prussia's character contributed."[19] Some of its effects, the author himself had the good luck to witness, and in a way of which he has left an amusing account. Having sent his satire to the newspaper, he immediately went down to the country-seat of his friend, Lord le Despencer, where among other guests happened to be Paul Whitehead, the poet. One morning while most of the company were chatting in the breakfast-parlor, Whitehead "came running in to us out of breath, with the paper in his hand. 'Here!' says he, 'here's news for ye! Here's the king of Prussia claiming a right to this kingdom!' All stared, and I as much as anybody; and he went on to read it. When he had read two or three paragraphs, a gentleman present said: 'Damn his impudence; I dare say we shall hear by next post, that he is upon his march with one hundred thousand men to back this.' Whitehead, who is very shrewd, soon after began to smoke it, and looking in my face said, 'I'll be hanged if this is not some of your American jokes upon us.' The reading went on, and ended with abundance of laughing, and a general verdict that it was a fair hit."[20] Indeed, Lord Mansfield, who, of course, was not in that company, called the satire "very able and very artful," and expressed the belief that it "would do mischief by giving here a bad impression of the measures of government, and in the colonies by encouraging them in their contumacy,"[21] all of which, certainly, was precisely the effect which it was intended to have.

The last of the three specimens of satire above mentioned, the Count de Schaumbergh's letter of instructions, seems to have been written by Franklin not long after his arrival in France in the latter part of 1776, and was intended to hold up to the execration of the civilized world both parties in the transaction by which the king of England bought of certain petty princes in Germany the troops with which to butcher his late American subjects. In some respects, this is the most powerful of all the satirical writings of Franklin. More, perhaps, than is the case with any other work of his, it displays, with marvelous subtlety and wit, that sort of genius which can reproduce with minute and perfect verisimilitude the psychological processes of some monstrous crime against human nature,—a crime which it thus portrays both to the horror and the derision of mankind. "Since the death of Swift," says John Bigelow in referring to this pretended letter of the Hessian trafficker in the bodies and souls of his subjects, "who, besides Franklin, was sufficiently a master of this kind of satire to have written it?"[22]

As Franklin was by far the greatest man of letters on the American side of the Revolutionary controversy, so a most luminous and delightful history of the development of thought and emotion during the Revolution might be composed, by merely bringing together detached sayings of Franklin, humorous and serious, just as these fell from his tongue or pen in the successive stages of that long conflict it would be a trail of light across a sea of storm and gloom.

Nevertheless, not by illustrative fragments of what he wrote or said, any more than by modern descriptions however vivid, can an adequate idea be conveyed of the mass, the force, the variety, the ease, the charm, of his total work as a writer during those twenty tremendous years. Undoubtedly, his vast experience in affairs and the sobriety produced by mere official responsibility, had the effect of clarifying and solidifying his thought, and of giving to the lightest products of his genius a sanity and a sureness of movement which, had he been a man of letters only, they could hardly have had in so high a degree. It is only by a continuous reading of the entire body of Franklin's Revolutionary writings, from grave to gay, from lively to severe, that any one can know how brilliant was his wisdom, or how wise was his brilliance, or how humane and gentle and helpful were both. No one who, by such a reading, procures for himself such a pleasure and such a benefit, will be likely to miss the point of Sydney Smith's playful menace to his daughter,—"I will disinherit you, if you do not admire everything written by Franklin."

Notes

1. *Works of Franklin*, Bigelow ed., iii. 407–450.
2. Ibid. iv. 28.
3. "The Gentleman's Magazine and Historical Chronicle," xxxvii. 368.
4. Reprinted in the Works of Franklin, Bigelow ed., iv. 97–111.
5. Ibid. iv. 98 note.
6. *Works of Franklin*, Bigelow ed., v. 323–338.
7. Ibid. 337–338.
8. *Works of Franklin*, Bigelow ed., vi. 118–122.
9. Ibid. 122–124.
10. Ibid. v. 416–417.
11. Ibid. 416–417.
12. *Works of Franklin*, Bigelow ed., iii. 378–379.
13. Ibid. i. 233–234.
14. Ibid. 214–220.
15. *Works of Franklin*, Bigelow ed., vi. 74–78. This, of course, is the English version of the letter; but it was a part of the jest to assume that the letter was originally written in German or in French—probably in French. The French version is given by M. de Lescure, in his "Correspondance secrète inédite sur Louis XVI.," etc., i. 31–33.
16. Ibid. 242–242.
17. *Works of Franklin*, Bigelow ed., v. 220.

18. Ibid. 219.
19. Ibid. 243.
20. *Works of Franklin*, Bigelow ed., v. 243.
21. Ibid. 224.
22. *Works of Franklin*, vi. 74 note.

D.H. Lawrence "Benjamin Franklin" (1923)

The Perfectibility of Man! Ah heaven, what a dreary theme! The perfectibility of the Ford car! The perfectibility of which man? I am many men. Which of them are you going to perfect? I am not a mechanical contrivance.

Education! Which of the various me's do you propose to educate, and which do you propose to suppress?

Anyhow I defy you. I defy you, oh society, to educate me or to suppress me, according to your dummy standards.

The ideal man! And which is he, if you please? Benjamin Franklin or Abraham Lincoln? The ideal man! Roosevelt or Porfirio Diaz?

There are other men in me, besides this patient ass who sits here in a tweed jacket. What am I doing, playing the patient ass in a tweed jacket? Who am I talking to? Who are you, at the other end of this patience?

Who are you? How many selves have you? And which of these selves do you want to be?

Is Yale College going to educate the self that is in the dark of you, or Harvard College?

The ideal self! Oh, but I have a strange and fugitive self shut out and howling like a wolf or a coyote under the ideal windows. See his red eyes in the dark? This is the self who is coming into his own.

The perfectibility of man, dear God! When every man as long as he remains alive is in himself a multitude of conflicting men. Which of these do you choose to perfect, at the expense of every other?

Old Daddy Franklin will tell you. He'll rig him up for you, the pattern American. Oh, Franklin was the first downright American. He knew what he was about, the sharp little man. He set up the first dummy American.

At the beginning of his career this cunning little Benjamin drew up for himself a creed that should "satisfy the professors of every religion, but shock none."

Now wasn't that a real American thing to do?

"*That there is One God, who made all things.*"

(But Benjamin made Him.)

"*That He governs the world by His Providence.*"

(Benjamin knowing all about Providence.)

"*That He ought to be worshipped with adoration, prayer, and thanksgiving.*"

(Which cost nothing.)

"*But—*" But me no buts, Benjamin, saith the Lord.

"*But that the most acceptable service of God is doing good to men.*" (God having no choice in the matter.)

"*That the soul is immortal.*"

(You'll see why, in the next clause.)

"*And that God will certainly reward virtue and punish vice, either here or hereafter.*"

Now if Mr. Andrew Carnegie, or any other millionaire, had wished to invent a God to suit his ends, he could not have done better. Benjamin did it for him in the eighteenth century. God is the supreme servant of men who want to get on, to *produce*. Providence. The provider. The heavenly store-keeper. The everlasting Wanamaker.

And this is all the God the grandsons of the Pilgrim Fathers had left. Aloft on a pillar of dollars.

"*That the soul is immortal.*"

The trite way Benjamin says it!

But man has a soul, though you can't locate it either in his purse or his pocket-book or his heart or his stomach or his head. The *wholeness* of a man is his soul. Not merely that nice little comfortable bit which Benjamin marks out.

It's a queer thing, is a man's soul. It is the whole of him. Which means it is the unknown him, as well as the known. It seems to me just funny, professors and Benjamins fixing the functions of the soul. Why the soul of man is a vast forest, and all Benjamin intended was a neat back garden. And we've all got to fit in to his kitchen garden scheme of things. Hail Columbia!

The soul of man is a dark forest. The Hercynian Wood that scared the Romans so, and out of which came the white-skinned hordes of the next civilization.

Who knows what will come out of the soul of man? The soul of man is a dark vast forest, with wild life in it. Think of Benjamin fencing it off!

Oh, but Benjamin fenced a little tract that he called the soul of man, and proceeded to get it into cultivation. Providence, forsooth! And they think that bit of barbed wire is going to keep us in pound forever? More fools them.

This is Benjamin's barbed wire fence. He made himself a list of virtues, which he trotted inside like a grey nag in a paddock.

1
TEMPERANCE
Eat not to fulness; drink not to elevation.

2
SILENCE
Speak not but what may benefit others or yourself;
avoid trifling conversation.

3
ORDER
Let all your things have their places;
let each part of your business have its time.

4
RESOLUTION
Resolve to perform what you ought;
perform without fail what you resolve.

5
FRUGALITY
Make no expense but to do good to others or yourself—
i.e., waste nothing.

6
INDUSTRY
Lose no time, be always employed in something useful;
cut off all unnecessary action.

7
SINCERITY
Use no hurtful deceit; think innocently and justly, and,
if you speak, speak accordingly.

8
JUSTICE
Wrong none by doing injuries,
or omitting the benefits that are your duty.

9

MODERATION
Avoid extremes, forbear resenting injuries
as much as you think they deserve.

10

CLEANLINESS
Tolerate no uncleanliness in body, clothes, or habitation.

11

TRANQUILLITY
Be not disturbed at trifles, or at accidents common or unavoidable.

12

CHASTITY
Rarely use venery but for health and offspring, never to dulness,
weakness, or the injury of your own or another's peace or reputation.

13

HUMILITY
Imitate Jesus and Socrates.

A Quaker friend told Franklin that he, Benjamin, was generally considered proud, so Benjamin put in the Humility touch as an afterthought. The amusing part is the sort of humility it displays. "Imitate Jesus and Socrates," and mind you don't outshine either of these two. One can just imagine Socrates and Alcibiades roaring in their cups over Philadelphian Benjamin, and Jesus looking at him a little puzzled, and murmuring: Aren't you wise in your own conceit, Ben?"

"Henceforth be masterless," retorts Ben. "Be ye each one his own master unto himself, and don't let even the Lord put his spoke in." "Each man his own master" is but a puffing up of masterlessness.

Well, the first of Americans practised this enticing list with assiduity, setting a national example. He had the virtues in columns, and gave himself good and bad marks according as he thought his behaviour deserved. Pity these conduct charts are lost to us. He only remarks that Order was his stumbling block. He could not learn to be neat and tidy. Isn't it nice to have nothing worse to confess? He was a little model, was Benjamin. Doctor Franklin. Snuff-coloured little man! Immortal soul and all! The immortal soul part was a sort of cheap insurance policy. Benjamin had no concern, really, with the immortal soul. He was too busy with social man.

1. He swept and lighted the streets of young Philadelphia.

2. He invented electrical appliances.

3. He was the centre of a moralizing club in Philadelphia, and he wrote the moral humorisms of Poor Richard.

4. He was a member of all the important councils of Philadelphia, and then of the American colonies.

5. He won the cause of American Independence at the French Court, and was the economic father of the United States.

Now what more can you want of a man? And yet he is *infra dig*, even in Philadelphia.

I admire him. I admire his sturdy courage first of all, then his sagacity, then his glimpsing into the thunders of electricity, then his common-sense humour. All the qualities of a great man, and never more than a great citizen. Middle-sized, sturdy, snuff-coloured Doctor Franklin, one of the soundest citizens that ever trod or "used venery."

I do not like him.

And, by the way, I always thought books of Venery were about hunting deer.

There is a certain earnest naïveté about him. Like a child. And like a little old man. He has again become as a little child, always as wise as his grandfather, or wiser.

Perhaps, as I say, the most complete citizen that ever "used venery."

Printer, philosopher, scientist, author and patriot, impeccable husband and citizen, why isn't he an archetype?

Pioneer, Oh Pioneers! Benjamin was one of the greatest pioneers of the United States. Yet we just can't do with him.

What's wrong with him then? Or what's wrong with us?

I can remember, when I was a little boy, my father used to buy a scrubby yearly almanack with the sun and moon and stars on the cover. And it used to prophesy bloodshed and famine. But also crammed in corners it had little anecdotes and humorisms, with a moral tag. And I used to have my little priggish laugh at the woman who counted her chickens before they were hatched, and so forth, and I was convinced that honesty was the best policy, also little priggishly. The author of these bits was Poor Richard, and Poor Richard was Benjamin Franklin, writing in Philadelphia well over a hundred years before.

And probably I haven't got over those Poor Richard tags yet. I rankle still with them. They are thorns in young flesh.

Because although I still believe that honesty is the best policy, I dislike policy altogether; though it is just as well not to count your chickens before they are hatched, it's still more hateful to count them with gloating when they are hatched. It has taken me many years and countless smarts to get out of that barbed wire moral enclosure that Poor Richard rigged up. Here am I now in tatters and scratched to ribbons, sitting in the middle of Benjamin's America looking at the barbed wire, and the fat sheep crawling under the fence to get fat outside and the watchdogs yelling at the gate lest by chance anyone should get out by the proper exit. Oh America! Oh Benjamin! And I just utter a long loud curse against Benjamin and the American corral.

Moral America! Most moral Benjamin. Sound, satisfied Ben!

He had to go to the frontiers of his State to settle some disturbance among the Indians. On this occasion he writes:

"We found that they had made a great bonfire in the middle of the square; they were all drunk, men and women quarrelling and fighting. Their dark-coloured bodies, half naked, seen only by the gloomy light of the bonfire, running after and beating one another with fire-brands, accompanied by their horrid yellings, formed a scene the most resembling our ideas of hell that could well be imagined. There was no appeasing the tumult, and we retired to our lodging. At midnight a number of them came thundering at our door, demanding more rum, of which we took no notice.

"The next day, sensible they had misbehaved in giving us that disturbance, they sent three of their counsellors to make their apology. The orator acknowledged the fault, but laid it upon the rum, and then endeavoured to excuse the rum by saying: 'The Great Spirit, who made all things, made everything for some use; and whatever he designed anything for, that use it should always be put to. Now, when he had made rum, he said: "Let this be for the Indians to get drunk with." And it must be so.'

"And, indeed, if it be the design of Providence to extirpate these savages in order to make room for the cultivators of the earth, it seems not improbable that rum may be the appointed means. It has already annihilated all the tribes who formerly inhabited all the seacoast . . ."

This, from the good doctor, with such suave complacency is a little disenchanting. Almost too good to be true. But there you are! The barbed wire fence. "Extirpate these savages in order to make room for the cultivators of the earth." Oh, Benjamin Franklin! He even "used venery" as a cultivator of seed.

Cultivate the earth, ye gods! The Indians did that, as much as they needed. And they left off there. Who built Chicago? Who cultivated the earth until it spawned Pittsburgh, Pa.?

The moral issue! Just look at it! Cultivation included. If it's a mere choice of Kultur or cultivation, I give it up.

Which brings us right back to our question, what's wrong with Benjamin, that we can't stand him? Or else, what's wrong with us, that we find fault with such a paragon?

Man is a moral animal. All right. I am a moral animal. And I'm going to remain such. I'm not going to be turned into a virtuous little automaton as Benjamin would have me. "This is good, that is bad. Turn the little handle and let the good tap flow," saith Benjamin and all America with him. "But first of all extirpate those savages who are always turning on the bad tap."

I am a moral animal. But I am not a moral machine. I don't work with a little set of handles, or levers. The Temperance-silence-order-resolution-frugality-industry-sincerity-justice-moderation-cleanliness-tranquility-chastity-humility keyboard is not going to get me going. I'm really not just an automatic piano with a moral Benjamin getting tunes out of me.

Here's my creed, against Benjamin's. This is what I believe:

"*That I am I.*"

"*That my soul is a dark forest.*"

"*That my known self will never be more than a little clearing in the forest.*"

"*That gods, strange gods, come forth from the forest into the clearing of my known self, and then go back.*"

"*That I must have the courage to let them come and go.*"

"*That I will never let mankind put anything over me, but that I will try always to recognize and submit to the gods in me and the gods in other men and women.*"

There is my creed. He who runs may read. He who prefers to crawl, or to go by gasoline, can call it rot.

Then for a "list." It is rather fun to play at Benjamin.

1

TEMPERANCE

Eat and carouse with Bacchus, or munch dry bread with Jesus,
but don't sit down without one of the gods.

2

SILENCE

Be still when you have nothing to say; when genuine passion moves you,
say what you've got to say, and say it hot.

3
ORDER
Know that you are responsible to the gods inside you and to
the men in whom the gods are manifest. Recognize your superiors and
your inferiors, according to the gods. This is the root of all order.

4
RESOLUTION
Resolve to abide by your own deepest promptings,
and to sacrifice the smaller thing to the greater. Kill when you must,
and be killed the same: the *must* coming from the gods inside you,
or from the men in whom you recognize the Holy Ghost.

5
FRUGALITY
Demand nothing; accept what you see fit.
Don't waste your pride or squander your emotion.

6
INDUSTRY
Lose no time with ideals; serve the Holy Ghost;
never serve mankind.

7
SINCERITY
To be sincere is to remember that I am I,
and that the other man is not me.

8
JUSTICE
The only justice is to follow the sincere intuition of the soul, angry
or gentle. Anger is just, and pity is just, but judgment is never just.

9
MODERATION
Beware of absolutes. There are many gods.

10
CLEANLINESS
Don't be too clean. It impoverishes the blood.

11
TRANQUILLITY

The soul has many motions, many gods come and go.
Try and find your deepest issue, in every confusion, and abide by that.
Obey the man in whom you recognize the Holy Ghost; command
when your honour comes to command.

12
CHASTITY

Never "use" venery at all. Follow your passional impulse,
if it be answered in the other being; but never have any motive
in mind, neither off-spring nor health nor even pleasure, nor even
service. Only know that "venery" is of the great gods. An offering-up
of yourself to the very great gods, the dark ones, and nothing else.

13
HUMILITY

See all men and women according to the Holy Ghost
that is within them. Never yield before the barren.

There's my list. I have been trying dimly to realize it for a long time, and only America and old Benjamin have at last goaded me into trying to formulate it.

And now I, at least, know why I can't stand Benjamin. He tries to take away my wholeness and my dark forest, my freedom. For how can any man be free, without an illimitable background? And Benjamin tries to shove me into a barbed-wire paddock and make me grow potatoes or Chicagoes.

And how can I be free, without gods that come and go? But Benjamin won't let anything exist except my useful fellow-men, and I'm sick of them; as for his Godhead, his Providence, He is Head of nothing except a vast heavenly store that keeps every imaginable line of goods, from victrolas to cat-o-nine tails.

And how can any man be free without a soul of his own, that he believes in and won't sell at any price? But Benjamin doesn't let me have a soul of my own. He says I am nothing but a servant of mankind—galley-slave I call it—and if I don't get my wages here below—that is, if Mr. Pierpont Morgan or Mr. Nosey Hebrew or the grand United States Government, the great US, US or SOMEOFUS, manages to scoop in my bit along with their lump—why, never mind, I shall get my wages HEREAFTER.

Oh Benjamin! Oh Binjum! You do NOT suck me in any longer.

And why oh why should the snuff-coloured little trap have wanted to take us all in? Why did he do it?

Out of sheer human cussedness, in the first place. We do all like to get things inside a barbed-wire corral. Especially our fellow-men. We love to round them up inside the barbed-wire enclosure of FREEDOM, and make 'em, work. "*Work, you free jewel, WORK!*" shouts the liberator, cracking his whip. Benjamin, I will not work. I do not choose to be a free democrat. I am absolutely a servant of my own Holy Ghost.

Sheer cussedness! But there was as well the salt of a subtler purpose. Benjamin was just in his eyeholes—to use an English vulgarism meaning he was just delighted—when he was at Paris judiciously milking money out of the French monarchy for the overthrow of all monarchy. If you want to ride your horse to somewhere you must put a bit in his mouth. And Benjamin wanted to ride his horse so that it would upset the whole apple-cart of the old masters. He wanted the whole European apple-cart upset. So he had to put a strong bit in the mouth of his ass.

"Henceforth be masterless."

That is, he had to break-in the human ass completely, so that much more might be broken, in the long run. For the moment it was the British Government that had to have a hole knocked in it. The first real hole it ever had: the breach of the American rebellion.

Benjamin, in his sagacity, knew that the breaking of the old world was a long process. In the depths of his own under-consciousness he hated England, he hated Europe, he hated the whole corpus of the European being. He wanted to be American. But you can't change your nature and mode of consciousness like changing your shoes. It is a gradual shedding. Years must go by, and centuries must elapse before you have finished. Like a son escaping from the domination of his parents. The escape is not just one rupture. It is a long and half-secret process.

So with the American. He was a European when he first went over the Atlantic. He is in the main a recreant European still. From Benjamin Franklin to Woodrow Wilson may be a long stride, but it is a stride along the same road. There is no new road. The same old road, become dreary and futile. Theoretic and materialistic.

Why then did Benjamin set up this dummy of a perfect citizen as a pattern to America? Of course he did it in perfect good faith, as far as he knew. He thought it simply was the true ideal. But what we *think* we do is not very important. We never really know what we are doing. Either we are materialistic instruments, like Benjamin or we move in the gesture of creation, from our deepest self, usually unconscious. We are only the actors, we are never wholly the authors of our own deeds or works. IT is the author, the unknown inside us or outside us. The best we can do is to try to hold ourselves in unison with the deeps which are inside us. And the worst we can do is to try to have things our own way, when we run counter to IT, and in the long run get our knuckles rapped for our presumption.

So Benjamin contriving money out of the Court of France. He was contriving the first steps of the overthrow of all Europe, France included. You can never have a new thing without breaking an old. Europe happens to be the old thing. America, unless the people in America assert themselves too much in opposition to the inner gods, should be the new thing. The new thing is the death of the old. But you can't cut the throat of an epoch. You've got to steal the life from it through several centuries.

And Benjamin worked for this both directly and indirectly. Directly, at the Court of France, making a small but very dangerous hole in the side of England, through which hole Europe has by now almost bled to death. And indirectly in Philadelphia, setting up this unlovely, snuff-coloured little ideal, or automaton, of a pattern American. The pattern American, this dry, moral, utilitarian little democrat, has done more to ruin the old Europe than any Russian nihilist. He has done it by slow attrition, like a son who has stayed at home and obeyed his parents, all the while silently hating their authority, and silently, in his soul, destroying not only their authority but their whole existence. For the American spiritually stayed at home in Europe. The spiritual home of America was and still is Europe. This is the galling bondage, in spite of several billions of heaped-up gold. Your heaps of gold are only so many muck-heaps, America, and will remain so till you become a reality to yourselves.

All this Americanizing and mechanizing has been for the purpose of overthrowing the past. And now look at America, tangled in her own barbed wire, and mastered by her own machines. Absolutely got down by her own barbed wire of shalt-nots, and shut up fast in her own "productive" machines like millions of squirrels running in millions of cages. It is just a farce.

Now is your chance, Europe. Now let Hell loose and get your own back, and paddle your own canoe on a new sea, while clever America lies on her muckheaps of gold, strangled in her own barbed-wire of shalt-not ideals and shalt-not moralisms. While she goes out to work like millions of squirrels in millions of cages. Production!

Let Hell loose, and get your own back, Europe!

WORKS

A collected edition of works is one of the greatest distinctions an author can receive. In this regard, Franklin was honored several times during his life and has been honored several times since. To present an original survey of Franklin's critical reception from the mid-eighteenth to the early twentieth centuries, this part of the volume is divided into six sub-sections. Some treat important individual editions of Franklin's writings. Others focus on multiple editions of his works.

The texts included in this section come from reviews of the individual editions. It was common for reviewers to quote large portions of text. Since Franklin's autobiography forms such an important part of his literary output, reviewers often devoted a great deal of space to retelling the story of his life. Consequently, many of the reviews included in this section have been abridged. Long quotations and redundant biographical information have been omitted.

Taken together, the reviews of Franklin's various collected editions tell the story of his critical reception from his recognition as the leading figure in electrical research in 1751 to 1906, the year celebrating the two hundredth anniversary of his birth with the release of a new collected edition of his works.

Since every new edition included little known or previously unpublished material, attitudes toward Franklin became more complex and more nuanced as each edition appeared. Franklin first became known to the world as an electrical researcher in the early 1750s, but the publication of *The Way to Wealth* later in that decade helped shape and determine popular perceptions of him. When Franklin's autobiography first appeared in the early 1790s, it became an instant classic. It has never been out of print. Jared Sparks's edition of Franklin's *Familiar Letters* exposed a more personal, intimate side of Franklin readers had never seen. The unknown documents included in the multivolume editions of the nineteenth and early twentieth centuries help readers recognize the originality and depth of Franklin's thought.

COLLECTED EDITIONS IN
FRANKLIN'S LIFETIME (1751–1787)

From the time he started the *Pennsylvania Gazette*, Benjamin Franklin developed a reputation in Philadelphia as a fine writer. Though his contributions to the *Gazette* were often reprinted in other colonial American newspapers, they were all or nearly all anonymous or pseudonymous, so they did nothing to extend his personal reputation as an author. Not until Franklin began writing about electricity did he establish an international reputation as an author and a scientist. As was typical, Franklin wrote descriptions and explanations of scientific experiments that he then sent to an English friend and a fellow of the Royal Society of London. The friend would then present these letters to the society. Once Franklin's correspondent, Peter Collinson, presented the letters before the society, they were included in its *Philosophical Transactions*. With the help of John Fothergill, Collinson collected the essays and published them as *Experiments and Observations on Electricity* (1751).

William Watson, Britain's leading expert on electricity, read his review of Franklin's *Experiments* before the Royal Society on June 6, 1751. At times technical, Watson's essay nevertheless demonstrates Franklin's international reputation as a scientist this early in his career. Discussing Franklin's research, Watson captures the excitement of his new discoveries. Besides showing Franklin's scientific abilities, Watson's essay also notes the American's concern for safety—but only to a point. Franklin was clearly willing to put himself at risk for the sake of new information. Recognizing Franklin's ingenuity as well as his charm, Watson retells his story of electrocuting a turkey, noting that Franklin thought that killing a turkey in this manner would make it "uncommonly tender."

Expanded editions of Franklin's *Experiments and Observations* followed. Franklin himself oversaw the publication of the fourth edition of *Experiments and Observations* (1769). The *Monthly Review*, a prominent London journal, took note of each new edition as did some other periodicals of the day, but these reviews largely consist of extracts or highly technical discussions. Besides Watson's lengthy notice, none of the other reviews of Franklin's electrical writings is included here, but it would be worthwhile for a student researcher to gather the reviews of each edition of and supplement to *Experiments and Observations* to track Franklin's burgeoning scientific reputation.

In the last two decades of his life, collected editions of Franklin's other writings appeared. In 1773 a French friend, Barbeu Dubourg, edited a two-volume collection of Franklin's works as *Oeuvres de M. Franklin*. In 1779 a British friend, Benjamin Vaughan, edited a collection of Franklin's writings, titled *Political, Miscellaneous, and Philosophical Pieces,* with his knowledge and consent. The fact that this British edition appeared in 1779, a time when Great Britain and the United States were at war, shows that British readers were able to separate Franklin's scientific and literary pursuits from his political work. The eighteenth century was the time of the Republic of Letters, a community that linked authors and scientists without regard to political boundaries.

Reviewing Vaughan's edition, William Bewley confirms the contemporary British appreciation of Franklin. The papers Vaughan included, Bewley observes, demonstrate Franklin's efforts to resolve the British-American conflict without war. Since the war had begun, however, the British are urged to take advantage of Franklin's ideas to aid their war effort. *The Way to Wealth*, for example, provides a prescription for personal economy that can be applied more broadly. Franklin's personal economy offered a model for British national economy. Bewley also compares Franklin to Swift. Numerous other authors have made the same comparison, but Bewley's may be the first published instance.

Prepared by Edward Bancroft and published by Charles Dilly, *Philosophical and Miscellaneous Papers* (1787) was the last collection of Franklin's writings to appear in his lifetime. A second volume of this edition was announced but never appeared. Dilly intended it as a supplement to the earlier collections. Published after the Revolutionary War, this edition was well received by the British reading public, as gauged by the contemporary reviews. The appreciative comments of the anonymous reviewer included here, for example, honor Franklin as a scientist but only because he truly understood the purpose of science: it is important only as a means to practical ends.

WILLIAM WATSON "AN ACCOUNT OF MR. BENJAMIN FRANKLIN'S TREATISE. LATELY PUBLISHED, INTITULED, *EXPERIMENTS AND OBSERVATIONS ON ELECTRICITY, MADE AT PHILADELPHIA IN AMERICA*" (1751)

Mr. Franklin's treatise, lately presented to the Royal Society, consists of four letters to his correspondent in England, and of another part intituled

"Opinions and conjectures concerning the properties and effects of the electrical matter arising from experiments and observations."

The four letters, the last of which contains a new hypothesis for explaining the several phaenomena of thunder gusts, have either in the whole or in part been before communicated to the Royal Society. It remains therefore, that I now only lay before the Society an account of the latter part of this treatise, as well as that of a letter intended to be added thereto by the author, but which arrived too late for publication with it, and was therefore communicated to the Society by our worthy brother Mr. Peter Collinson.

This ingenious author, from a great variety of curious and well-adapted experiments, is of opinion, that the electrical matter consists of particles extremely subtil; since it can permeate common matter, even the densest metals, with such ease and freedom, as not to receive any perceptible resistance: and that if any one should doubt, whether the electrical matter passes through the substance of bodies, or only over and along their surfaces, a shock from an electrified large glass jar, taken through his own body, will probably convince him.

Electrical matter, according to our author, differs from common matter in this, that the parts of the latter mutually attract, and those of the former mutually repel, each other; hence the divergency in a stream of electrified effluvia:[1] but that, tho' the particles of electrical matter do repel each other, they are strongly attracted by all other matter.

From these three things, *viz.* the extreme subtilty of the electrical matter, the mutual repulsion of its parts, and the strong attraction between them and other matter, arises this effect, that when a quantity of electrical matter is applied to a mass of common matter of any bigness or length within our observation (which has not already got its quantity) it is immediately and equally diffused thro' the whole.

Thus common matter is a kind of sponge to the electrical fluid; and as a sponge would receive no water, if the parts of water were not smaller than the pores of the sponge; and even then but slowly, if there was not a mutual attraction between those parts and the parts of the sponge; and would still imbibe it faster, if the mutual attraction among the parts of the water did not impede, some force being required to separate them; and fastest, if, instead of attraction, there were a mutual repulsion among those parts, which would act in conjunction with the attraction of the sponge: so is the case between the electrical and common matter. In common matter indeed there is generally as much of the electrical as it will contain within its substance: if more, is added, it lies without upon the surface,[2] and forms what we call an electrical atmosphere; and then the body is said to be electrified.

'Tis supposed, that all kinds of common matter do not attract and retain the electrical with equal force, for reasons to be given hereafter; and that those called electrics *per se*, as glass, &c. attract and retain it the strongest, and contain the greatest quantity.

We know, that the electrical fluid is in common matter, because we can pump it out by the globe or tube; and that common matter has near as much as it can contain; because, when we add a little more to any portion of it, the additional quantity does not enter, but forms an electrical atmosphere and we know, that common matter has not (generally) more than it can contain; otherwise all loose portions of it would repel each other, as they constantly do when they have electric atmospheres.

The form of the electrical atmosphere is that of the body, which it surrounds. This shape may be render'd visible in a still air, by raising a smoke from dry resin dropp'd into a hot tea spoon under the electrised body, which will be attracted and spread itself equally on all sides, covering and concealing the body. And this form it takes, because it is attracted by all parts of the surface of the body, though it cannot enter the substance already replete. Without this attraction it would not remain round the body, but be dissipated in the air.

The atmosphere of electrical particles surrounding an electrified sphere is not more disposed to leave it or more easily drawn off from any one part of the sphere than from another, because it is equally attracted by every part. But that is not the case with bodies of any other figure. From a cube it is more easily drawn at the corners than at the plane sides, and so from the angles of a body of any other form, and still most easily from the angle that is most acute; and for this reason points have a property of drawing on, as well as throwing off the electrical fluid, at greater distances than blunt bodies can.

From various experiments recited in our author's treatise, to which the curious may have recourse, the preceding observations are deduced. You will observe how much they coincide with and support those which I some time since communicated to the Society upon the same subject.

To give even the shortest account of all the experiments contained in Mr. Franklin's book, would exceed greatly the time allowed for these purposes by the Royal Society: I shall content myself therefore with laying a few of the most singular ones before you.

The effects of lightning, and these of electricity, appear very similar. Lightning has often been known to strike people blind. A pigeon, struck dead to appearance by the electrical shock, recovering life, drooped several days, eat nothing, tho' crumbs were thrown to it, but declined and died. Mr. Franklin did not think of its being deprived of fight; but afterwards a pullet, struck dead in like manner, being recovered by repeatedly blowing into its lungs, when set down on the floor, ran headlong against the wall, and on examination appeared perfectly blind: hence he concluded, that the pigeon also had been absolutely blinded by the shock. From this observation we should be extremely cautious, how in electrising we draw the strokes, especially in making the experiment of Leyden, from the eyes, or even from the parts near them.

Some time since it was imagined, that deafness had been relieved by electrising the patient, by drawing the snaps from the ears, and by making him undergo the electrical commotion in the same manner. If hereafter this remedy should be fantastically applied to the eyes in this manner to restore dimness of sight, I should not wonder, if perfect blindness were the consequence of the experiment.

By a very ingenious experiment our author endeavours to evince the impossibility of success, in the experiments proposed by others of drawing forth the effluvia of non-electrics, cinamon, for instance, and by mixing them with the electrical fluid, to convey them with that into a person electrified: and our author thinks, that tho' the effluvia of cinamon and the electrical fluid should mix within the globe, they would never come out together through the pores of the glass, and thus be conveyed to the prime conductor; for he thinks, that the electrical fluid itself cannot come through, and that the prime conductor is always supplied from the cushion, and this last from the floor. Besides, when the globe is filled with cinamon, or other non-electrics, no electricity can be obtained from its outer surface, for the reasons before laid down. He has tried another way, which he thought more likely to obtain a mixture of the electrical and other effluvia together, if such a mixture had been possible. He placed a glass plate under his cushion, to cut off the communication between the cushion and the floor: he then brought a small chain from the cushion into a glass of oil of turpentine, and carried another chain from the oil of turpentine to the floor, taking care, that the chain from the cushion to the glass touched no part of the frame of the machine. Another chain was fixed to the prime conductor, and held in the hand of a person to be electrified. The ends of the two chains in the glass were near an inch from each other, the oil of turpentine between. Now the globe being turned could draw no fire from the floor through the machine, the communication that way being cut off by the thick glass plate under the cushion: it must then draw it through the chains, whose ends were dipp'd in the oil of turpentine. And as the oil of turpentine being in some degree an electric *per se*, would not conduct what came up from the floor, the electricity was obliged to jump from the end of one chain to the end of the other, which he could see in large sparks; and thus it had a fair opportunity of seizing of the finest particles of the oil in its passage, and carrying them off with it: but no such effect followed, nor could he perceive the least difference in the smell of the electrical effluvia thus collected, from what it had when collected otherwise; nor does it otherwise affect the body of the person electrified. He likewise put into a phial, instead of water, a strong purging liquid, and then charged the phial, and took repeated shocks from it; in which case every particle of the electrical fluid must, before it went through his body, have first gone thro' the liquid, when the phial is charging, and returned through it when discharging; yet no other effect followed than if the phial had been charged with water. He has also smelt the electrical fire, when drawn thro' gold, silver, copper, lead, iron, wood, and the human body, and could perceive no difference; the odour being always the same, where the spark does not burn what it strikes; and therefore he imagines, that it does not take that smell from any quality of the bodies it passes through. There was no abridging this experiment, which I think very well conceived, and as well conducted, in a manner to make it intelligible; and therefore I have laid the author's words nearly before you.

As Mr. Franklin, in a letter to Mr. Collinson some time since, mentioned his intending to try the power of a very strong electrical shock upon a turkey, I desired Mr. Collinson to let Mr. Franklin know, that I should be glad to be acquainted with the result of that experiment. He accordingly has been so very obliging as to send an account of it, which is to the following purpose. He made first several experiments on fowls, and found, that two large thin glass jars gilt, holding each about 6 gallons, and such as I mentioned I had employed in the last paper I laid before you upon this subject, were sufficient, when fully charged, to kill common hens outright; but the turkeys, though thrown into violent convulsions, and then, lying as dead for some minutes, would recover in less than a quarter of an hour. However, having added three other such to the former two, though not fully charged, he killed a turkey of about ten pounds weight, and believes that they would have killed a much larger. He conceited, as himself says, that the birds kill'd in this manner eat uncommonly tender.

In making these experiments, he found, that a man could, without great detriment, bear a much greater shock than he imagined: for he inadvertently received the stroke of two of these jars through his arms and body, when, they were very near fully charged. It seemed to him an universal blow throughout the body from head to foot, and was followed by a violent quick trembling in the trunk, which went gradually off in a few seconds. It was some minutes before he could recollect his thoughts, so as to know what was the matter; for he did not see the flash, tho' his eye was on the spot of the prime conductor, from whence it struck the back of his hand; nor did he hear the crack, tho' the bystanders said it was a loud one; nor did he particularly feel the stroke on his hand, tho' he afterwards found it had raised a swelling there of the bigness of half a swan-shot, or pistol-bullet. His arms and the back of his neck felt somewhat numbed the remainder of the evening, and his breast was sore for a week after, as if it had been bruised. From this experiment may be seen the danger, even under the greatest caution, to the operator, when making these experiments with large jars; for it is not to be doubted, but that several of these fully charged would as certainly, by increasing them, in proportion to the size,, kill a man, as they before did the turkey.

Upon the whole, Mr. Franklin appears In the work before us to be a very able and ingenious man; that he has a head to conceive, and a hand to carry into execution, whatever he thinks may conduce to enlighten the subject-matter, of which he is treating: and altho' there are in this work some few opinions, in which I cannot perfectly agree with him, I think scarce any body is better acquainted with the subject of electricity than himself.

Notes

1. As the electric stream is observed to diverge very little, when the experiment is made *in vacuo*, this appearance is more owing to the resistance of the atmosphere, than to any natural tendency in the electricity itself. *W.W.*
2. The author of this account is of opinion, that what is here added, lies not only without upon the surface, but penetrates with the same degree of density the whole mass of common matter, upon which it is directed.

WILLIAM BEWLEY
"FRANKLIN'S POLITICAL, MISCELLANEOUS, AND PHILOSOPHICAL PIECES" (1780)

Though these cannot properly be called the posthumous works, yet—when we reflect on the Author's present situation, and that he has entered on his 75th year,—we cannot help considering, and lamenting over them, as the relict of the great philosopher, politician, and *prophet*, as the event has turned out, whose name is prefixed to them, and who, notwithstanding the present hostile character that he bears to this country, appears, from many papers contained in this collection, to have taken sincere pains, before the American dispute arrived at its present formidable magnitude, to preserve the *unity* of the British empire—or, to use his own apposite allusion, who 'long endeavoured with unfeigned and unwearied zeal; to preserve from breaking that fine and noble *china vase*—the British empire:'—well knowing, that 'being once broken, the separate parts could not retain even their *share* of the strength and value that existed in the whole; and that a prefect *re-union* of those parts could scarce ever be hoped for;'—Dead to use, however, as we have just now represented him, we shall still indulge the expectation, that his great talents may yet be employed in arranging and *cementing* the parts of this shattered vase; and of giving to the whole all the solidity of which it is now capable.

The anonymous Editor, who has taken pains thus to collect, and preserve—their own intrinsic merit will perpetuate—the scattered productions of the American patriot and philosopher, appears to be a zealous friend of Dr. Franklin; but at the same time, a friend who will not disgrace him. *Tam Marti quam Mercurio*; he appears well qualified to attend him both in his political and his philosophical capacity. In the former, by annotations subjoined to each piece, he gives the reader all the information which he has been able to procure, with respect to the occasion on which it was written, and other circumstances relating to it. In the latter, the philosophical Editor appears likewise a fit companion for his Author; and in the last piece particularly, on the *Aurora Borealis*, adds many pertinent observations or conjectures, in the form of notes.

* * *

As another specimen of this division of the work, we shall select some parts of a popular and useful production of the Author; which, we are told, his countrymen read with much avidity and profit; intitled, '*The Way to Wealth*, as clearly shewn in the preface of an old Pennsylvanian. Almanack, intitled, *Poor Richard improved*,' Dr. Franklin, who is said for many years to have published *Poor Richard's Almanack*, in Pennsylvania, furnished it with various sentences and proverbs, principally relating to the topics of industry, attention to one's own business, and frugality. The whole, or chief of these sentences and proverbs, says the Editor, he at last collected and digested in the above-mentioned general preface.—As he is at present our enemy, we naturally wish, as *British* patriots, to turn his arms against himself, by applying them to our own defence. And as the present situation of our country will render more taxes, as well as more economy, necessary; and certain murmurings on that account are, at this time, growing louder than usual; we shall first select what our late countryman says on the article of industry.

* * *

If every one of us, in our respective stations, would attend to, and immediately put in practice, the excellent advice given by poor Richard in this paper; each individual would, we apprehend, soon find a much more sensible alleviation of the weight that he bears in the burthens imposed by the state, than is to be expected from even the present endeavours to procure relief, by the abolition of sinecures, and the reduction of exorbitant emoluments, how proper forever.—Be this as it may, we are glad to circulate a part of poor Richard's plain and wholesome precepts; and to extend the knowledge of them farther, by intimating that the whole of this excellent little piece has been printed on a single sheet of paper, of a small size, fit for framing, and may be had of the publisher of the present volume, at the small price of *two-pence*.

In perusing the political pieces in this collection, though the Reader will frequently be reminded of Swift, when treating of the interests of Ireland; yet no two characters will be found more different in several respects. Except in those parts of his writings where he treats of what may be called *General Politics*, Swift exhibits every mark of a disappointed, passionate, and even caustic party man; execrating ministers, and in short, almost constantly venting his spleen in personalities against those who differ from him. Dr. Franklin, on the contrary, in the political writings now before us, appears almost on every occasion the placid and dispassionate *philosopher*;—as much a philosopher, at least, as one, who is at the same time a *public man*, and on very trying occasions, can be expected to be. His writings, before the American troubles commenced, every where breathe the spirit of peace and conciliation. They express an anxious desire to unite and blend the interests of the parent country and its colonies, in one common mass of vigour and public felicity; and to prevent every measure that shewed a tendency to alienate the two countries from each other. It is evident likewise, from some papers in this collection, that he earnestly wished to preserve the natural connection between this country and *his own*; even after certain proceedings—(on *both sides*, it must be acknowledged) had created a distinction between them.

* * *

We meet with no personalities in our Author's productions respecting
the American contest. Indeed a candid looker on will perhaps infer, that the
measures that have been pursued, in this country, with respect to America,
are not to be wholly ascribed to any particular set of men, *in* or *out* of place;—
for persons of both these descriptions have contributed to the bringing
matters to the present formidable crisis:—but to the monopolising spirit
of a rich, proud, warlike, and commercial Nation, operating with the spirit
of their rulers for the time being. The nation will perhaps, to a philosophic
eye, appear to have been equally criminal with the ministers of the day, in
anticipating a catastrophe which must, however, probably have taken place,
under any management whatever, though at a later period.

Anonymous "Philosophical and Miscellaneous Papers" (1787)

Among the numerous writers who submit their speculations to the public,
fortunately there are some whose works always receive, because they always
merit, public approbation, and a Reviewer has little more to do than to
announce their publications. In this class, and indeed in the foremost of this
class, is to be ranked Dr. Franklin; a man whose literary effusions have ever
tended to some useful end, the communication of some profitable knowledge,
or the dissemination of some liberal principle.

A great part of the present production is employed on what may be termed
one of the most troublesome and unpleasant of domestic evils—a smoky
chimney; an evil which from the ignorance of builders, and the quackery of
chimney-doctors, contributes not a little to the uncomfortableness of many
dwellings, and to which many people quietly submit, under an idea that, a
smoky chimney, like a scolding wife, is incurable: But however ungovernable
may be the tongue of a woman, Dr. F. makes it appear, that smoky chimnies
are to be controlled by the laws of philosophy. Great advances have lately
been made in the knowledge of the properties of air, from which ingenious
systems have been formed, and useful discoveries reduced to experience,
and rendered subservient to the benefit of mankind. This, indeed, is the true
end of philosophy; and to this end are directed all the papers contained in
the publication before us. In those on chimnies, the Doctor inquires into the
causes of, and points out the remedies for, their smoking; and this in so plain
and simple a manner as cannot fail to be of universal utility, provided the
ignorant prejudices and obstinate stupidity of common builders can be made
to give way to scientific knowledge.

The rest of the philosophical tracts in this production, consist of meteorological and maritime observations, in the latter of which are many excellent directions for the preservation of ships, and the prevention of accidents at sea, and for promoting the swift sailing of vessels. It is a great misfortune, that very useful discoveries are frequently made a long time before they are adopted; but we trust that the name of Dr. F. will recommend his dissertations to immediate notice, that the world at large may reap the benefit of those philosophical talents which have been so long and so successfully exerted in favour of general happiness.

The philosophical papers are succeeded by—"Information to those who would remove to America."—"Remarks concerning the savages of North-America;"—"The internal state of America;" and a "Letter from Dr. Franklin, on the criminal laws, and the practice of privateering."—The Information to those who would remove to America, it is highly necessary should be universally disseminated. In this paper, Dr. F. points out the reception and encouragement which different classes of people may expect to find in America; and states, that the man who is neither rich, a husband-man, an artificer, nor a mechanic, would find himself a very useless and despised member of the community on the other side of the Atlantic.—From Dr. F.'s "Remarks concerning the savages of North-America," and which, of course, are made from actual observation, some will be induced to think but meanly of that decorum and politeness which it is the ambition of many to acquire, and which, they will be surprized to find savages possessing, in several instances, in a greater degree than themselves, elucidate our meaning.

* * *

In his paper on the "Internal State of America," Dr. F. has given a description of the interest and policy of that vast continent; enriched with many just and seasonable remarks, peculiarly necessary for those who inhabit, or have any communication with that country.

The last article is a "Letter from Dr. F. to B.V. Esq. on the criminal laws, and the practice of privateering." In this letter he is particularly and justly severe on a pamphlet, published in this country, intitled, "Thoughts on Executive Justice;" the author of which, Dr. F. observes, is for hanging all thieves, instead of proportioning punishments to offences." A disregard to this proportion is surely productive of very serious evils.

* * *

This disproportion between crimes and punishments is a matter of serious contemplation. It is not only wicked, but impolitic. Few persons suffer on the gibbet, who might not be made useful to the community. The death of a robber can afford small consolation to him that is robbed: whereas, by the labour of the malefactor, the property might, in time, be restored, even "fourfold;" and that labour might also be greatly conducive to the penitence of the thief. There is, indeed, no good plea for sanguinary laws. It is thought, by some that example may effect prevention; but this, besides being no excuse for injustice, will depend on the progress of corruption in the community where such laws are promulgated, and such executions are authorized. We have reason to conclude, from what we daily observe, that not only the example of one, but even of one thousand, has not the least effect in regard to prevention.

* * *

It is high time, for the sake of humanity, that the enormities which form the subjects of the last two articles were abolished; and we have been the more diffusive in our remarks, though we wish our limits would permit us to be still more diffusive in what so materially concerns the welfare of mankind, in order that principles like these may be generally adopted: that the lives of our fellow creatures may no longer be sacrificed to impolitic laws; nor their property exposed to the merciless depredation of legal plunderers.

It is needless to add any thing by way of critique on these papers: there is no error to detect; and the highest commendation we can bestow upon them is, that they come from the pen of Dr. FRANKLIN.

AUTOBIOGRAPHY AND
COMPLETE WORKS (1793–1806)

Benjamin Franklin bequeathed his library and personal papers to his grandson William Temple Franklin. After his grandfather's death, Temple Franklin traveled to England, in part to prepare an edition of his grandfather's writings. He left the library behind but took the manuscripts with him. Temple Franklin's editorial incompetence and general distractions delayed the edition for decades. His hesitance to bring out a collected edition gave others the opportunity to publish Franklin editions of their own. This subsection consists of critical reviews of Franklin editions ranging from 1793, the year the first English edition of his autobiography appeared, to 1806, the one hundredth anniversary of his birth.

Multiple copies of Franklin's autobiography were circulating in manuscript at the time of his death in 1790. The following year, Jacques Gibelin published a French translation of part 1 of the autobiography as *Mémoires de la vie privée de Benjamin Franklin*, which constitutes the first edition of the autobiography. In 1793 the Gibelin translation was retranslated back into English and supplemented with a biography of Franklin by Dr. Henry Stuber. This, the first English edition, appeared as the initial volume of *Works of the Late Doctor Benjamin Franklin: Consisting of His Life Written by Himself, Together with Essays, Humorous, Moral and Literary*. Though Temple Franklin possessed the most complete and authoritative manuscript of his grandfather's autobiography, his reluctance to publish it meant that this other edition of Franklin's autobiography became the standard. It was in this version that the text became canonized as a classic of American literature. Another retranslation of the Gibelin text, by Alexander Stevens, appeared in 1793 as *The Private Life of the Late Benjamin Franklin*.

The first document included in this subsection is a review of *Works* that appeared in the *British Critic*. The anonymous reviewer recognizes how different Franklin's life was from the lives of other great men. Unlike so many men in power, Franklin exemplified hard work and honest dealings. His literary career paralleled his political one in terms of its movement from modest beginnings to extraordinary stature. This reviewer enjoys the variety of Franklin's literary output, especially his late, short writings and the autobiography's unforgettable sketch of his entry into Philadelphia. While recognizing the influence of Joseph Addison on Franklin, the reviewer asserts that Addison's writings remain superior. This contention is worth refuting. A detailed comparison of the two may reveal that in terms of literary complexity, generic virtuosity, and sheer number of uniquely defined personas, Franklin far surpasses Addison.

In 1806 William Marshall, a prolific agricultural writer, set about assembling the fullest edition of Franklin's works produced to that time. Marshall had help. Since Benjamin Vaughan was still alive, Marshall consulted him. The care with which this edition was prepared affirms the profound respect the British maintained for Franklin. Published as *The Complete Works in Philosophy, Politics, and Morals, of the Late Dr. Benjamin Franklin*, the edition prompted extensive reviews in the British press.

Francis Jeffrey's review of *Complete Works* first appeared in *Edinburgh Review* and was later collected with his other contributions to the journal, the source of the next selection. Jeffrey, the editor of the *Edinburgh Review*, applauds Franklin's rationality and his common sense. Franklin's career demonstrates that regular education can hinder originality. While the importance of regular education to society is undeniable, what is good for society is not necessarily good for individual genius. Jeffrey sees Franklin as the founder of a modern, journalistic style. He specialized in writing short compositions because he was a busy man who did not have time for long, leisurely essays. Franklin's style suited his contemporary readers. They, too, were busy people who did not have time for long compositions. Franklin's brevity prompted him to write with force and clarity.

Jeffrey also recognizes Franklin's stylistic virtuosity and his skill at making scientific writing insightful and entertaining. He specifically appreciates *The Interest of Great Britain Considered* (1760), or the "Canada pamphlet," so called because in it Franklin argued for the strategic and economic importance of Canada to both Great Britain and the American colonies. Jeffrey has only one major critique: he questions Franklin's ideas on political economy. Jeffrey's challenge to Franklin's thoughts on political economy should prompt modern readers to reconsider Franklin's ideas. Do they apply today? If so, how? Jeffrey also critiques the trifling details of Franklin's autobiography, but overall he finds the work useful reading for young people.

The next selection presents another review of *Complete Works*, this one from an annual British review. In direct contradiction to Jeffrey, this anonymous reviewer applauds Franklin's economic writing. The terms Franklin coined to talk about electrical polarity—*negative* and *positive*—come under scrutiny: a reactionary perspective. By this time, Franklin's terms had not only become commonplace in the scientific discourse, they had also entered the figurative language, as Henry Tuckerman would later recognize. Here is another good research topic: how soon after Franklin introduced the terms *positive* and *negative* were they begin being used figuratively to describe mood, outlook, and attitude?

This reviewer appreciates Franklin's political writings most. He finds many ideas applicable to British policy: another intriguing notion that deserves further analysis. To what extent did *Complete Works* influence British policy and political theory? Check for references to *Complete Works* in the writings of early-nineteenth-century political theorists and in nineteenth-century library catalogs. Comparing Franklin to other important thinkers of the day, the reviewer offers additional opportunities for consideration. Franklin's writings on population, for instance, resemble Malthus's. The clarity and forcefulness of Franklin's writings also compare to those of Thomas Paine; high praise indeed. Both comparisons could be developed further.

Anonymous "Works of the Late Dr. Benjamin Franklin" (1794)

The curious reader cannot but be interested in the perusal of the two volumes before us, slender as their contents are, since they present him with a nearer view of a character, whose prominent and striking features have long been contemplated at a distance. The career of most men, who from obscurity arrive at eminence, is marked either by the intrigues of meanness, or the dangerous designs of ambition; while the reputation of Dr. Franklin appears to have been earned by the indefatigable exercise of good talents, a course of upright dealings amongst men, and with some few exceptions, a regular adherence to moral rectitude. This tribute of approbation, the rancour even of political animosity will not refute him; while those who enjoyed the benefit of his counsel, those who were leagued with him in the intercourse of business, and those who partook in the pleasure of his conversation, may find other sources of panegyric, and agree to applaud the sagacity of the politician, the scrupulous integrity of the man of business, and the sociable and amiable qualities of their companion. His literary character may be said to bear a striking resemblance to his political one: each sprung from a beginning, which gave no particular hopes of future greatness, and each, certainly became distinguished at its close. While other youths are trained to the cultivation of knowledge by the arts of persuasion, or the threats of an instructor, he appears without many opportunities of gathering information, except such as a vigilant mind could steal from the intervals of business, to have risen to an eminence in the science of natural philosophy, which few, who have devoted their whole life to that study, have arrived at. Nor does this pursuit seem to have engaged him, from the hopes of attaining to the celebrity of a professor, but of becoming more useful to society. The occupations of the Philosopher have then a double value, when they not only tend to humanize the mind, but can be applied to the immediate service of mankind. In his writings Dr. Franklin was a professed imitator of Addison, and inasmuch as he united conciseness with perspicuity, and energy with simplicity, he may be said to have been successful; yet it must be acknowledged that in the stores of classical erudition, the playfulness of elegant wit, and in the sublimer and more dignified departments of composition, he is far behind his original.—"Sequiturque patrem non passibus aequis." Thus while we do not consider Dr. Franklin as the rival of that matchless writer, Addison, we heartily applaud his choice of him as the model of his style, and are of opinion, that, only by the aid of good sense, good taste, and unwearied application, he arrived at that rank which he holds in the lists of moral philosophers and political writers.

We cannot but repeat our regret, that after the variety of political tracts, and of didactic, moral, and prudential treatises which are known to have flowed from the active pen of Dr. Franklin, this publication, which professes to collect them, should be comprised in two small volumes. Our business, however, is to consider them as they are.

The first volume is composed of essays on various subjects, with a few letters to different friends; through the whole of which the amiable qualities of the author dispose us to wish for a more intimate acquaintance with him.

* * *

His letter, with the signature of Historicus, on the Slave-trade, contains some forcible reasoning, not without a mixture of that severe sarcasm which Dr. Franklin appears, upon proper occasions, to have been capable of applying with great effect. His Observations on War proclaim rather the benevolence of the man, than the sagacity of the politician; since, though every person of feeling will unite with him in wishing to deprive war of its attendant calamities, the observation of every one must point out to him, that the indulgence of such a wish is confident only with a system of Utopian society. His Necessary Hints to those that would be rich (p. 60), and his Directions to "make money *plenty* in every man's pocket," contain the maxims of an experienced observer.—His "Information to those who would remove to America," has, we believe, upon trial, been proved accurate and authentic.

* * *

The last essay in this volume is entitled the "Sketch of an English School," of which, perhaps, it may be observed, that more attention is given to one object than is altogether necessary, since a boy is to be moved through six classes in the accomplishment of only one language. But the Doctor's attention to the subject is highly honourable, and we do not mean to decide upon it as positively injudicious.

Vol. II. consists of a sketch of the earlier part of the Doctor's life, written by himself, which is continued, we cannot say, perfected, by Dr. Stuber, and the volume concludes with some extracts from his will.

That part of this work which is written by Dr. Franklin, brief as it is (containing 190 pages), is replete with scenes which are rendered highly interesting by the peculiar skill of the hand which drew them. Perhaps the following picture, which exhibits his entrance into that city, where he was afterwards placed in so distinguished a situation, cannot, in colouring, keeping, and truth, be any where exceeded.

* * *

But we will not anticipate the pleasure of our readers by presenting them with detached pieces of a story, which we wish them to peruse entire.

FRANCIS JEFFREY "FRANKLIN" (1806)

This self-taught American is the most rational, perhaps, of all philosophers. He never loses sight of common sow in any of his speculations; and when his philosophy does not consist entirely in its fair and vigorous application, it is always regulated and controlled by it in its application and result. No individual, perhaps, ever possessed a juster understanding, or was so seldom obstructed in the use of it, by indolence, enthusiasm, or authority.

Dr. Franklin received no regular education; and he spent the greater part of his life in a society where there was no relish, and no encouragement for literature. On an ordinary mind, these circumstances would have produced their usual effects, of repressing all sort of intellectual ambition or activity, and perpetuating a generation of incurious mechanics; but to an understanding like Franklin's, we cannot help considering them as peculiarly propitious, and imagine that we can trace back to them, distinctly, almost all the peculiarities of his intellectual character.

Regular education, we think, is unfavourable to vigour or originality of understanding. Like civilization, it makes society more intelligent and agreeable; but it levels the distinctions of nature. It strengthens and assists the feeble; but it deprives the strong of his triumph, and casts down the hopes of the aspiring. It accomplishes this, not only by training up the mind in an habitual veneration for authorities, but, by leading us to bestow a disproportionate degree of attention upon studies that are only valuable as keys or instruments for the understanding, they come at last to be regarded as ultimate objects of pursuit; and the means of education are absurdly mistaken for its end. How many powerful understandings have been lost in the Dialectics of Aristotle! And of how much good philosophy are we daily defrauded, by the preposterous error of taking a knowledge of prosody for useful learning! The mind of a man, who has escaped this training, will at least have fair play. Whatever other errors he may fall into, he will be safe at least from these infatuations. If he thinks proper, after he grows up, to study Greek, it will be for some better purpose than to become acquainted with its dialects. His prejudices will be those of a man, and not of a schoolboy; and his speculations and conclusions will be independent of the maxims of tutors, and the oracles of literary patrons.

The consequences of living in a refined and literary community, are nearly of the same kind with those of a regular education. There are so many critics to be satisfied—so many qualifications to be established—so many rivals to encounter, and so much derision to be hazarded, that a young man is apt to be deterred from so perilous an enterprise, and led to seek for distinction in some safer line of exertion. He is discouraged by the fame and the perfection of certain models and favourites, who are always in the mouths of his judges, and, "under them, his genius is rebuked," and his originality repressed, till he sinks into a paltry copyist, or aims at distinction by extravagance and affectation. In such a state of society, he feels that mediocrity has no chance of distinction: and what beginner can expect to rise at once into excellence? He imagines that mere good sense will attract no attention; and that the manner is of much more importance than the matter, in a candidate for public admiration. In his attention to the manner, the matter is apt to be neglected; and, in his solicitude to please those who require elegance of diction, brilliancy of wit, or harmony of periods, he is in some danger of forgetting that strength of reason, and accuracy of observation, by which he first proposed to recommend himself. His attention, when extended to so many collateral objects, is no longer vigorous or collected;—the stream, divided into so many channels, ceases to flow either deep or strong;—he becomes an unsuccessful pretender to fine writing, and is satisfied with the frivolous praise of elegance or vivacity.

We are disposed to ascribe so much power to these obstructions to intellectual originality, that we cannot help fancying, that if Franklin had been bred in a college, he would have contented himself with expounding the metres of Pindar, and mixing argument with his port in the common room; and that if Boston had abounded with men of letters, he would never have ventured to come forth from his printing-house, or been driven back to it, at any rate, the sneers of the critics, after the first publication of his Essays in the Busy Body.

This will probably be thought exaggerated; but it cannot be denied, we think, that the contrary circumstances in his history had a powerful effect in determining the character of his understanding, and in producing those peculiar habits of reasoning and investigation by which his writings are distinguished. He was encouraged to publish, because there was scarcely any one around him whom he could not easily excel. He wrote with great brevity, because he had not leisure for more voluminous compositions, and because he knew that the readers to whom he addressed himself were, for the most part, as busy as himself. For the same reason, he studied great perspicuity and simplicity of statement. His countrymen had no relish for fine writing, and could not easily be made to understand a deduction depending on a long or elaborate process of reasoning. He was forced, therefore, to concentrate what he had to say; and since he had no chance of being admired for the beauty of his composition, it was natural for him to aim at making an impression by the force and the clearness of his statements.

His conclusions were often rash and inaccurate, from the same circumstances which rendered his productions concise. Philosophy and speculation did not form the business of his life: nor did he dedicate himself to any particular study, with a view to exhaust and complete the investigation of it in all its parts, and under all its relations. He engaged in every interesting inquiry that suggested itself to him, rather as the necessary exercise of a powerful and active mind, than as a task which he had bound himself to perform. He cast a quick and penetrating glance over the facts and the data that were presented to him; and drew his conclusions with a rapidity and precision that have not often been equalled; but be did not stop to examine the completeness of the *data* upon which he proceeded, nor to consider the ultimate effect or application of the principles to which he had been conducted. In all questions, therefore, where the facts upon which he was to determine, and the materials from which his judgment was to be formed, were either few in number, or of such a nature as not to be overlooked, his reasonings are, for the most part, perfectly just and conclusive, and his decisions unexceptionably sound; but where the elements of the calculation were more numerous and widely scattered, it appears to us that he has often been precipitate, and that he has either been misled by a partial apprehension of the conditions of the problem, or has discovered only a portion of the truth which lay before him. In all physical inquiries; in almost all questions of particular and immediate policy; and in much of what relates to the practical wisdom and the happiness of private life, his views will be found to be admirable, and the reasoning by which they are supported most masterly and convincing. But upon subjects of general politics, of abstract morality, and political economy, his notions appear to be more unsatisfactory and incomplete. He seems to have wanted leisure, and perhaps inclination also, to spread out before him the whole vast premises of these extensive sciences, and scarcely to have had patience to hunt for his conclusions through so wide and intricate a region as that upon which they invited him to enter. He has been satisfied, therefore, on every occasion, with reasoning from a very limited view of the facts, and often from a particular instance; he has done all that sagacity and sound sense could do with such materials: but it cannot excite wonder, if he has sometimes overlooked an essential part of the argument, and often advanced a particular truth into the place of a general principle. He seldom reasoned upon these subjects at all, we believe, without having some practical application of them immediately in view; and as he began the investigation rather to determine a particular ease than to establish a general maxim, so he probably desisted as soon as he had relieved himself of the present difficulty.

There are not many among the thorough-bred scholars and philosophers of Europe, who can lay claim to distinction in more than one or two departments of science or literature. The uneducated tradesman of America has left writings that call for our attention, in natural philosophy,—in politics,—in political economy,—and in general literature and morality.

Of his labours in the department of *Physics*, we do not propose to say much. They were almost all suggested by views of utility in the beginning, and were, without exception, applied, we believe, to promote those views in the end. His letters upon *Electricity* have been more extensively circulated than any of his other writings; and are entitled to more praise and popularity than they seem ever to have met with in this country. Nothing can be more admirable than the luminous and graphical precision with which the experiments are narrated; the ingenuity with which they are projected; and the sagacity with which the conclusion is inferred, limited, and confirmed.

The most remarkable thing, however, in these, and indeed in the whole of his physical speculations, is the unparalleled simplicity and facility with which the reader is conducted from one stage of the inquiry to another. The author never appears for a moment to labour, or to be at a loss. The most ingenious and profound explanations are suggested, as if that were the most natural and obvious way of accounting for the phenomena; and the author seems to value himself so little on his most important discoveries, that it is necessary to compare him with others, before we can form a just notion of his merits. As seems to be conscious of no exertion, he feels no partiality for any part of his speculations, and never seeks to raise the reader's idea of their importance, by any arts of declamation or eloquence. Indeed, the habitual precision of his conceptions, and his invariable practice of referring to specific facts and observations, secured him, in a great measure, both from those extravagant conjectures in which so many naturalists have indulged, and from the zeal and enthusiasm which seems so naturally to be engendered in their defence. He was by no means averse to give scope to his imagination, in suggesting a variety of explanations of obscure and unmanageable phenomena; but he never allowed himself to confound these vague and conjectural theories with the solid results of experience and observation. In his Meteorological papers, and in his Observations upon Heat and Light, there is a great deal of such bold and original suggestions: but the author evidently sets little value upon them; and has no sooner disburdened his mind of the impressions from which they proceeded, than he seems to dismiss them entirely from his consideration, and turns to the legitimate philosophy of experiment with unabated diligence and humility.

* * *

Our limits will not permit us to make any analysis of the physical papers contained in this collection. They are all admirable for the clearness of the description, the felicity and familiarity of the illustrations, and the singular sagacity of the remarks with which they are interspersed. The theory of whirlwinds and water-spouts, as well as the observations on the course of the winds and on cold, seem to be excellent. The paper called Maritime Observations is full of ingenuity and practical good sense; and the remarks on Evaporation, and on the Tides, most of which are contained in a series of letters to a young lady, are admirable, not merely for their perspicuity, but for the interest and amusement they are calculated to communicate to every description of readers. The remarks on Fire-places and Smoky Chimneys are infinitely more original, concise, and scientific, than those of Count Rumford; and the observations on the Gulph-stream afford, we believe, the first example of just theory, and accurate investigation, applied to that phenomenon.

Dr. Franklin, we think, has never made use of the mathematics, in his investigation of the phenomena of nature; and though this may render it surprising that he has fallen into so few errors of importance, we conceive that it helps in some measure to explain the unequalled perspicuity and vivacity of his expositions. An algebraist, who can work wonders with letters, seldom condescends to be much indebted to words, and thinks himself entitled to make his sentences obscure, provided his calculations be distinct. A writer who has nothing but words to make use of, must make all the use he can of them: he cannot afford to neglect the only chance he has of being understood.

We should now say something of the political writings of Dr. Franklin,— the productions which first raised him into public office and eminence, and which will be least read or attended to by posterity. They may be divided into two parts: those which relate to the internal affairs and provincial differences of the American colonies, before their quarrel with the mother country; and those which relate to that quarrel and its consequences. The former are no longer in any degree interesting: and the editor has done wisely, we think, in presenting his readers with an abstract only of the longest of them. This was published in 1759, under the title of an Historical Review of the Constitution of Pennsylvania, and consisted of upwards of 500 pages, composed for the purpose of showing that the political privileges reserved to the founder of the colony had been illegally and oppressively used. The Canada pamphlet, written in 1760, for the purpose of pointing out the importance of retaining that colony at the peace, is given entire; and appears to be composed with great force of reason, and in a style of extraordinary perspicuity. The same may be said of what are called the Albany Papers, or the plan for a general political union of the colonies in 1754; and of a variety of other tracts on the provincial politics of that day. All these are worth preserving, both as monuments of Dr. Franklin's talents and activity, and as affording, in many places, very excellent models of strong reasoning and popular eloquence: but the interest of the subjects is now completely gone by; and the few specimens of general reasoning which we meet with, serve only to increase our regret that the talents of the author should have been wasted on such perishable materials.

There is not much written on the subject of the dispute with the colonies; and most of Dr. Franklin's papers on that subject are already well known to the public. His examination before the House of Commons in 1766, affords a striking proof of the extent of his information, the clearness and force of his *extempore* composition, and the steadiness and self-possession which enabled him to display these qualities with so much effect upon such an occasion. His letters before the commencement of hostilities, are full of grief and anxiety; but no sooner did matters come to extremities, than he appears to have assumed a certain keen and confident cheerfulness, not unmixed with a seasoning of asperity, and more vindictiveness of spirit than perhaps became a philosopher.

Of the merit of this author as a political economist, we have already had occasion to say something, in the general remarks which we made on the character of his genius; and we cannot now spare time to go much into particulars. He is perfectly sound upon many important and practical points;—upon the corn-trade, and the theory of money, for instance; and also upon the more general doctrines, as to the freedom of commerce, and the principle of population. In the more elementary and abstract parts of the science, however, his views seem to have been less just and luminous. He is not very consistent or profound in what he says of the effects of luxury; and seems to have gone headlong into the radical error of the *Economistes*, when he maintains, that all that is done by manufacture, is to embody the value of the manufacturer's subsistence in his work, and that agriculture is the only source from which a real increase of wealth can be derived. Another favourite position is, that all commerce is *cheating*, where a commodity, produced by a certain quantity of labour, is exchanged for another, on which more labour has been expended; and that the only *fair* price of any thing, is some other thing requiring the same exertion to bring it to market. This is evidently a very narrow and erroneous view of the nature of commerce. The fair price to the purchaser is, whatever he deliberately chooses to give, rather than go without the commodity;—it is no matter to him, whether the seller bestowed much or little labour upon it, or whether it came into his possession without any labour at all;—whether it be a diamond, which he picked up, or a picture, at which he had been working for years. The commodity is not valued by the purchaser, on account of the labour which is supposed to be embodied in it, but solely on account of certain qualities, which he finds convenient or agreeable: he compares the convenience and delight which he expects to derive from this object with the convenience and delight which in afforded by the things asked in exchange for it; and if he And the former preponderate, he consents to the exchange, and makes a beneficial bargain. We have stated the case in the name of a purchaser, because, in barter, both parties are truly purchasers, and act upon the same principles; and it is easy to show, that all commerce resolves itself, ultimately, into barter. There can be no unfairness in trade, except where there is concealment on the part of the seller, either of the defects of the commodity, or of the fact that the purchaser may be supplied with it at a cheaper rate by another. It is a matter of *fact*, but not of *morality*, that the price of most commodities will be influenced by the labour employed in producing them.—If they are capable of being produced in unlimited quantities, the competition of the producers will sink the price very nearly to what is necessary to maintain this labour; and the impossibility of continuing the production, without repaying that labour, will prevent it from sinking lower. The doctrine does not apply at all to cases where the materials, or the skill necessary to work them up, are scarce in proportion to the demand. The author's speculations on the effects of paper-money, seem also to be superficial and inaccurate. *Statistics* had not been carefully studied in the days of his activity; and, accordingly, we meet with a good deal of loose assumption, and sweeping calculation, in his writings. Yet he had a genius for exact observation, and complicated detail; and probably wanted nothing but leisure, to have made very great advances in this branch of economy.

As a writer on morality and general literature, the merits of Dr. Franklin cannot be estimated properly, without taking into consideration the peculiarities that have been already alluded to is his early history and situation. He never had the benefit of any academical instruction, nor of the society of men of letters;—his style was formed entirely by his own judgement and occasional reading; and most of his moral pieces were written while he was a tradesman, addressing himself to the tradesmen of his native city. We cannot expect, therefore, either that he should write with extraordinary elegance or grace; or that he should treat of the accomplishments, follies, and occupations of polite life. He had no great occasion, as a moralist, to expose the guilt and the folly of gaming or seduction; or to point a poignant and playful ridicule against the lighter immoralities of fashionable life.

His account of his own life, down to the year 1730, has been in the hands of the public since 1790. It is written with great simplicity and liveliness, though it contains too many trifling details and anecdotes of obscure individuals. It affords a striking example of the irresistible force with which talents and industry bear upwards in society; as well as an impressive illustration of the substantial wisdom and good policy of invariable integrity and candour. We should think it a very useful reading for all young persons of unsteady principle, who have their fortunes to make or to mend in the world.

Upon the whole, we look upon the life and writings of Dr. Franklin as affording a striking illustration of the incalculable value of a sound and well-directed understanding, and of the comparative uselessness of learning and laborious accomplishments. Without the slightest pretensions to the character of a scholar or a man of science, he has extended the bounds of human knowledge on a variety of subjects, which scholars and men of science had previously investigated without success; and has only been found deficient in those studies which the learned have generally turned from in disdain. We would not be understood to say any thing in disparagement of scholarship and science; but the value of these instruments is apt to be overrated by their possessors; and it is a wholesome mortification, to show them that the work may be done without them. We have long known that their employment does not insure its success.

Anonymous "The Works of Dr. Benjamin Franklin" (1806)

The life and the other works of Dr. Benjamin Franklin will circulate long and far. His discoveries in science were important; his attention to economics popularly instructive; and his practical efficacy in preparing and consolidating the American revolution conspicuous and decisive. His autobiography, if published without mutilation, would no doubt illuminate many recesses of the human heart, and of the political theatres: it is here not given entire, but extends to the day of his marriage in 1730.

* * *

Such are the principal incidents of a life, of which the first half is here given in Dr. Franklin's own words; and the second in those of Dr. Stuber, of Philadelphia.

To the biography succeeds a collection of tracts and pamphlets: and first, the papers on electricity. Dufaye, chief gardener to the king of France, had discovered two kinds of electricity, which he called *vitreous* and *resinous*, from the substances by which he supposed them to be furnished. Recent experiments prove that the vitreous electricity has a tendency to produce oxygen, and that the resinous electricity has a tendency to produce *hydrogen*. They are, therefore, distinct in kind, and might fitly be called *oxygenous* and *hydrogenous*. But Dr. Franklin rashly and mistakenly substituted the denominations positive and negative to vitreous and resinous, which were nearer the truth. This is not making a discovery in science, but the reverse: it was an obfuscation of truth, which has delayed its detection. These papers on electricity are sufficiently numerous to fill the first volume: they are admirable for the clearness of intellect they display, for the natural method of philosophizing they inculcate, and for the great results they reveal;

among which especially is to be remembered, the identity of electricity and lightning.

The second volume continues the collection of philosophic letters and papers.

The dissertation on smoaky chimneys is one of the most complete, and forms an admirable example of the art of turning the observations of science to purposes of immediate practical utility. The commentaries on innovations in language display less of the appropriate abounds less with reading and with knowledge and sagacity than any other essays in the collection.

At length occur the papers on general politics, which are in every view the most important and the most excellent of Franklin's works, and which we shall therefore enumerate one by one.

I. Observations on Population. This pamphlet contains the germ of Mr. Malthus's celebrated work: it teaches the same doctrines in a more pregnant and concise form, but illustration. Dr. Franklin supplies such original information concerning North America as Mr. Malthus gives concerning Scandinavia. Dr. Franklin more willingly notices the phenomena of unpeopled countries, Mr. Malthus more willingly notices those of overpeopled countries. Both writers well deserve, not merely the perusal, but the study of the statesman. To this paper is appended a plan for extending the civilization of the earth, by transplanting and transferring to distant countries the vegetables and animals locally deficient.

II. National Wealth is the next topic of discussion. The notes to a pamphlet entitled, The Principles of Trade, printed in 1774, were, in our opinion, not written by Dr. Franklin, but by Dr. Adam Smith. The fourth note is transcribed almost word for word into the Wealth of Nations.

III. The Dissertation on the Price of Corn is written with humorous popularity of manner: it teaches the doctrine, still to be learnt in Great Britain, that entire freedom of exportation and importation, in all circumstances and in all extremities of price, is most advantageous to any country, whether agricultural or no.

IV. On Luxury. An excellent paper, both for argument and handling. The art of writing to the people, of being both clear and stimulant, was possessed by Dr. Franklin in as high a degree as by Thomas Paine, and was exerted with more taste and more discernment.

V. The duty is enforced of not buying Smuggled Wares.

VI. Observations on War. These remarks propose a further softening of the law of nations, so as to confine the miseries of war to the fighting classes.

It is humanely recommended that cultivators, fishermen, traders, mechanics, should have the protection of both sides: that the hospitals of enemies should be unmolested and assisted; and that the practice of privateering, or of robing merchants, on the high seas, should be abandoned.

VII. Marginal Comments on Foster's Argument in Favour of Impressing Seamen. This concludes with an admirable piece of irony, which cannot be read too often. Why will the present ministry not try the experiment of manning first a peculiar fleet, and, if practicable, the whole navy, by an increase of the wages of seamen, without compulsory enrolment? By abolishing tellerships and auditorships of the exchequer, a fund might be raised adequate to the deliverance of thousands from the unjust burden of forced service. High wages would give us the command of all the seamen in the world, and found the defence of our wealth on its very abundance.

VIII. On Criminal Laws. Again, an humane and well-reasoned paper. How long benevolent doctrines have been circulated, without producing the slightest practical effect on legislation!

IX. Parable against Persecution. This parable is only a republication of what Jeremy Taylor derived from his rabbinical learning, and appended to the later editions of his Liberty of Prophesying. It is still a dead letter. The declaration against transubstantiation is yet extorted from members of the House of Commons, although the church of England consecrates that doctrine by maintaining that "the body and blood of Christ are verily and indeed received by the faithful at the Lord's Supper." This may be called consubstantiation by Lutheran sophistry, but it only removes the transubstantiation of the sacramental elements from the chalice of the priest to the mouth of the communicant. We comprehend not how any evangelical Christian, or other sincere member of the established Church, how Mr. Wilberforce or Mr. Thornton, for instance, can assent to this declaration without feeling the remorse of perjury. The laws against anti-trinitarian writers and thinkers still subsist, although laxly executed. The corporation and test acts still subsist. The grievances of the Irish Catholics still subsist. In short, half a century of knowledge has been lost to English legislation, in this, as in other departments of criminal law. And we wonder at discontent. O let us praise the patience of the people under the indolence or bigotry of their less enlightened rulers. The parable is accompanied by historical comments on the conduct of dissenter, which deserve the recollection of the ecclesiastical historian.

X. Slave Trade. This topic has awakened in Great Britain the desirable attention.

XI. Freedom of the Press. A Piece of Socratic irony not sufficiently specific in its drift to be wisely dwelt upon.

The third volume consists, 1, Of Papers on Colonial Grievances prior to the revolutionary troubles; 2, Of Papers on American Topics, written during the Revolution; 3, Of Papers concerning the condition and constitution of America, after the recognition of its independence.

Among these papers occurs (p. 59) an historical review of Pennsylvania, which is merely an abridgement of a more extensive work of five hundred pages, printed in 1759. We should have preferred the preservation of the entire original work to a collection of this kind.

A characteristic speech is Dr. Franklin's final address to the Federal Convention.

This speech is an unusual lesson of political modesty. We believe it is generally understood that Dr. Franklin contended for the unity of the legislative, and the plurality of the executive power. He would have preferred a directory of three persons, of whom one was to rote out triennially and alternately, to a solitary president. This organization would have intercepted a danger, which has already occurred, of the separation of North America into geographical parties. The southern states, which have a black peasantry, were nearly unanimous in the choice of Jefferson; the northern states, which have a white peasantry, were nearly as unanimously attached to Adams. Had the latter possessed a military and independent spirit, like Burr, it is likely that he could have accomplished a division of the country into two distinct nations; and such a division is, perhaps, expedient, now that the extent of empire is become so unwieldy. Boston is adapted for the northern metropolis. The Tennessee is fitter than the Patowmak for the imperial river of the southern metropolis. The agricultural population, which pours its produce down the Mississippi, requires other laws, and tends to other manners, than the commercial settlers of the maritime provinces. The infidelity, the libertinism, the negro vassalage of the south, amalgamate ill with the Calvinism, the moral discipline, and the civic equality of the north. A federal union might continue to subsist between these regions; if it were to become necessary to consolidate, under distinct legislatures, the two sets of provinces. And such a form of union might perhaps be devised, as should facilitate an alliance with Canada, and even with the British isles, for several purposes of legislation and jurisdiction, in which all these countries have a joint interest. It would be expedient to concede to some common amphictyonic council the arbitration of various questions of cosmopolitical law, such as neutral rights of navigation, the adjudication of captured property, the reciprocal customhouse duties, the reclamation of emigrants, and the concession of denizenship. Why may not a purer, milder, more philanthropic law of nations be devised between the children of one family, than has hitherto prevailed in Europe. A common language has prepared common principles of equity: it remains to give them the sanction of concerted discussion and solemn acceptation.

Next follow various papers on the minor morals, and the economy of life. Of these, the most conspicuous is The Way to Wealth. There are paltry maxims in this gnomology. Such are: Fools make feasts, and wise men eat them: a ploughman on his legs is higher than a gentleman on his knees: get what you can, and what you get hold: he that murders a crown piece, destroys all that it might have produced, even scores of pounds: a penny sav'd is two-pence clear; a pin a day's a groat a year. The very popular circulation of these low-life sentiments has evidently impaired the American national character, has taught a sordid, tricking, selfish, unfeeling, mean cast of conduct, and has introduced a bigoted one-sided appreciation of merit, an exclusive value for success in money-making. Why have the Americans so little literature, and so little of the lofty, the heroic, the generous in public sentiment or personal proceeding; but because their very boys are taught to read in Poor Richard's Almanack?

An appendix contains some writings of Dr. Franklin omitted in their proper place. Of these, an ordinary pamphlet, called Plain Truth, is the most considerable. It also compiles some letters illustrative of his pursuits, conduct, and character.

The writings of Dr. Franklin are justly admired for a plain popularity of style, for the distinct picturesque character of idea, for humorous Socratic irony, and for the art of arguing *to the selfishness*. The reader is constantly put in mind of the *use* that will accrue to him, and such as him, from the adoption of Dr. Franklin's premises. Even a question of science is never handled as a question of curiosity, where to evolve the truth is the disinterested end in view: it must be hooked to some petty practical purpose of private accommodation before it is held worthy of being investigated. This concatenation of the *cui bono* to every footstep is a clog for excellence. It illiberalizes science; but it seems to be the characteristic of American philosophy. The national foible is readily forgotten in Dr. Franklin, when his vast efficacy is contemplated. History will class him among her great men; among the strong minds employed in directing the important events. He had, perhaps, more of craft than of boldness, more of prudence than of magnanimity; but he attained his ends without harshness or waste of effort. He early saw the scope of his pursuit, and proceeded toward it, step by step, with a singleness of purpose, and an undeviating perseverance, that rarely accompany a comprehensive mind. Indeed, Dr. Franklin's range of attention and idea, was but narrow. The classical, poetical, and elegant writers, had employed little of his leisure; the moral, sublime, the heroic delineations of the Muse, seldom tinged his sentiments or actions; nor had the luxuries and refinements of social life attraction enough to encroach much on his habits of snug sufficiency. He allowed himself time to think, and time to say but little: that little was always hitting: and what especially will consecrate his memory to the grateful veneration and growing applause of the remotest posterity is, that he belonged among those worthies who have assisted the people to obtain liberty; and not among those cringelings who have assisted sovereigns to extend their power.

AUTHORITATIVE EDITIONS (1809–1818)

When, after more than two decades, William Temple Franklin had failed to bring out a collected edition of his grandfather's works, William Duane could wait no longer. As a member of Benjamin Franklin's extended fam-ily, Duane also had access to a wealth of original manuscript material. In Philadelphia he had worked for Franklin's grandson and namesake, Benjamin Franklin Bache, helping issue the *Aurora*, the well-respected newspaper Bache edited and published. After Bache died of yellow fever in 1798, his widow, Margaret Bache, continued publishing the *Aurora* herself and hired Duane as editor. The two married in 1800. His profound respect for his wife's grandfather-in-law, combined with his growing family's continual need for money and Temple Franklin's apparent inabil-ity to produce the edition he had promised, motivated Duane to prepare a Franklin edition himself. Duane planned a six-volume edition, issuing volumes two through five in 1808 and 1809 under the general title *The Works of Dr. Benjamin Franklin, in Philosophy, Politics, and Morals.*

Before Duane released the two remaining volumes, he and Temple Franklin reached an agreement. Duane consented to not releasing his last two volumes until Temple Franklin finished preparing his edition. In 1816 Temple Franklin published his first volume, *The Private Correspondence of Benjamin Franklin*. The edition is dated 1817, but it was ready as early as December 18, 1816, when he sent James Monroe a copy. In 1818 Temple Franklin published two additional volumes, one titled *Private Correspondence* and the other *Memoirs of the Life and Writings of Benjamin Franklin*.

Though Temple Franklin had finally delivered his long-promised edition of his grandfather's writings, it left much to be desired. As part of the manuscript material he inherited, Temple Franklin had possessed the original manuscript of the autobiography in four parts in Benjamin Franklin's hand, but he inexplicably traded it away for a manuscript copy containing only the first three parts of the work. Still, Temple Franklin's edition represents the initial publication of the second part in English and the initial publication of the third part. Temple Franklin also tinkered with the text in many places, decorously toning down his grandfather's racy language and graphic imagery. In 1818, the same year Temple Franklin published his edition of the autobiography in London, Duane issued Temple Franklin's text of the autobiography as the first volume of his edition of Franklin's *Works*. Duane also published another volume of correspondence as the sixth volume of his edition.

In January 1817 an anonymous contributor to the *Critical Review*, a British periodical, presented the earliest known review of Temple Franklin's edition. In the extract included here, the reviewer applauds Franklin's character and his honesty, especially compared to other politicians and diplomats. The reviewer finds evidence in Franklin's correspondence supporting his religious beliefs. Many early-nineteenth-century readers were uneasy about Franklin's attitudes toward organized religion. This reviewer, however, took comfort in what Franklin had to say. The reviewer also praises Franklin's efforts to bring the Revolutionary War to a close, favorably comparing him to George Washington. This is another comparison that could be developed further: how do Franklin and Washington differ? As a start, look at their letters to each other.

The *Analectic Magazine*, an American review edited by Thomas Isaac Wharton and patterned after the British quarterlies, devoted considerable attention to both Duane's and Temple Franklin's editions. Contemporary American intellectuals—including Thomas Jefferson—recognized the *Analectic Magazine* as an important development in the history of American periodical literature. In 1817 the anonymous reviewer, possibly Wharton himself, discussed the first four volumes of Duane's edition and the first volume of Temple Franklin's edition. This review provides the source for the next selection. Though critical of Duane's editorial method, the reviewer there recognizes Duane's most original inclusion, a selection of several pieces Franklin had published in the *Pennsylvania Gazette* but which had not appeared in any previous edition of his works.

Duane's inclusion of these pieces reflects his dedicated efforts to collect and preserve books from Franklin's library. Franklin saved a file of the *Pennsylvania Gazette* in several volumes, each annotated to show who wrote which articles. Most of these volumes no longer survive.

Duane's inclusion of these pieces added a new dimension to Franklin's literary reputation, demonstrating his early ability to bring fine writing to scientific subjects. This reviewer's appreciation suggests another topic for critical exploration: to what extent can scientific writing be considered literature? The reviewer also compares Franklin with Francis Bacon: yet another comparison worth exploring.

John Foster, a wayward Baptist minister and prolific English essayist, reviewed *Private Correspondence* for the *Eclectic Review* in 1818. This article was republished with Foster's other reviews in a collected edition, the source of the present text. Foster emphasizes Franklin's importance as a letter writer, another rich topic for discussion. What made Franklin an excellent letter writer? How did he shape his materials to suit individual correspondents? In his published writings, Franklin frequently assumed different personas. Does he take on different literary presences in his letters too? To what extent can Franklin's letters be taken at face value? To what extent must they be recognized as artfully crafted literary works?

Foster also notes Franklin's love of the useful. In early-nineteenth-century Britain, utilitarianism was becoming an influential mode of thought. How did Franklin's thought affect the rise of utilitarianism? Foster further suggests that there are many political lessons that can be learned from Franklin's letters. Can the same be said today? Are there any new political lessons that can be learned from Franklin? Foster's only critique of Franklin is that his writings lacked sublimity. The sublime was considered a key element in much of the esteemed literature of the eighteenth century. Foster's critique begs the question: what was Franklin's relation to literary trends of his time?

Andrews Norton, best known as a biblical scholar, reviewed Temple Franklin's edition of *Memoirs* and *Private Correspondence* for the staid and stuffy Boston quarterly, the *North American Review*. Unsurprisingly, Norton critiques Franklin's life and his religious beliefs. As part of his edition, Temple Franklin included his grandfather's 1726 journal of his trip from England back to America. This journal introduced readers to another dimension of Franklin's character. The man who would be an internationally famous scientist and diplomat was quite a mischievous young man, as he dawdled along the south coast of Britain waiting for the wind.

The last text in this subsection also comes from the *Analectic Magazine*. The reviewer examines the third and final volume of Temple Franklin's edition. This reviewer, too, emphasizes the importance of analyzing Franklin's literary style and notices Franklin's extensive knowledge of history. The reviewer does not go into specifics, but additional research into Franklin's knowledge of history is now possible with the publication of *The Library of Benjamin Franklin* (2006), a catalog of Franklin's library by Edwin Wolf, 2d and Kevin J. Hayes. Look at what history books Franklin had in his library to see what he read and then analyze how those books influenced his thought.

ANONYMOUS "PRIVATE CORRESPONDENCE OF DR. FRANKLIN" (1817)

In order without delay to gratify our readers with the extracts from the Correspondence, we shall only premise, that the author of these letters, unshackled by the fetters of education, has shewn the superiority of knowledge over mere learning; has discovered the progress that may be made, both in natural and moral science, by the unassisted efforts of a sound and clear understanding; and has reduced to humiliation and shame, by the candour, the simplicity, and the manliness of his political conduct, those feeble and pigmy statesmen who would accomplish by chicane, intrigue, and falsehood, that in which the means should be noble as the purpose, *the independence, the happiness, and the glory of mankind.*

The first extract we make is a sort of confession of faith, with respect to which the Doctor enjoined secrecy to the Reverend President Stiles, to whom it is addressed: and it is the more interesting, as it was the only general declaration of his opinions on such a subject, and was made within less than six weeks before his death. The firmness of his belief in every essential article connected with an overruling Providence, with the perfect system of morals and religion taught by Jesus, and with the consolatory doctrine of a future state, will be a full answer to the calumnies which probably led to the inquiry of the American professor.

* * *

Having already gone to so much length in our review of this volume, we shall pass over very cursorily both the subject of general politics, and the particular application of the science as it referred to the war with America. Very opprobrious language is applied to our venerable Sovereign, whose conscientious discharge of his exalted duties is known to every Englishman, and as the errors of his reign will now be attributed to an infirmity, which no rectitude of heart could prevent, we shall not sully our pages by quoting the offensive paragraphs.

It is said that the great obstruction to the peace with America was, that we endeavoured to detach her from her allies; and it might be so without any imputation on the honour of this country: which, single-handed and unsupported in the sequel, maintained a contest with four distinct powers. We have, however, under all the circumstances, no doubt of the injustice and impolicy of that war; and if any uncertainty with regard to it rests on the mind of man, it will be effectually removed by the letters before us, which unfold the whole circumstances of the protracted negociation, by which that war was terminated. The great work of peace was accomplished by this best friend of humanity, to whom the attention of our readers has been invited. What Washington was in the camp Franklin was in the cabinet; and it is to this day problematical, whether America be indebted for the early acquisition of her independence more to the valour of the one, or to the wisdom of the other: certain it is, that different as were their occupations, there was a great resemblance between them in their natural vigour of mind, and in their general character founded upon it.

Anonymous "Life and Writings of Benjamin Franklin" (1817)

In reading these publications we have, on more than one account, had occasion to admire the wisdom of Sir Walter Raleigh, in throwing his historical manuscripts into the fire. It is a sufficient mortification, that, of an event which happens at noon-day, perhaps no two eyewitnesses will make the same report:—it is still more disparaging, that transactions, of which we imagine ourselves to know the origin, are carried on with closed doors and by secret correspondence: but when, in addition to the disagreement of reporters and the privacy of negotiators, we have the misstatements of editors and the blunders of typographers, we are nearly prepared to give up all hopes of coming at the truth of history. Before we entered upon the task of reviewing the works of Dr. Franklin, we had no adequate idea of the changes, falsifications, and errors, which are incident to successive republication. It may be, that, in general, a celebrated author does not fall into hands so very unskilful as those which have been in the habit of republishing our philosopher's writings. We believe no edition was ever published under his own supervision, or even with his own consent; and those, accordingly, which have found their way into the world, are put together in the most clumsy and inattentive manner.

* * *

The remaining forty pages of this volume [the fourth volume of Duane's edition] consist of Essays which, with the exception of the last, have never before been collected into a book. The authorship seems to be pretty clearly fastened upon Dr. Franklin;—and, indeed, our Editor has here shown a disposition to honest and accurate reference, which sorts but ill with this previous uniformity of error and disingenuousness. He tells us plainly (p. 367)—'that in the two first volumes of the Pennsylvania Gazette, which are in the possession of the Philadelphia Editor, these pieces are noted on the inner side of the cover, in pencil writing, which writing is that of the author—The words are—"*Pieces written by B.F.*" and the several articles are there stated by their titles, with a reference to the number of the paper in which each was first published.' In part, this is as it should be;—but why is this same Philadelphia Editor constantly alluding to books in Dr. Franklin's library, without telling us how those books came into his possession? Why was it necessary to give us a constant and repeated impression of his unfair play, by dealing out here and there an obscure hint only of the matter,—by loving darkness rather than light? We have read these eight Pieces with considerable pleasure; but then we could not get rid of the vexation and the doubt which the Editor's half-way information was calculated to produce. The Essays on the Waste of Life—on Discoveries—and on Earthquakes—are peculiarly good. They breathe a spirit of retrospection and of generalization—along with a cheerfulness and sanguinity about the progress of knowledge—which are the only things that can promote it; and they are written in a liveliness and impetuosity and force of stile, which are very rarely to be found in philosophical composition. We have no doubt there are many other interesting essays of the Doctor's in the Pennsylvania Gazette; and we cannot but think it would be an edifying employment for the Philadelphia Editor, to ascertain how many Numbers of *The Plain Dealer*, particularly, were the production of his pen.

* * *

With these exceptions, we know not that any late work has afforded us more pleasure, than the Private Correspondence of Dr. Franklin. Here are letters upon subjects of every sort—written to persons of almost every character; and yet the whole correspondence is carried on with such an easy and practised hand, that we are hardly capable of discerning what part is executed the best. We certainly think no writer has ever displayed more versatility of powers. Hardly any person suggests an inquiry which he does not seem to have anticipated, or which he does not satisfactorily answer: And when we reflect upon the inadequacy of his early attainments, and the scanty opportunities which public business afforded him of augmenting them afterwards, we are almost astonished at the knowledge which he every where displays, and are sometimes ready to think, that he overtook the learning of the eighteenth century, by the native force of his own original thought. In many things, indeed, he went beyond it; and, though perhaps the physical sciences are the most indebted to him, the moral have to acknowledge the receipt of many valuable improvements at his hands. In the writings of other philosophers, it is common to find the labour of investigation proportioned to the difficulty of the subject; but we believe it is generally conceded to Dr. Franklin—that, upon whatever he undertook to treat, he was equally familiar and at home. In the moral sciences, indeed, he was not comparatively so much at his ease; for, as we learn from many parts of his writings, he had no very exalted idea of the progress which they had already made,—nor was he oversanguine as to that which they might hereafter make. In physics, however, he delighted beyond measure. Even while yet the humble Editor of the Pennsylvania Gazette, he began to take the globe familiarly in his hand;—and it is particularly amusing to read his early speculations upon those meteorological phenomena, which he afterwards elucidated with so much success. He was always desirous to get leisure for the prosecution of these studies; and, when he received the permission of Congress to return from France, he expresses his joy on the occasion in this apostrophic language:—'I shall now be free from politics for the rest of my life. Welcome again, my dear philosophical amusements!'—*Priv. Cor.* p. 72.

In his love of physical study, Dr. Franklin was not altogether singular; but in his style of treatment, we believe he was. Over his strongest and most durable speculations, there was a playfulness and jocularity, which commended it to the understandings of all readers—and which not more than one or two eminent scientific men, besides himself, have ever been able to display. We may be considered as extravagant, when we venture to think that Lord Bacon, and Dr. Franklin, were almost the only two philosophers of great name, who have ever exercised a vivid and lively imagination with a powerful and solid understanding. In saying this, however, we must not be understood as intimating a complete parallelism between the two greatest luminaries of the eastern and western hemispheres. The imagination of Lord Bacon was employed in superintending the general concerns of universal science; whereas, that of Dr. Franklin entered into the minutest particulars of several departments. The former exercised the same faculty in telling how to do a thing, which the latter employed in doing it. Neither of them was, by any means, a thorough mathematician: And perhaps it is to this circumstance alone, that we must attribute the freedom and liveliness of their imaginative powers. The mathematics have—we must say it—a very peculiar property of suppressing the imagination, and of turning all the strength of our minds into the single faculty of reasoning. Indeed, when our chief employment is to deal only with the ideas that are suggested by the figures of the decade, or the letters of the alphabet, we are not likely to encourage the entertainment of those which we get by the study of polite literature, and the exercise of imagination. Whatever might have been the case with Lord Varulam, we are pretty sure, it was the comparative neglect of pure mathematical study, that enabled Dr. Franklin to be a polished wit, at the same time that he was a profound reasoner.—We do not mean that his imagination, like that of too many others, was exercised without government and without use. We may compare it, indeed, with the humble instrument of some of his best experiments; which, though it soared into the clouds, was never suffered to go out of his controul,—and, instead of being sent up for vain amusement, was always employed in some profitable discovery. The sociable and story-telling wit of Dr. Franklin, too, had the singular property of being reconcileable with great dignity of character. He had not that constitutional levity, which made him lose his equilibrium. The gusts of jocularity which so often swept across him, might agitate the foliage, but could seldom shake the trunk, of his understanding. Lord Bacon, also, had exquisite wit; but it was a wit, which never descended to be jocular. According to our ideas of the two philosophers, the latter could say many witty things, which would make others laugh, without moving one of his own muscles; but, when the former set the table in a roar, his own sides, we suspect, could not help partaking in the general convulsion. Lord Bacon, we should say, would never attempt a witticism, till he saw there was no chance of miscarriage:—Dr. Franklin essayed too often; and sometimes said a thing that was silly.

The fame of such men is constantly augmenting. And the reason is—that they outstrip their own age; and accumulate, during the short period of their lives, a multiplicity of wise plans to ameliorate the world, which its slow and gingerly adoption of improvement, takes a long course of years to exhaust. Both the philosophers we now speak of, were sensible of this. Lord Bacon even made it an article of his will—that his name should belong to posterity, after the lapse of some generations; and Dr. Franklin often intimates, with something like impatience, that his schemes of amelioration would never be adopted, till the world 'had more sense.' 'I begin to be almost sorry, (says he to Sir Joseph Banks, *Priv. Cor.* p. 44,) I was born so soon, since I cannot have the happiness of knowing what will be known an hundred years hence.' The same regret is expressed in other places;—but it must be understood as relating to physical knowledge merely. He was sometimes on the borders of desperation, with regard to politics. See his letter to Dr. Priestley, dated from Passy, June 7, 1782; when he was 'weary of talking to inattentive heads,' and, for the first time, had fairly got out of patience with mankind.

* * *

The conclusion we draw from the foregoing review—is—that a skilful edition of Dr. Franklin's complete works is still a *desideratum* in English literature. And we had rather it might always remain a *desideratum*, than to have an inadequate hand undertake to supply it. The editor of Dr. Franklin's works should be somewhat like Dr. Franklin himself,—a man of great penetration—of versatile abilities—of considerable research—of inexhaustible patience—and of irrefragable integrity. He should at least have penetration enough to enter into his author's train of thought—abilities enough to be at home on almost every sort of subject—research enough to ascertain when, and where, and how, the different treatises were published—patience enough to set them in proper order—and integrity enough to reject such as are not genuine. Almost all the Doctor's works appeared originally in the newspapers; the editors of which, we have no doubt, took the liberty of making many alterations in such as were political, and often misprinted, because they did not understand, such as were philosophical. Neither as a politician, nor as a philosopher, therefore, is he adequately represented in our collections of his writings; and we are afraid he never will be adequately represented, till we have ascertained how many of his papers have been thus mutilated, and how much mutilation they have undergone. We hope, that, some day or other, we may be able to notice an edition, which will satisfy us upon all these subjects. And, in the mean time, we think we can ourselves communicate some facts, not commonly known, respecting three of his productions.

JOHN FOSTER
"FRANKLIN'S CORRESPONDENCE" (1818)

This ample assemblage of letters is intended as a sequel to the Memoirs of Dr. Franklin, written by himself. Or rather, it appears as constituting the latter half of that work, and is designated as the second volume, though preceding by a considerable interval of time the publication of the regular narrative.

The reader will feel little disposition to complain of the withholding of all information relative to the manner in which these letters could have been collected, the repository where many of them must long have lain, the proportion, in number, of those that have been suppressed, to that of these which are produced, or the question whether any considerable liberties have been taken in suppressing parts and passages of these. He will acknowledge that quite a sufficient number, and perhaps somewhat more, are given, that they embrace a considerable diversity of subjects, that they afford decisive internal evidence of authenticity, and that they very effectually display the talents and character of the writer.

The collection is distributed into three parts,—letters on miscellaneous subjects—letters on American politics—and letters on the negotiations for peace. In each part they are put in chronological series, and therefore they are placed as far as the shorter series extend back in time, in three parallel courses, thus bringing the writer thrice through the same states of his life and employments; and that, too, after the reader may be presumed to have passed through them once already in the narrative. This is the best arrangement for facilitating the reader's acquisition of the historical information to be derived from the political portions of the correspondence; but it less comports with a strictly biographical purpose, since, instead of our beholding, during the progress, the whole character and the diversified agency of the man, we are shown only one section or side, if we may so express it, of that character and agency at once, and are brought back to go with him again, and yet again, through the same periods of his life, in order to have another and still another view of the same person. We would rather, if we conveniently might, take our whole view of the man in one progress, beholding him exhibited, at each step and stage, in each and all of his capacities, characteristics, and occupations.

Perhaps, however, when a large portion of a man's letters relate solely to a grand national affair, which they very greatly elucidate, it may, after all, be as well to let the biographical purpose and interest become secondary, and make such a disposition of them as will be most advantageous for understanding that affair of history. Indeed, if the display of the man were to be regarded as the chief object in this part of the correspondence, we are apprehensive that most readers might wish it retrenched, as less than one half the number of letters would have sufficed for that; but let the object be a disclosure of the secret history of the American Revolution, and nearly all of them may be found to have their pertinence and value.

Taken all together, this collection of letters would, we think, in the absence of all other documents and representations, afford sufficient means for a competent estimate of the writer. The character displayed by them is an unusual combination of elements. The main substance of the intellectual part of it, is a superlative good sense, evinced and acting in all the modes of that high endowment; such as,—an intuitively prompt and perfect, and steadily continuing apprehension; a sagacity which with admirable ease strikes through all superficial and delusive appearances of things, to the essence and the true relations; a faculty of reasoning in a manner marvellously simple, direct, and decisive; a power of reducing a subject or question to its plainest principles; an unaffected daring to meet whatever is to be opposed, in an explicit, direct manner, and in the point of its main strength; a facility of applying familiar truths and self-evident propositions, for resolving the most uncommon difficulties; and a happy adroitness of illustration by parallel cases, supposed or real, the real ones being copiously supplied by a large and most observant acquaintance with the word. It is obvious how much this same accurate observation of the world would contribute to that power of interpreting the involuntary indications of character, and of detecting motives and designs in all sorts of persons he had to deal with, and to that foresight of consequences in all practical concerns, in which he was probably never surpassed. It is gratifying to observe how soon he would see to the very bottom of the characters and schemes of plausible hypocrites and veteran statesmen, proud as they might be of the recollected number of their stratagems and their dupes, and so confident of their talents for undermining and overreaching, that it took some of them a considerable time to become fully aware of the hazard of attempting their practice upon the republican. Not one of their inadvertencies, or of their over-done professions, or of the inconsistencies into which the most systematic craft is liable to be sometimes betrayed, was ever lost upon him. There are in the course of these letters, curious and striking instances of personages of great pretension, and of other personages, seeking to effect their purposes, under the guise of making no pretension, putting him in full possession of their principles and designs, by means of circumstances which they little suspected to be betraying them, and for which he, if it was necessary, could be discreet enough to appear never the wiser. In process of time, however, courtiers, ministers, intriguers, and the diplomatic gentry, had the mist cleared from their faculties sufficiently to understand what kind of man it was they had to do with.

There is one thing deficient in this collection, for the perfect illustration of the independence of Dr. Franklin's judgment. He resided a long course of years in France, in the exercise of the most important official functions for the American States, both during and after the war; and a great majority of the letters are dated at Passy, near Paris. As the French government was a most efficient friend to America in that momentous and perilous season, and her minister at the French Court experienced there all manner of respect and complaisance, it was natural enough he should speak in terms of considerable favour of that people and their governors,—of favour to certain extent—*quoad hoc*. But we are in vain curious to know whether this complacency was any thing like limited by justice. We are compelled to doubt it, from observing the many unqualified expressions of partiality to the French and their rulers, and from nowhere finding any terms appropriate to the frivolity of the nation, and the despotism and ambition of the government. Why do we find none such? Are there no preserved letters manifesting that the republican philosopher maintained a clear perception and a condemnatory judgment of such things, in spite of the Parisian adulation to himself, and the aid given to the rising republic by a tyrannic monarchy? And as to that aid itself, it would be one of the most memorable examples of the weakness of strong minds, if Franklin could ever for a moment mistake, or estimate otherwise than with contempt, the motive that prompted it; a motive which, in any case in which he had not been interested, would have placed the whole affair of this alliance and assistance in a quite different light from that in which he seemed so gratified to regard it.—A profligate and tyrannic court, a disinterested friend to a people asserting their freedom, and in the form of a republic! And could the American ambassador, though gratified, of course, by the fact of powerful assistance, affect to accept from that court, without a great struggle with his rising indignant scorn, the hypocritical cant and cajolery about co-operation against oppression, respect for the virtuous and interesting patriots of the new world, and the like, as expressive of its true principles in seizing so favourable an occasion for giving effect to its hatred against England? And could he, into the bargain, contemplate an enslaved and debased people, pass in the front of the Bastille, and behold the ruinous extravagance and monstrous depravity of that court, with feelings which required nothing to keep them in the indulgent tone, but the recollection of French troops and French money employed in America?

If the editor had in his possession any letters or other manuscripts tending to prove that no such beguilement took effect upon a judgment on which so many other kinds of persons and things attempted in vain to impose, it was due to Franklin's reputation for independence of judgment, to have given them, even though they should have brought some impeachment upon his sincerity in the grateful and laudatory expressions repeatedly here employed respecting France, and its interference in the contest.

In a general moral estimate of his qualities, insincerity would seem to find very little place. His principles appear to have borne a striking correspondence, in simplicity, directness, and decision, to the character of his understanding. Credit may be given him for having, through life, very rarely prosecuted any purpose which he did not deliberately approve; and his manner of prosecution was distinguished, as far as appears, by a pain honesty in the choice of means, by a contempt of artifice and petty devices, by a calm inflexibility, and by a greater confidence of success than is usually combined with so clear and extended a foresight of the difficulties;—but indeed that foresight of the difficulties might justify his confidence of the adaptation of his measures for encountering them.

He appears to have possessed an almost invincible self-command, which bore him through all the negotiations, strifes with ignorance, obstinacy, duplicity, and opposing interest, and through tiresome delays and untoward incidents, with a sustained firmness, which preserved to him in all cases the most advantageous exercise of his faculties, and with a prudence of deportment beyond the attainment of the most disciplined adepts in mere political intrigue and court-practice. He was capable, indeed, of feeling an intense indignation, which comes out in full expression in some of the letters, relating to the character of the English government, as displayed in its policy toward America. This bitter detestation is the most unreservedly disclosed in some of his confidential correspondence with David Hartley, an English member of parliament, a personal friend of Franklin, a constant advocate, to a measured extent, of the Americans, and a sort of self-offered, clandestine, but tacitly recognized medium for a kind of understanding, at some critical periods, between the English government and Dr. Franklin, without costing the ministers the condescension of official intercourse and inquiry. These vituperative passages have a corrosive energy, by virtue of force of mind and of justice, which perfectly precludes all appearance of littleness and mere temper in the indignation. It is the dignified character of Cato or Aristides. And if a manifestation of it in similar terms ever took place in personal conference with such men as were its objects, it must have appeared any thing rather than an ungoverned irritability; nor would it have been possible to despise the indignant tone in which contempt was mingled with anger, as far as the two sentiments are compatible. Believing that the men who provoked these caustic sentences did for the most part deserve them, we confess we have read them with that sort of pleasure which is felt in seeing justice made to strike, by vindictive power of mind, on the characters of men whose stations defended their persons and fortunes from the most direct modes of retribution.

When, at length, all was accomplished that, with long and earnest expostulation, he had predicted, and been ridiculed for predicting, to the English statesmen, as the certain consequence of persisting in their infatuated course, we find no rancorous recollection, no language of extravagant triumph at the splendid result, nor of excessive self-complacency in the retrospect of his own important share in conducting the great undertaking to such a consummation. His feelings do not seem to have been elated above the pitch of a calm satisfaction at having materially contributed to the success of a righteous cause, a success in which he was convinced he saw not simply the vindication of American rights, but the prospect of unlimited benefit to mankind.

And here it may be remarked, that his predominant passion appears to have been a love of the useful. The useful was to him the *summum bonum*, the supreme fair, the sublime and beautiful, which it may not perhaps be extravagant to believe he was in quest of every week for half a century, in whatever place, or study, or practical undertaking. No department was too plain or humble for him to occupy himself in for this purpose; and in affairs of the most ambitious order this was still systematically his object. Whether in directing the constructing of chimneys or of constitutions, lecturing on the saving of candles or on the economy of national revenues, he was still intent on the same end, the question always being how to obtain the most of solid tangible advantage by the plainest and easiest means. There has rarely been a mortal, of high intelligence and flattering fame, on whom the pomps of life were so powerless. On him were completely thrown away the oratorical and poetical heroics about glory, of which heroics it was enough that he easily perceived the intention or effect to be, to explode all sober truth and substantial good, and to impel men, at the very best of the matter, through some career of vanity, but commonly through mischief, slaughter, and devastation, in mad pursuit of what amounts at last, if attained, to some certain quantity of noise, and empty show, and intoxicated transient elation. He was so far an admirable spirit for acting the Mentor to a young republic. It will not be his fault if the citizens of America shall ever become so servile to European example, as to think a multitude of supernumerary places, enormous salaries, and a factitious economy of society, a necessary security or decoration of that political liberty which they enjoy in pre-eminence above every nation on earth. In these letters of their patriarch and philosopher, they will be amply warned, by repeated and emphatical representations, of the desperate mischief of a political system in which the public resources shall be expended in a way to give the government both the interest and the means to corrupt the people.

* * *

It would, however, have been but fair to have acknowledged how inconsiderable a portion of the nation they are whose venality it is that, on these occasions, has the effect of selling the whole people; and that, the case being so, the fact of the nation's being sold does not prove its general venality. How perverse is its fortune! that in such a state of its representation it might be sold, though a vast majority of its people were of the sternest integrity; whereas, in an enlarged and more equalized state of its representation, with a more frequent return of elections, it could not be sold, though every living thing in the land were venal, for the plain reason that the buyers could not come into such a market. They could not afford to purchase such a number of articles miscalled consciences, even at the low rate apiece which is the utmost worth of most of them, upon any calculation of three years' chances of indemnification, by obtaining some moderately remunerated office, with the additional chances as to the duration of their occupancy. And, by the way, is not this obvious view of the matter, more than an answer to all that sophistry and corruption can say for things as they are? Can there be any more decided test of a bad or a good construction of political institutions, than that they appear framed expressly to promote corruption and venality, and to avail themselves of them, like our present system of representation; or that they disappoint and discourage corruption, by being of a constitution the least capable that human wisdom can contrive, of finding their advantage in that corruption?

The political portion (the larger portion) of this correspondence, will be a valuable addition to the mass of lessons and documents which might have been supposed long since sufficient to disenchant all thinking men of their awful reverence for state-mystery, and cabinet-wisdom and ministerial integrity, and senatorial independence. We would hope, in spite of all appearances, that the times may not be very far off, when the infatuation of accepting the will of the persons that happen to be in power, as the evidence of wisdom and right, will no longer bereave nations of their sense, and their peace, and the fruits of their industry and improvements,—no longer render worse than useless, for the public interests,—the very consciences of men whose conduct relative to their individual concerns bears a fair appearance of sound principle and understanding. We will hope for a time when no secret history of important events will display the odious spectacle of a great nation's energies and resources, and the quiet of the world, surrendered without reserve, to the mercy, and that mercy "cruel," of such men as Franklin had to warn in vain of the consequences of their policy respecting America.

The correspondence gives an exhibition of almost every thing that ought to enforce on a nation the duty of exercising a constitutional jealousy of the executive. English readers may here see how worthily were confided the public interest of their forefathers, involving to an incalculable extent of their own. They may see how, while those forefathers looked on, many of them for a great while too infatuated with what they called loyalty to dare even a thought of disapprobation, those interests were sported with and sacrificed by men who cared not what they sacrificed, so long as their own pride, and resentment, and emolument, could stand exempted. They may see how fatally too late those forefathers were in discovering that their public managers had begun their career in the madness of presumption; and that warning, and time, and disastrous experiments, and national suffering, had done nothing towards curing it. They will see how, while a show of dignity, and a talk of justice, national honour, and so forth, were kept up before the people, there were no expedients and tricks too mean, no corruptions too gross, no cabals and compromises of disagreeing selfishness too degrading, to have their share in the state-machinery which was working behind this state-exhibition. What is the instruction resulting from all this, but the very reverse of what we have so often heard inculcated on the one hand by interested and corrupt advocates, and on the other by good men of the quietist school? What should it be but that nations ought to maintain a systematic habitual jealousy and examination relative to the principles and schemes of their rulers; that especially all movements toward a war should excite a ten-fold vigilance of this distrust, it being always a strong probability that the measure is wrong, but a perfect certainty that an infinity of delusions will be poured out on the people to persuade them that it is right.

But to return to an honest politician. Great admiration is due to the firm, explicit, and manly tone, with which he meets the inquiries, the insidious propositions, or the hinted menaces, of the hostile government and its agents; to the patience with which he encounters the same overtures, and attempted impositions, in a succession of varied forms; to the coolness and clearness with which he sometimes discusses, and the dignified contempt with which he sometimes spurns. Very many of the political letters afford examples; we are particularly struck with one, (p. 250, 4to.) addressed from Paris to a person who had written to him from Brussels, without a genuine name, and with other circumstances of mystery, suggesting also a mysterious mode, which the Doctor did not adopt, of transmitting a reply. The letter was designed to obtain Franklin's opinion of certain unofficially proposed terms of accommodation, and his answer shows that he believed the writer to be a person of more importance than the ordinary sort of agents that now and then made their attempts upon him. It is far too long for us to insert a fourth part of it; but it is an example of vigorous thought, compressed composition, and high-toned feeling.

* * *

His perfect superiority to all envy of this sort of honours, under any circumstances, is shown, not by laborious depreciation, but by the transient casual expressions of slight which give the more genuine indications of contempt,—of that easy and true contempt which it costs a man no trouble to maintain. The only instance in which we recollect his taking pains about the matter, is in reference to that little whim of the transatlantic republicans, the order of the Cincinnati, which some of them wished to make an hereditary distinction; in humble imitation of the European institution of nobility. He felt it due to the character of their revolution and their republican polity, to set himself in earnest to explode, by ridicule and argument, this piece of folly. If for the honour of their own persons the aspirants liked such a bauble, even let them have it, he said, at whatever it was worth; but he had no mercy on the absurdity of pretending to transmit down honorary distinctions to persons who by the nature of the case cannot have earned them.

It has been hinted already that, as a matter of general reading, the political portion of these letters will perhaps be thought too large. But it may be presumed that documents illustrating the American Revolution, may excite more interest now than they would have done between twenty and thirty years since. About that time the old world appeared to be on the eve of such a revolution in favour of liberty, as would have rendered, at least for a time, that of the American colonies a comparatively inconsiderable event. The military process through which it had been accomplished, was already begun to be spoken of as "the little war;" and the republican confederation of a number of scantily inhabited farming districts, was ceasing to be an imposing spectacle, when European monarchies, of immense population, and ancient fame for literature, arts, arms, and royal and aristocratic magnificence, were seen melting and moulding, amid volcanic fires, into new forms, bearing a transient, indeed, and dubious, but at first hopeful semblance of beauty and vigour. The long and tremendous tumult of all the moral elements, involving such a cost of every human interest, as could be repaid by no less a result, than a mighty change for the better of the whole political and social condition of Europe, has subsided in the consolidation of the very system by which its commencement was provoked, with the addition of an infinite account of depravity and poverty. But America, all this while has been exulting in the consequences of her revolution, and still triumphs in freedom undiminished, in an administration of government of which it is not the grand business to squander or devour her resources, and in a prosperity and power continually enlarging, with unlimited capabilities and prospects. Here then is the revolution that has succeeded, while all things else have failed: it eclipses, now, the importance of all the events by which its own importance appeared about to be eclipsed; and the interest which it claims to excite, will be progressive with its magnificent consequences. The proprietor, therefore, of these papers, has been wise or fortunate in reserving them to become old in his possession.

The most entertaining, however, and by no means an uninstructive division, of the letters, will be the first part, called "miscellaneous," and consisting chiefly of letters of friendship, abounding in tokens of benevolence, sparkling not unfrequently into satiric pleasantry, but of a bland good-natured kind, arising in the most easy natural manner, and thrown off with admirable simplicity and brevity of expression. There are short discussions relating to various arts and conveniences of life, plain instructions for persons deficient in cultivation, and the means for it; condolences on the death of friends, and frequent references, in an advanced stage of the correspondence, to his old age and approaching death. Moral principles and questions are sometimes considered and simplified; and American affairs are often brought in view, though not set forth in the diplomatic style.

It is unnecessary to remark that Franklin was not so much a man of books as of affairs; but he was not the less for that a speculative man. Every concern became an intellectual subject to a mind so acutely and perpetually attentive to the relation of cause and effect. For enlargement of his sphere of speculation, his deficiency of literature, in the usual sense of the term, was excellently compensated by so wide an acquaintance with the world, and with distinguished individuals of all ranks, professions, and attainments.

It may be, however, that a more bookish and contemplative employment of some portion of his life, would have left one deficiency of his mental character less palpable. There appears to have been but little in that character of the element of sublimity. We do not meet with many bright elevations of thought, or powerful enchanting impulses of sentiment, or brilliant transient glimpses of ideal worlds. Strong, independent, comprehensive, never remitting intelligence, proceeding on the plain ground of things, and acting in a manner always equal to, and never appearing at moments to surpass itself, constituted his mental power. In its operation it has no risings and fallings, no disturbance into eloquence or poetry, no cloudiness of smoke indeed, but no darting of flames. A consequence of this perfect uniformity is, that all subjects treated, appear to be on a level, the loftiest and most insignificant being commented on in the same unalterable strain of a calm plain sense, which brings all things to its own standard, insomuch that a great subject shall sometimes seem to become less while it is elucidated, and less commanding while it is enforced. In discoursing of serious subjects Franklin imposes gravity on the reader, but does not excite solemnity, and on grand ones he never displays or inspires enthusiasm.

Andrews Norton "Dr. Franklin" (1818)

We have read through these volumes, with mixed and somewhat contradictory feelings, respecting the very extraordinary man to whom they relate. The volume first mentioned commences with that portion of Franklin's life, written by himself, which has been long before the public. It is now, for the first time, printed from his original manuscript; but differs in nothing essential from the copy before in circulation. We have been surprised at the manner in which this piece of biography has been sometimes spoken of. It has been recommended as a work particularly proper to be generally read; and adapted to promote good morals, especially among the uneducated class of the community, by the beneficial influence of Franklin's example. We think very differently of it. It is the history of a young man, professedly without any religious, and obviously without much moral principle, making his way in the world, by the force of his talents, sharp-sightedness, industry, resolution, and address, all which properties he possessed in a very uncommon degree. The groundwork of his character, during this period, was bad; and the moral qualities, which contributed to his rise, were of a worldly and very profitable kind. Let us consider some of the facts which he relates of himself. At the age of seventeen, he ran away from home, and left his parents for several months ignorant of his situation, apparently very indifferent to the anxiety which they must have suffered respecting him; though it does not appear that he had any cause of complaint against them. He habitually neglected all the duties of religion; was a professed infidel; and perverted the principles of two of his associates. He gained the affections of a young woman; entered into an engagement of marriage with her; left the country for England; and while there, sent her but one letter, the object of which was to let her know, that he was not likely soot to return. While in England, he wrote and printed a pamphlet, for the purpose of proving, that 'nothing could possibly be wrong in the world; and that vice and virtue were empty distinctions, no such things existing.' Here likewise, he attempted to share with Ralph, one of his friends, in the favours of his mistress, which produced a quarrel between Ralph and himself. From England he returned to this country; and two of the last things which he relates of himself, in this portion of his biography, are, that he was engaged in a sort of bargain for a wife, which was broken off, because he insisted upon what were considered too hard terms; and that he had 'frequent intrigues with low women who fell in his way, which were attended with some expense, and great inconvenience; beside a continual risque to leis health, by a distemper which, above all things, he dreaded.'

Subsequently to the period of which we have spoken, there were undoubtedly important changes in the character of Franklin; as will appear by the extracts and remarks, which we shall have occasion to make in the course of our review. He returned from England in the summer of 1726, when he was in the 21st year of his age. The journal which he kept on the voyage is now for the first time published, and is rather curious; as exhibiting some of his powers and intellectual habits in their development, and formation; and discovering likewise occasionally an amusing contrast between what his character was at this time, and what it subsequently appeared to be. It is full of those details and remarks which indicate an observing; active, and clear-sighted mind. It is very remarkable, also, as a piece of composition, considering the age, and previous advantages of the author; and shows that the style of Franklin was formed at this early period.

Resolution, perseverance, and physical hardihood were characteristics of Franklin. There is an adventure mentioned in his journal, by which this remark is exemplified; and by which we think our readers will be amused; especially if they bear in mind, that the young man who relates it of himself, was afterward familiar in the courts of princes, and honoured by the learned throughout Europe.

* * *

In one of the foreign reviews, Franklin has been celebrated for his religious character, and his sincere and habitual piety. He certainly was far from being destitute of religious principles or feelings. There is no evidence, however, that at any subsequent period, he recovered from the infidelity into which he fell early in life, so as to become a Christian. Indeed, as far as indirect and presumptive evidence will go, there is proof of the contrary in the volumes before us. The inference drawn from them is also confirmed by information from other sources. 'It is much to be lamented,' says Dr. Priestley, in his Memoirs, 'that a man of Dr. Franklin's general good character, and great influence, should have been an unbeliever in Christianity, and also have done so much as he did to make others unbelievers. To me, however, he acknowledged that he had not given so much attention as he ought to have done to the evidences of Christianity, and desired me to recommend to him a few treatises on the subject, such as I thought most deserving of his notice, but not of great length, promising to read them, and give me his sentiments on them. Accordingly, I recommended to him Hartley's evidences of Christianity in his Observations on Man, and what I had then written on the subject in my Institutes of natural and revealed religion. But the American war breaking out soon after, I do not believe that he ever found himself sufficiently at leisure for the discussion.'

Franklin, however, was educated a Christian, in the midst of a religious community; and the early and probably very deep impressions which he thus received, though they might be afterward obscured, were never effaced. Subsequently to that period in his life, when his opinions were in a very unsettled state, he never seems to have indulged himself in scepticism respecting the being and attributes of God, the immortality of man, or a future state of rewards and punishments. But it may be doubted, whether his belief in the two last mentioned truths, was not more the result of education, than of any inquiry into the evidence, by which they may be maintained without the support of revelation. Without this support, indeed, there is no sure and sufficient foundation for the structure of our religious belief. But he who has been educated a Christian, may, if he cease to be so, still retain the belief of truths, which he has been taught as derived from revelation, and still be influenced by sentiments dependent upon these truths. Though he reject the evidence by which they are established and justified; yet they may still survive in his mind; as a plant will continue to live, for a certain time, after being separated from its root. To Franklin's early education, is to be attributed, we think, that frequent recurrence of his mind to religious topics, which appears in his writings. He had, at the same time, a great deal too much practical good sense, and too much love of the useful, not to be, very strongly sensible, at least in the latter part of his life, of the importance to society of religious belief. One of the letters contained in his correspondence is addressed to the author of a skeptical work, dissuading him from its publication on account of the pernicious effects it was adapted to produce. We do not, however, put any great value upon such a regard for religion, when it exists alone. He who is ready to acknowledge religion to be useful, may, if he please, find it to be true; and he has not that excuse for neglecting its evidence, which arises from any gross mistake respecting its character.

* * *

But religion when not identified with Christianity, and when, of consequence, it derives no support from revelation, holds but an insecure, and disputed authority in the mind. Of Franklin's morals, there are not materials enough in the two quarto volumes before us, to enable us to form a full and fair judgment; and the information which we have derived from other sources is so general, or so indirect, that we cannot with propriety make it the ground of any public statement. Of some parts of his political conduct, we have already sufficiently expressed our opinion. He seems to have been regarded by many of his contemporaries, as having had too much of that simulation and dissimulation, which is taught by Lord Bacon. The libertinism of his early life is related by him in his memoirs, without any expression of shame or repentance. Of his wife and children, there is but little account in the present volumes; and very little that may enable us to judge of his character in the domestic relations.

But whatever charges may be brought against him, it is to be recollected, that he was preeminently distinguished from ordinary men by his zeal and talents for being useful. There was nothing, it is true, of a very high character in his exertions or sacrifices, except the continuance and frequency of the former. It is a quite different kind of praise to which he is entitled, from that which is due to such men as Howard or Clarkson. He had, it may be remarked at the same time, little of the spirit of a reformer. He did not attempt to remove moral and physical evils, by entering into a difficult and dangerous conflict with the prejudices by which they are produced. But he very industriously made use of common means for the attainment of very beneficial purposes; and sedulously directed the attention of men to valuable objects, which might be secured without any struggle against prevailing errors. 'I have always,' he says, 'set a greater value upon the character of a doer of good, than upon any other kind of reputation.' He appears to have taken sincere pleasure in contemplating and promoting the well-being of his fellow men.

* * *

Dr. Franklin was distinguished by great practical good sense respecting the common affairs of the world; and by a freedom from extravagant and visionary calculations. But these excellencies were accompanied, though certainly not necessarily accompanied, by corresponding defects. There are some men, who see objects clearly as they are in themselves, and who observe likewise their nearest and most obvious relations; but who pay little regard to their relations to higher objects, to the invisible and the remote; men whose thoughts are never conversant in the world of the imagination, and busy with forms of ideal perfection. They regard man principally as a being of this life with certain natural wants and desires, and enjoying or suffering a certain quantity of good or evil, generally proportioned to his external circumstances; but they think little of those capacities which in the greater part are but imperfectly developed, and scarcely conceive of him as 'infinite in reason, noble in faculties, and in apprehension like a God.' They fix upon objects of pursuit, the value of which is recognised by all; and in their endeavours to attain them, keep the open road which is trodden by the multitude. They are never led to venture into untried and hazardous paths, by the prospect of opening the way to some distant, unappreciated good. To them, that utility which is obvious to all, constitutes beauty. They are desirous to do good; but they are equally or more desirous to have the reputation of doing good; and therefore what they propose to effect, must be something, the advantage of which may be understood by the generality. But it is not more a matter of calculation, than the habit of their own minds, to put but little value upon improvements, which can not be weighed or measured, and which make no show in a statistical table. The character of Franklin resembled, we conceive, in some of its traits, that which we have just been describing. His mind was defective, in the higher class of conceptions and feelings. He was not a man to distinguish himself by bold efforts or thankless sacrifices.

Dr. Franklin's high reputation as a man of literature and science is perfectly well established. As a man of science, he was not, indeed, as some of his eulogists seem to have thought, the rival of Newton; but though he devoted but a small part of his life to scientific pursuits, he is entitled to a distinguished place among philosophers of the second class. As a fine writer, though he formed himself without the benefit of a literary education, or the society of literary men, he may be compared with Addison or Goldsmith. He is their equal in wit and humour, in nice observation, and in ease and naïveté of language; and he possessed far more acuteness and force of mind than either. He had but little imagination as a writer; though he occasionally discovers some play of fancy, both in the conception of a piece, and in particular expressions; as when he speaks of 'fine promises being forgotten like the forms of last year's clouds.' We will not vouch however that the figure is not stolen, for he was not very conscientious about committing such petty larcenies. In his style, we meet occasionally, though but rarely, with some trifling blemishes, which may be supposed to be occasioned by his want of early education. But it is always admirable for its precision and perspicuity. It is as transparent as the atmosphere; and his thoughts lie before us like objects seen in one of our finest and, clearest days, when their very brightness and distinctness alone give us pleasure. Exclusive of his papers on Electricity, he treats in his other works of various subjects of natural philosophy, morals, politics, and political economy; and he shows a mind which might have enabled him to attain the highest reputation as an author upon almost any one of these subjects, if he had directed to it a greater share of attention. There are thoughts and discussions in some of his letters and papers, which an inferior writer would have manufactured into a volume, without adding any essential argument or illustration. Those of his writings, also, in which such a character is to be expected, have, generally speaking, a decidedly moral tendency; and are adapted to form correct habits of thinking and action. From this praise, however, we must except, as formerly mentioned, the first part of the memoirs of his own life; which however is a curious and valuable document in the study of human nature.

In speaking of the fame of Franklin, as a man of literature and science, we cannot help recollecting how few men of this class our country can toast of, as having distinguished themselves by their writings. We are looking forward, indeed, to better things; but there is much; very much, yet to be done, to accelerate the approach of what we hope for. A great nation without literature, or whose literature is bad, is like a great man, who cannot converse, or who converses idly. Strangers will form but a mean opinion of his merits. Literary men, and not an hereditary aristocracy, are the 'Corinthian capital of polished society.' But such men are wanted by us more for use than ornament. We want men formed among us, formed to love and value their country, formed under the influence of our institutions; our manners, and our religious and moral habits, whose writings may perpetuate, and give efficacy to those feelings and principles, from which our present blessings are derived, and without which they cannot subsist. We want men among us, who may counteract the libertinism, irreligion, and looseness of principle, which appear in one class of European writers, and the bigotry to established prejudices, which is found in another. We owe too something to the world, as well as to ourselves. If we have really attained to a degree of political happiness, and intellectual freedom, without example, we are placed in a situation to become the instructors of other nations. We have lessons of more importance to communicate than to receive.—This subject of our literature is one, on which it is not irreverent to apply the language of scripture, and to say that we ought to be *instant in season, and out of season*. No man, at the present day, can give better proof of his patriotism, or serve his country more effectually, than by promoting its literature. There is no secret about the manner in which this is to be done. There is but one thing wanting—ENCOURAGEMENT.

ANONYMOUS "LIFE AND WRITINGS OF BENJAMIN FRANKLIN" (1818)

We shall not dilate upon the unequalled perspicuity, the 'quick and poignant brevity,' the unremitting vividness, and rich variety of his style, about which so much has been said, with such warmth of panegyric, by the European critics. The reproach of vulgarity thrown out against it by some of them, appears to us, we must confess, to have little foundation; not more, certainly, than exists for a similar one against almost any English writer equally voluminous. Coarse terms occur indeed, from time to time, in his practical and familiar compositions; but only, we are inclined to think, when they are indispensable, or best adapted for the occasion. The great English writers of the reign of queen Anne, have sinned against delicacy in language in a thousand instances, to one that can he proved upon the 'American tradesman;' and if we took an example among the more modern authors of celebrity, say Mr. Burk or the magnates of the Edinburgh Review, our countryman could but gain by the comparison. Franklin is eminently a moral writer, in every sense of the phrase; he indulges in no allusions or imagery, fitted to inflame and vitiate the imagination; we question whether he any where falls into grossness of expression, without having it at the same time directly in view to recommend purity of conduct.

There is a striking, perhaps exclusive distinction, which may he claimed for his writings considered as models of literary excellence—it is that this excellence though the effect of early preparation of the most laborious sort, was not immediately intentional; in no one of them, does he appear to have aimed at displaying his powers or acquiring literary fame: We are justified in supposing that he would willingly, like Socrates, have confined himself to oral discussion and exhortation, had his ends of business or philanthropy been attainable in this course.

* * *

The paper respecting a plan of studies for the University of Pennsylvania, dated in the year 1789, and extant in the present volume, shews that this apostle of the useful, retained to the last, a keen solicitude for the proficiency of his countrymen in English composition. It evinces, also, how great was the variety and refined the choice of his reading; how carefully he had investigated and practised the best modes of forming an elegant style. His writings generally afford ample proof that he had an intimate acquaintance with the classical authors of his own tongue, and had accomplished himself in all the higher branches of an English education. His frequent and happy references to history, both ancient and modern, imply a minute knowledge of it, drawn from the best sources. It is evident also, that he was familiar with the philosophical doctrines of antiquity, and versed in the Latin language. His scholarship was not indeed, profound or critical; but he had, probably, more than is commonly imagined, and enough for his purposes.

The absence of all declamation, paradox and fine-spun, metaphysical morality—of heroics of whatever kind, from his writings, accords with his consummate character as a citizen and philosopher. Though he took the lead in a mighty revolution, there was nothing *revolutionary* in his temper or doctrines; he has left no line that gives the least countenance to anarchy, disorder, or any species of licentiousness. Nothing sets out in stronger relief the superiority of his understanding and the firmness of his principles, than his total exemption from the follies and weaknesses of the sect of politicians and philosophers, by whom he was surrounded, during his residence in France. His social, his political, his religious creed, remained the opposite of all that was preached by the oracles of the day. He returned to America without having admitted into his mind a single ray of the 'newborn light.' He lived long enough to hear of the first movements of the French revolution, and, as we are credibly informed, often expressed in conversation, serious alarms for the issue.—His letter to M. Le Roy, at Paris, of November 13, 1789, contains phrases which give an insight into his feelings and opinions on this subject. ''Tis now more than a year since I have heard from my dear friend Le Roy. What can be the reason? Are you still living? or have the mob of Paris mistaken the head of a monopoliser of knowledge, for that of a monopoliser of corn, and paraded it about the streets on a pole? Great part of the news we have had from Paris, for near a year past, has been very afflicting. I sincerely wish and pray it may all end well and happily both for the king and the nation. The voice of philosophy, I apprehend, can hardly he heard among those tumults.'

'He who gives glory to his country,' says an English orator, Mr. Wyndham, 'gives it that which is far more valuable to it than any acquisition whatever.

Glory alone is not to he taken away by time or accident. It is that fine extract, that pure essence which endures to all ages, while the grosser parts, the residuum, may pass away and be lost in the course of time.' In this point of view thus exalted, above all others, in importance, Franklin was, if we except Washington, the greatest benefactor of America. He has won for her more and brighter trophies than any other of her sons. Europe has acquiesced, almost unanimously, in the pre-eminence of his genius, and virtue, and usefulness. To desecrate his name, would therefore, be to despoil his country of some of her most precious honours; and the American who should attempt it, under whatever pretence, would be guilty of a sort of treason and sacrilege.

FAMILIAR LETTERS (1833)

Jared Sparks, the indefatigable nineteenth-century historian and editor, assembled an impressive personal collection of manuscript material pertaining to American history, especially the history of the revolutionary period. As part of his collection, he had more than a hundred of Franklin's personal letters. Sparks realized that these letters, as a whole, could provide a much different picture of Franklin than the one supplied by his known, published writings. Fueling his interest in Franklin, Sparks came across a number of books at the Philadelphia Athenaeum that had formerly been in Franklin's personal library.

In 1822 William Duane had sold several books he had purchased from Franklin's library to the Athenaeum, including many Revolutionera pamphlets. What made these pamphlets uniquely valuable was that their margins were filled with manuscript annotations in Franklin's hand. Sparks recognized the value of Franklin's marginalia and transcribed several passages from the margins of his books. Sparks's personal manuscript collection, combined with the notes from his research at the Philadelphia Athenaeum, convinced him that he had the makings of an original edition of previously unknown Franklin writings. He combined the letters with the marginalia, added a few other pieces, and published the whole in 1833 as *A Collection of Familiar Letters and Miscellaneous Papers of Benjamin Franklin*. The London edition appeared the same year under the title, *Familiar Letters and Miscellaneous Papers of Benjamin Franklin*. The book was widely reviewed.

In his notice of *Familiar Letters*, the first document in this subsection, O.W.B. Peabody recognizes a disparity between Franklin's public image and the personality these private letters suggest. *Familiar Letters* gave readers a view of Franklin they had never seen before, a softer side. Peabody's comments point toward an important research topic: what is the relationship between the public Franklin and the private one? People often equate the two, but the private Franklin differed from the self he portrayed in print and in public.

Several nineteenth-century readers of *Familiar Letters* recognized the value of ephemeral writings. For example, the contributor who reviewed *Familiar Letters* for the *American Quarterly Observer* asserted that since genius touches everything, the slightest writings of a great mind are worth consideration for the nuggets of wisdom they may contain. Is this true? Can you find evidence of Franklin's genius in the letters to friends and family or in his marginalia? Could Franklin's familiar letters be used as a model for letter writing? How does the style of his correspondence reflect its substance?

The anonymous contributor to the *New England Magazine*, whose review forms the next selection, finds that Franklin's familiar letters, though slight, nonetheless confirm his greatness. This reviewer refers to Peabody's review of *Familiar Letters* but disputes his conclusion regarding the importance of the letters. These familiar letters also reveal Franklin's relationship with women. In *The Life of Benjamin Franklin* (2006), J.A. Leo Lemay recognizes Franklin's forward-thinking feminism. Lemay argues that Franklin's female personas and his public writings advocated greater public roles for women. To what extent do his private letters affirm Lemay's idea? How did Franklin shape himself for his female readers? And what do his letters say about his attitudes toward women?

This New England reviewer really dislikes the second part of this edition—the miscellaneous papers—which he finds little more than waste paper. The reviewer misses the significance of Franklin's marginalia, however. The margins of a book are where author and reader meet. Inscribed with marginalia, a book stops being a one-sided discourse: it becomes a dialogue. Franklin did not write in his books very much, but when he did, his comments, as Sparks recognized, were worth studying. The Yale edition of Franklin's *Papers* transcribes marginalia from some of Franklin's surviving books. *The Library of Benjamin Franklin* transcribes marginalia from others. What kind of comments did Franklin make in the margins of his books? What conclusions about his reading process can be drawn from his marginal comments?

The anonymous contributor to *New Monthly Magazine*, a London periodical, also reviewed a work by Horace Walpole in the same issue. The coincidence prompted him to compare Franklin and Walpole. The correspondence of both men reveals their wit, their playfulness, and their grace. In addition, this London reviewer comments on the historical image of Franklin. Traditionally, we think of him as an old man, but many of these letters show him as a much younger man and thus help to dispel the traditional image.

In a way, the anonymous contributor to the *American Monthly Review* continues a dialogue established by O.W.B. Peabody in his essay. This reviewer suggests that Franklin's familiar letters catch him in unguarded moments, revealing his character in ways his published writings do not. They show his tenderness. They also show that his characteristic thriftiness never made him miserly. They do not really reveal anything new about his attitude toward Christianity, however. In other words, they do not help dispel the idea that he was a skeptic when it came to matters of religion.

Contemporary women's conduct books were often written as letters to a daughter. Collected together, Franklin's letters to female relatives read like a conduct book. Or so this reviewer suggested. To what extent is this suggestion valid? Compare *Familiar Letters* with contemporary female conduct manuals to test this idea. The last document in this subsection, which comes from an anonymous review in the *American Ladies' Magazine*, reinforces the idea that *Familiar Letters* is a ladies' book. Of the 128 letters included, 95 are written to women. Taken together, they show that Franklin appreciated the hearts and minds of women.

Sparks's *Familiar Letters* inspired others to extend his research. Taking a hint from Sparks, William Duane, Jr., the grandson of William Duane, went to the Philadelphia Athenaeum, transcribed several of Franklin's essays from manuscript, and sent them to Edgar Allan Poe who published them in the *Southern Literary Messenger* (2 [1836]: 293–296, 349–352, 411–412). Duane's contributions to the *Messenger* show that much editorial work remained.

O.W.B. Peabody
"Franklin's Familiar Letters" (1833)

The impression has always prevailed to a considerable extent, that Franklin was a selfish man, and that he took no interest in any thing which did not tend either to flatter his vanity, or advance the purposes of his ambition. It was sufficiently evident that the philosophic repose, which has always been ascribed to him, by no means prevented him from observing others; and that, instead of being indifferent to them, he was one of the most shrewd and sarcastic of men: but there are no traces of bitterness,—no appearances of envy or jealousy,—no attempts to injure the standing of others, in any of his writings which the world has ever seen; so that this impression concerning him seems rather traditional and indefinite, than sustained either by the spirit of his familiar writings, the records of his life, or the testimony of those who knew him best.

Political men may have been prejudiced against him from personal motives, and their hostile feelings would, of course, be shared by all the members of their party. The impression, too, would be confirmed by inferences drawn from the spirit of some of his writings. He gave practical rules for the government of life; he recommended a thriving, minute attention to the details of business, a close regard to small gains, which, to many, would have an air of selfishness about them, since they seem to concentrate upon one's own prosperity all the powers of the mind and the affections of the heart. But those who are acquainted with men, know full well that so far from being inconsistent with generous feeling, this habitual exactness is necessary, to make generosity of any value: without this practical sagacity, it spends itself in feeling, or runs to waste, and neither benefits its possessor nor the world. He was in the habit of attaching conditions to his gifts, which sometimes seemed to lessen his reputation for liberality: but it was afterwards found, that the favor had been doubled instead of diminished, by a compliance with the conditions which had been exacted. We have seen more instances than one, of princely benefactions, thus accompanied with conditions, which at first seemed embarrassing and impracticable, but which afterwards proved to be so judicious, and tended so much to the prosperity of the receiver, that he felt as much gratitude to his benefactor for those conditions, as for the donation itself. That kind of liberality, which secures as far as possible the right use of its gifts, is the most desirable in the world. It is true, that there are those, who insist upon doing favors in their own way as they call it, and make it manifest that they are thinking all the while more of themselves than of others. Such, however, was not the case with Franklin.

Those who have indulged the suspicion that the integrity of Franklin was apt to be overcome by self-interest, have brought forward certain passages in his published correspondence, in which he alludes to a proposed grant from the crown, which, they imagined was solicited for himself and his son. Mr. Sparks, however, has removed all the mystery of this transaction. It appears, that while Franklin was residing in England, as agent for Pennsylvania, a company was formed by Sir William Johnson and others in America, who requested Dr. Franklin to use his influence to procure for them a grant of land in the Ohio country. This bore the name of *Walpole's Grant*, so called from Mr. Walpole, a banker in London, who was placed at the head of the company. All the petitions and other proceedings of this company were public, and Franklin had no more personal interest, than any other individual of the numerous proprietors. The plan succeeded so far as respected the grant, but the disorders of the country, which were their beginning, prevented its execution.

But those who have never doubted the uprightness of Dr. Franklin, and have given him credit for general liberality, and good feeling, have not, we believe, regarded him as a warm-hearted man or an active friend. This book will serve to give a different impression. There is something exceedingly pleasing in the interest which he expresses for his connexions, the kind attention and advice which he gives them, the forbearance with which he treats their faults, and the pleasure with which he encourages their virtues. Some of these letters were written more than a century ago, when he was poor and unknown they therefore show the man as he was,—not when he lived in the broad sunshine of life, where it is easy to be generous,—but as he was when struggling with difficulties, and laden with cares, which seem to have left him little time to think of others. But we will let them speak for themselves. They will bear a favorable testimony to the character of Franklin.

* * *

Our limits have restricted us to a very cursory notice of this interesting volume, which is rendered more valuable by the fact, that a small portion only of the familiar correspondence of Dr. Franklin has heretofore been given to the world. Mr. Sparks, its editor, has placed the public under new obligations to himself, for the ability and diligence with which he is laboring to preserve from oblivion the facts and documents that may serve to illustrate our history, and of the characters of our distinguished men.

Anonymous
"Franklin's Familiar Letters" (1833)

The Letters and Miscellaneous Papers of Dr. Franklin, contained in this volume, and now for the first time published, came into the hands of Mr. Sparks, from various sources, while prosecuting researches for other objects. We are glad that he has given them to the public.

Genius always imparts life and interest to whatever it touches, so that the great reason why the public have so strong a desire to look into the familiar

and private writings of really eminent men, is not mere curiosity to become acquainted with their private history—it arises from the fact, that a pen, which is really skilful on any subject, will throw a charm over any one which it touches. In fact, the principles which guide in one case, will guide in all. This is shown, very distinctly, in the work before us. The clear view of human character and conduct—the forcible and lucid expression—the sound, irresistible reasoning, and the dexterous appeal—illuminate these letters, relating often to the merest minutiae of family arrangements, as brightly as they do discussions, by the same writer, of the most important questions of politics and science.

The perusal of these letters is calculated to have a good influence, in many respects. First, in style and language. Like all of Franklin's writing, the book is a model of simplicity, ease and force. The great, we may say, the almost universal fault, of American writers, is affectation of eloquence. Writing can never be of any permanent interest, except from the thought it conveys; and the more simply, and tersely, and sententiously, this thought is expressed, the better. Some of our leading writers, such as Franklin, Rush, Jefferson, and others, have been models in this respect. It has been said of Rush, for example, that a quotation from his works makes a bright spot on the page to which it is transferred. It is so with Franklin. He makes use of language, merely as a medium by which to convey his thoughts. Many other writers employ thought, only as a groundwork on which to display language.

Again, the letters are written in a great variety of circumstances, and relate to a great variety of subjects in common life; so that they teach wisdom, by a practical exhibition of it. No one can read them, attentively and thoughtfully, without learning lessons of prudence and good management from them. We give an example, by extracting a letter. The circumstances were these. Franklin was at Philadelphia, a printer, and he had interested himself in getting his nephew, whom he calls Benny, apprenticed to a printer in New York. In process of time, difficulties arose between the young apprentice and his master. The former complained to Franklin, and to his mother, at Boston; and this letter is an effort of our author's to allay the rising irritation. It is a model, worthy of the study of many a father and master, in our days. Firmness and good sense, united with good humor and dexterity, characterise his management. It seems, too, to have been successful.

* * *

The first part of the volume is occupied chiefly with letters to the various branches of his family, and were written previously to his first going to England, on political business. While in England, he resided in the family of Mrs. Stevenson, whose daughter seems to have been a favorite with him. The volume contains many of his letters to her, on a great variety of topics, amusing and instructive.

As years move on, the correspondence becomes gradually involved with political events; and many of the letters on these subjects, written in France, are highly interesting, especially those relating to the movements and operations of the celebrated John Paul Jones.

The volume is concluded with what are called Miscellaneous Pieces—chiefly arguments, and memoranda of arguments, on the political controversies in which Franklin was engaged. The spirit and force of his writing gives interest to what would otherwise, now, deserve little attention; and the whole closes with a very amusing article, entitled the "Craven-street Gazette," in which the occurrences of a few days, in the family in which he resided at London, are pompously described, in the technical phraseology used by the newspapers, in recording the measures of a ministry. The whole is highly interesting and instructive, and of decidedly good moral tendency.

Anonymous "Literary Notices" (1833)

As regards *eye-sight*, the human race are divided into three classes, *near-sighted* people, *far-sighted* people, and people whose eyes are as they should be; and we may make a similar classification with regard to the *mental* character of our fellows. We see some whose minds are constantly engrossed by objects near at hand, by humble and familiar objects, who can perceive these in their full or more than their full proportion; but to whom all beyond, great truths, far-reaching relations, general laws and important results, are shrouded in impenetrable mist. This is by far the largest class. Then there are some, whose mental vision is constantly strained to its utmost keenness, who can look deep, and high, and far, to whom objects immense and obscure appear in well-defined proportions; but who are blind to the daily occurrences, the daily duties, and the common-place relations of life, who are dead weights upon all the minor machinery of society, and who, while the path of their spirits is among the clouds, fairly cumber the ground on which they vegetate. These are vulgarly called great men, but, notwithstanding all their services to science and to literature, they are great nuisances; for their example leads new aspirants after greatness to commence their career by neglect of duty. The truly great man is, in our apprehension, a much rarer phenomenon. He, only, deserves that name, to whom, great and small things, things terrestrial and spiritual, things visible and invisible, duties, pleasures and privileges, appear each in its just proportions, each in its full importance. To this third and small class, Dr. Franklin indubitably belongs. In this we have always assigned him a high rank, and the chief value of the work before us, is, that it confirms him in that rank. These letters are such as delicacy and justice ought to have kept forever unpublished. They make the reader shudder for the fate of his own unburned letters; for there is hardly any man, who can spell decently and write grammatically, whose every-day epistles are not as well worth printing as Franklin's *Familiar Letters*. These are simply letters to near relatives or intimate friends, such as every man must write from time to time to save appearances, or will write frequently from the promptings of affection. They generally relate to family affairs, often trivial, often delicate, often of the most unedifying kind. Nor does the circumstance, that they are discussed by his pen, magnify their importance. He treats trifles as trifles, expresses his regards, and makes friendly inquiries as any other printer would have done, and gives good advice as sparingly and modestly as every wise man ought to. If Franklin had belonged to our *second* class of great men, his (so called) familiar letters might have been interesting from their eccentricity and irrelevancy. Thus, had he been a Byron, he would have berated his mother instead of reverencing her gray hairs; or, had he resembled Tom Moore, we should have found a donation of cash to his relatives enveloped in half a dozen lines of highly wrought poetry, rather than in a letter stating the simple fact that the money was sent. But for the very reason that they are just what they should be, the major part of these epistles will be deemed not worth the perusal.

These letters, as we have already observed, show the true greatness of the author's *mind*. In the last number of the North-American Review, a high value is attached to this volume, as relieving Franklin's *moral* character from the charge of *selfishness* and *irreligion*. That he was, throughout life, a selfish man,—that he governed his appetites, obeyed the laws, and served his country, because he deemed it his best policy so to do,—we have never doubted. We discern traces of supreme selfishness in the very letter quoted in that journal, as proof positive of his generosity. We will quote the entire letter, since it will serve as a fair specimen of the volume.

* * *

It appears that this sister Douse was aged, infirm, and destitute, and therefore had strong claims upon the sympathy and liberality of her relatives. And how does her philosophic brother proceed on these premises? Does he express any fraternal sympathy? No. He might have spoken as tenderly, had the subject of the letter been an old family drudge, or even a worn-out horse. Does he send her pecuniary aid from his own already ample resources? No; not a word of this. But yet he is lavish of his good advice; and to what does he advise her? Forsooth, not to sell those superfluities by which she might procure the money which he does not see fit to offer her. "Be thou warmed and be thou comforted," says he; "yet, my dear sister, do not expect from my bounty, and do not procure for yourself the means of warmth and comfort." But Dr. Franklin, if not himself beneficent, like a skilful engineer, brings fuller fountains of beneficence to play upon his poor sister. Mrs. Mecom is urged to pay her assiduous attention. Cousin Williams is directed to continue his care. A loud appeal is made to the selfishness, (a principle in which Franklin's own experience seems to have given him great confidence,) of *that* person, (an ill-fed domestic, we presume.) And we cannot but hope that, blessed with a sister's frequent visits, a cousin's constant care, and a discontented servant's all-grasping cupidity, sister Douse finished her mortal sojourn without feeling the want of her brother Benjamin's advice or aid. *Expressions* of affectionate interest abound in the letters to his sisters; but they seem too mechanical and business-like to have been prompted by deep feeling, and are sufficiently accounted for by the following judicious remark in one of those letters: "The more affectionate relations are to each other, the more they are respected by the rest of the world."

The best letters in this collection are those addressed to two ladies, with whom Franklin commenced a correspondence when they were young girls, and continued it after they became matrons. The first of these ladies was Miss Catharine Ray, afterwards wife of Governor Green, of Rhode-Island. She seems to have been a sprightly, good-humored girl, ready, in the abundance of her *philanthropy*, to make any man happy for the time being, whether he were single or married, young or old. Franklin was captivated by her gaiety of spirit, and her devoted affection to himself,—then so far advanced in age, as to make the attachment of a young lady a high compliment to his mental graces. She seems not to have been a lady of cultivation,—hardly one of decent education; for we find the following rather suspicious comment on her orthography in one of his letters to her. "As to your spelling, don't let those laughing girls put you out of conceit with it. "'Tis the best in the world; for every letter of it stands for something." Franklin's earlier letters to her are written in a playful style, full of compliments, so artfully set forth as to show that he had already sunk the mechanic in the courtier.

The other lady with whom he corresponded was Miss Stevenson, daughter of his hostess at London, and afterwards the wife of Dr. Hewson. She was an amiable, interesting, intelligent, and highly educated young lady, in whose progress in knowledge and prospects in life, Dr. Franklin took a deep interest. His letters to her are of a much more serious character than those to the mirthful Miss Ray. They are such as a judicious and well-informed parent would write to a daughter, whose mind and morals were his chief care. He gives her good advice as to her reading, study, and conduct; writes interesting sketches of his residence at France; and occasionally discusses literary and moral subjects. Very nearly one half of the letters are addressed to her.

The *miscellaneous papers*, which occupy the last eighty pages of this volume, seem to have been copied from odd pieces of waste paper found under Franklin's table. The first of them is a paper of such memoranda as a man holds in his hand to refresh his memory when about to address a deliberative assembly; and neither of them, (with a single exception) could ever have been issued from the press by any but an incorrigible book-maker. The exception is the Craven Street Gazette, in which the pompous annunciations of Court movements are ridiculed by a journal of the trivial household affairs at Mrs. Stevenson's mansion in Craven-street, drawn up in an equally pompous style.

Though no American can read this volume without interest, we must, in conclusion, express our willingness that Mr. Sparks may lose money by this act of literary sacrilege; and remind him that, unless he repent of this before he dies, every one of his *billets-doux*, every college theme, every thing which he would the most anxiously desire to bequeath to the flames, may, through the officiousness of his surviving admirers, be presented to a frowning public.

Anonymous
"Franklin's Familiar Letters" (1833)

It is singular enough that, just after finishing an article, which will be found in another part of this number, upon the gentleman Walpole, some new letters, just published in America, and not yet made known in this country, should be put into our hands, written at various epochs of his life by the citizen Franklin; and what, perhaps, will strike some of our readers as rather extraordinary, we find in the correspondence of the one, as of the other, great wit, playfulness, and grace. But the wit and playfulness of Franklin are of the homely and republican order we might expect. His thoughts appear very frequently to be lively and gay; but, generally speaking, they are without the tinsel and ornament of gaiety; and as, in the correspondence of the one, the mind of the courtier is everywhere perceptible, so, in the correspondence of the other, it is impossible not to see, at every page, that the writer had been educated without the precincts of a court; but then you do not regret it. The coarseness which occasionally occurs is not of the mind; and, therefore, instead of shocking as vulgarity, it charms as simplicity.

We cannot help first quoting a paper [*The Craven Street Gazette*], which, though published with the correspondence, does not, of course, form a part of it—not, we own, on account of its simplicity,—for it bears rather a contradiction to the theory we have been laying down, and which we believe to be generally correct,—but for the singular manner in which it resembles, even in flighty fineness, the similar productions of Horace Walpole. Considering the total dissimilarity in the characters, pursuits, habits of thought, and habits of writing of these two persons, it is almost a literary curiosity when looked at in this point of view—a point of view in which we should never, but for the preceding criticism, have thought of regarding it.

* * *

There are two or three other pieces of the same kind which follow and which are remarkable—as this is remarkable—for a vein of wit and humour. But the correspondence is of another kind: its charm—and it has a peculiar charm—is in its quiet and steady good sense and unaffected good-nature. The first letter we shall quote was written when Franklin was twenty years old, and is only noticeable for its *naïve* simplicity, and the kind of contrast which it forms to our general idea of the character of the grave philosopher and statesman. At the time of the second he was thirty-six years old; this was just previous to his first appearance in political life, and the appointment offered to him, and refused by him, of Colonel of the Philadelphia regiment. Its interest is in the opinions it expresses, and the admirable spirit of toleration which, with bigots and fanatics, has naturally passed for a spirit of irreligion. The third, to which we shall give a place, is mainly remarkable for the practical sense and the keen habit of investigation it displays on the merest trifles of ordinary life. The picture of the boy's unwillingness to go to church,—of his shuffling, and delaying, and complaining of his clothes on Sunday,—is, in its way, excellent, and shows, in a touch, the character of the writer. These letters the reader will find at the end of our remarks.

We find a remark in another letter which, though we do not quote the letter itself, we cannot pass over in silence; there is a simple and unaffected spirit of high and genuine honesty in it which the wittiest phrase of Walpole cannot compete with. He is speaking of the conduct of a Mr. Parker to his nephew.

"Mr. Parker," he says, "has, in every respect, done his duty by him, and in this affair has really acted a generous part; therefore I hope if Kenny succeeds in the world, he will make Mr. Parker a return *beyond what he promised.*"

There is, in this short sentence of the printer's apprentice, a nobility which all the herald's art did not furnish to the honourable member of the House of Orford.

The fourth and last letter which we now quote,—for it is intended to continue the notice of this correspondence,—is to a young lady, and has all the gallantry and grace that might be expected from a *preux chevalier.*

"Persons," says the old Philosopher, "complain of the north-east wind as increasing their malady, but since you promised to send me kisses in that wind,—and I find you as good as your word,—'tis to me the gayest wind that blows, and gives me the best spirits. I write this during a north-east storm of snow, the greatest we have had this winter. Your favours come mixed with the snowy flakes, which are pure as your virgin innocence, white as your lovely bosom, and—as cold."

Match us, reader, in the most gallant memoirs of the happiest French court a prettier paragraph.

But we have turned to Franklin after Walpole, not so much to draw a comparison between their writings as between their lives.

Franklin,—sprung from a low origin, the citizen of a colony which swelled into an active republic, in which every path was open to ability,—passed through each gradation of useful and ambitious life. Read the account of his arrival at Philadelphia—the commencement of his career!—

"I arrived at Philadelphia in my working-dress, my best clothes being to come by sea. I was covered with dirt; my pockets were filled with shirts and stockings; I was unacquainted with a single soul in the place, and knew not where to find a lodging. Fatigued with walking, rowing, and having passed the night without sleep, I was extremely hungry, and all my money consisted of a Dutch dollar and about a shillings-worth of coppers, which I gave to the boatmen for my passage. As I had assisted them in rowing, they refused it at first, but I insisted on their taking it. *A man is sometimes more generous when he has little than when he has much*; probably because, in the first case, he is desirous of concealing his poverty."

He then goes on, we remember, to tell how he bought three large rolls, and "with one under each arm walked on, eating the third. Passing, in this manner, the house of Mr. Read, the father of my future wife, she, standing at the door, observed me, and thought, with reason, that I made a very singular and grotesque appearance."

Beginning thus, and not stopping in his laborious career, he did not end it until he had successively been the apprentice to the printer, the editor of the newspaper, the clerk of the General Assembly of Philadelphia, the representative of that city, the philosopher, celebrated for his discoveries in science, the diplomatist. You see him through life,—now employed in improving his almanack—now in making his experiments in electricity— now in taking part in the debates of a public assembly—now in conducting a treaty, and settling the basis of national independence for his country. Contrast this useful and laborious life with the epicurean and softened existence which smoothed down and wore off the energies of Horace Walpole! In his writing—in his speeches—simple, unadorned, and concise, the grace of Franklin (for he also had that charm) was the grace of an antique statue; while Walpole's more frequently resembles that of a French painting. They were both men of various and extraordinary talents; but the one, living only for pleasure, produced nothing that could do more than contribute to the idle amusement, while the other engaged in everything that could add to the solid happiness and moral dignity of his countrymen. Walpole, afraid of peeping without the pale of good society, clipped his talents down into accomplishments; Franklin, with the wide range of the world before him, took an easy flight into its various paths;—the one could hardly have been more, the other could not have been less, than he was. We aim at no moral; and our tale, if we had any, is finished.

Anonymous "Franklin's Letters" (1833)

The scanty memorials which many distinguished philosophers and statesmen have left behind them relating to their private history and character have often called forth expressions of great regret. Curiosity is always alive, when men who have filled a large place in the republic of letters or in the affairs of state, have ceased from their labors, to know all about their habits, their social and domestic characters, their virtues and vices, their strong and weak points as neighbours and every day companions. Few men of the class to which we have adverted, have put it to the power of posterity to know so much concerning them as Franklin did. "The memoirs of his life and writings, written by himself to a late period, and continued to the time of his death by his grandson, William Temple Franklin," do much to answer the inquiries of the curious—how such a great man was formed; how much he did for society; how he conducted himself in practical matters; and what were the qualities of his mind and heart. The "Familiar Letters," recently collected and published by Mr Sparks, add to the means of gratifying our curiosity in those respects. "They must have been written," as Mr Sparks says, "without the remotest thought on the part of the author, that they would ever be made public." Hence, being little on his guard, we may look for the expressions of the undisguised workings of his understanding, passions, and affections, in regard to his family and friends, and as a man living and moving among other men.

We shall endeavour to illustrate in a few particulars, from a cursory reading of these "Familiar Letters," the bearing they have upon the character of the author.

It is natural to look in these letters for the indications of the author's character in the domestic relations. The collection, however, contains but three letters to his wife, and these were written in the year 1756, during short absences from home. His terms of affectionate address begin with "dear child," and end with "dear Debby," and "dear girl."

The first letter is dated at Gnadenhutten, a frontier place, whither he had gone to build forts. He speaks of the good provisions which his wife had prepared, and of the more perfect enjoyment of good eating "when the kitchen is four score miles from the dining room;" and concludes with the hope that he shall soon return to his wife and family, and "chat things over." In a letter from another place, towards the close of the year we have mentioned, he expresses his disappointment at not hearing from his wife, adds a good natured reproof, and concludes—"I think I won't tell you that we are well, nor that we expect to return about the middle of the week, nor will I send you a word of news; that's poz."—"P.S. I have *scratched out the loving words*, being writ in haste by mistake, when I *forgot I was angry*."

In one of his letters to Miss Catharine Ray, of Rhode Island, in 1755, there is a casual and unstudied tribute to the virtues and good dispositions of his wife, which fully proves the happiness of the relation. He speaks of his pleasure in receiving some presents from this female correspondent, and among others of an "excellent cheese."

* * *

There is one point in regard to which Franklin's character has suffered we suppose with many, and that is, in his notions about saving and thrift upon a small scale. It has been thought that his minute attention to such matters indicated in his writings, and especially that the acuteness and particularity of his maxims about economy and gain in respect to time and money, are calculated to produce a mean and penurious spirit; and that in general, those only will heed those maxims, who are already imbued with their spirit, and who are liable to be encouraged by them to regard the end kept in view, with such singleness and sagacity, as the great end of human wisdom and foresight. This view of the case is not altogether groundless. But we should remember that Franklin, like most young tradesmen, had to struggle, in the outset, against poverty, and that his maxims are the result of his own experience. The effects of them in his own case do not appear to have reached beyond the emergency; for when he had prospered so far as to lose all reasonable anxiety about competence, we do not perceive the reign of a penurious spirit.

* * *

Much curiosity, not to say anxiety, has been shown at different times by different individuals to ascertain Dr Franklin's views of Christianity. It is deeply to be regretted that a man of so great a mind, and on most subjects so ingenuous, never thought it worth his while to satisfy himself, by thorough investigation, concerning the truth and inspiration of Christianity. There is nothing in these letters, perhaps, which throws any new light upon the subject. They contain repeated confirmations of what was well known before, namely, that he was a firm believer in a paternal God, in a superintending Providence, and in a future life. Nor are there any unfavorable reflections on Christianity itself. He was disgusted with seeing many things overacted, and in general with sectarian disputes as they were conducted, and too proudly, as we think, looked on as a philosophical spectator, without heeding that better part of philosophy which looks deeply into the truth of things.

Anonymous
"Books and Authors" (1834)

A wise head and a warm heart is the perfection of the human character: every one allowed that Doctor Franklin possessed the first, but till these 'Letters' appeared, there was not very good evidence of the last requisite. But here we have his heart and all its emotions laid open as though he were in the Palace of Truth—and strange enough it is to find that 'to love and be beloved,' was the dearest happiness of the Philosopher, who

'Grasped the lightning's fiery wing'—
the 'Poor Richard,' whose soul seemed all absorbed in saving pence and farthings.

The 'Letters' have been for some months before the public, and we hope have been generally read. The book is truly a 'lady's book,' *ninety-five* out of the one hundred and twenty-eight Letters it contains being addressed to the female friends of this great statesman; and the tone of entire confidence in these letters shows that he appreciated the mind as well as the heart of women. The letters to his mother and sisters display the most tender and considerate affection; he enters into all their plans, pleasures, and cares, consoling, encouraging, and assisting, as though to promote their happiness was the main object of his life. This is showing the perfection of the prudent philosophy he taught in his writings, namely, making the best use of every earthly advantage. Many a man who prides himself on his profound sagacity and splendid talents, devotes these entirely to the world, and takes little heed to secure the affections of those whom nature has made his friends, and whose tender love would far more effectually contribute to his happiness than would the loudest notes of the trumpet of fame. It is not the rushing cataract, but the gentle dew that gives life and loveliness to nature.

* * *

One thing deserves particular remark—these letters exhibit no trace of the infidel. On the contrary, the spirit of Christian trust in and submission to God is manifested in a manner which shows that in heart Doctor Franklin was never an unbeliever, however in some of his speculations, the pride of reason may have shown itself in doubts and cavils.

LIFE AND *WORKS* (SPARKS) (1840–1844)

When Jared Sparks was in Philadelphia in 1831 gathering material for an edition of George Washington's writings, a member of the Historical Society of Pennsylvania escorted him to Champlost, the estate of the Fox family just outside Philadelphia, to view Franklin material pertaining to

Washington and located among a huge cache of Franklin manuscripts. The visit provided the impetus for Sparks's next big project, an edition of Benjamin Franklin's writings. Edgar Allan Poe imagined Sparks as "a man who was very busy among a great pile of books and papers huddled up in confusion around him" (*Southern Literary Messenger* 2 [1836]: 601). Poe's image is not far from wrong. Sparks returned to Champlost in 1837, when Charles Pemberton Fox helped him organize the Franklin papers and let him take away two large trunks filled with manuscripts. Sparks must have almost buried himself in Franklin documents as he worked. By the time he was through he had created a ten-volume edition, which added more than four hundred new Franklin documents to what had already appeared in print: an impressive achievement. Sparks's first Franklin volume appeared in 1836, the last in 1840. His first volume, which consisted of Franklin's autobiography and Sparks's continuation of the story of Franklin's life, was republished separately in 1844.

In nineteenth-century British quarterlies, it was common for reviewers to use a newly published book as a pretense for launching a discussion of a much larger subject. The book under review merely provided a starting point for the essay. Such is the case of the review of Sparks's edition that appeared in the *Eclectic Review*. This reviewer used Franklin's writings as an opportunity to discuss British colonial rule, emphasizing the importance of applying lessons learned during the American Revolution to suit colonial rule in the Victorian era, as the British empire expanded throughout much of the world. The reviewer suggested that a copy of Sparks's edition of Franklin should be given to public functionaries of all ranks as an object lesson in good governance and diplomacy. What Franklin wrote in the eighteenth century was crucial to the nineteenth. The *Eclectic* reviewer identifies parallels between the settling of Ohio and the settling of New Zealand. Could similar kinds of things be said today? In other words, does what Franklin says about good governance apply to modern-day situations? If so, how?

Sandwiched between two more extensive reviews in this collection, the anonymous review of Sparks's edition of Franklin's *Autobiography* that appeared in the *Columbia Lady's and Gentleman's Magazine* may seem slight, but it is worth noticing because it captures a childhood memory of reading Franklin's *Autobiography*. Since people seldom recorded their childhood reading experiences, the accounts of those who did provide important details for reconstructing the literary culture of the time. The fond memories of reading Franklin's autobiography as an adolescent recorded here contrast with Mark Twain's portrayal of how nineteenth-century children reacted to Franklin.

In his discussion of Sparks's edition for the *North American Review*, Francis Bowen offers a fine appreciation of Franklin's autobiography, comparing it with such literary classics as *Pilgrim's Progress* and *Robinson Crusoe*. All three can be read in youth and returned to in adulthood. Oliver Goldsmith's *Vicar of Wakefield* is another classic English novel that bears comparison to Franklin's autobiography. The friends Franklin describes, according to Bowen, resemble characters in a novel. Franklin's minuteness of detail also links his autobiography to the novel. These connections between Franklin's autobiography and the novel are worth developing further. Are there other eighteenth-century novels it resembles? What deliberately novelistic techniques does Franklin use to tell his personal story?

Bowen sees the figure of Poor Richard as a key to understanding the autobiography: *The Way to Wealth* provides a précis of Franklin's moral philosophy. It is, Bowen asserts, the "true manual of utilitarianism." Bowen links Franklin to ethical doctrine as well as to Bentham, Cicero, Hobbes, Hume, Paley, and Socrates. These associations provide several additional topics for further critical exploration.

Anonymous "Founding, Misruling, and Losing Colonies" (1843)

Emigration by the advance of public funds is a subject of the utmost importance, involving several great difficulties; but upon this theme we do not at present intend to enter. The subject of colonial government, which we shall discuss, is quite independent of emigration, and affects established interests far too extensive to be fairly or prudently treated with the neglect which it has hitherto encountered. A survey, therefore, of some of the stores furnished by colonial experience for the improvement of colonial government, may be well timed. Of those stores, none are more useful than the writings of Franklin; and to the numerous valuable publications, for which the United States of North America and the world at large are indebted to Mr. Sparks, the volumes now before us make an addition more important to the British public than any others of the same class with which we are acquainted. To the reader who is interested in colonial affairs, a large portion of this fine work has also the merit of being at this moment singularly *opportune*, for the following reasons, which will be appreciated in every corner of our colonies.

Franklin's writings treat in great detail of the way in which British colonies are founded and flourish, as well as of the errors of the government, which, in aiming at an unjust domination over the thirteen old American colonies, impeded their prosperity and provoked the sanguinary struggle so fatal to the supremacy of Great Britain. They further exhibit a full display of the means by which the outraged colonists succeeded in establishing their independence, after they had most reluctantly resorted to arms in vindication of their ancient rights. The lesson, however, to be learned from the utter failure of the Machiavellian policy attempted to be enforced over those colonies, has been absolutely thrown away upon our government, as it has been long disregarded by the public, at whose expense it was taught.

Through various pretences since 1782 (the date of the independence of the thirteen old colonies), the same policy has been established over many new ones,[1] in which despotism prevails to a degree unparalleled in British history. The evil consequences of this have been enormous, and it is the duty of every lover of his country to call for a reform of the system which has led to so gross an abuse of power. The experience of half a century may thus become a beacon to the future; and the new empires fast forming under British auspices be consolidated by the avoidance of past errors.

The necessity of a deep searching inquiry into this matter will be admitted by all who reflect on those evil consequences, coupled with the fact, that however the acquisitions of the crown abroad since the American revolution differ in other points, they all agree in being thus despotically governed. In the purely British settlements of the Australias, equally with our conquests in the West Indies, in Africa, and in the Indian Ocean, also in various other quarters of the globe the supreme rule has everywhere been—*the despotism of the Colonial Office*. Indeed, so complete is the success of this office, that even the New Zealand Colony, founded in a great degree by a powerful body of ardent reformers of Colonial policy, has accepted an arbitrary constitution to begin their young British empire upon in the Southern Ocean. It does not however require the gift of second sight to perceive that this *crown* colony is destined to be one of the first scenes of the early coming struggle for a return to our ancient principle of free colonial government.

We cannot stop to trace the arts by which the Colonial Office has succeeded by playing parties against each other so as to derive aid from all—from Tories, Whigs, and Radicals,—nay, even from religious and philanthropic bodies, although their leaders have long been thoroughly convinced of the iniquity of the system. It is enough to justify a call for reform, that the results in modern colonies are—general discontent among the whites, and ruin to the aborigines, abroad; and at home, prodigality in the place of the economy, which for the most part prevailed in managing the affairs of the old free colonies.

These evils must in existing circumstances be remedied by very different measures from those which saved the old colonies. Forming one block of territory, and inhabited chiefly by one nation, they were able to combine in order to resist by fighting; whilst, on the contrary, the misgoverned colonists of modern times are separated from each other by oceans, and by various manners and languages, so that, happily, military combination for such a purpose is impossible. But resistance of another character is in our power; and vigorous, judicious discussion in every possible form, with bills and other proceedings in parliament, and private enterprises of various kinds, cannot fail beneficial effects.

The writings of Franklin are invaluable in aid of such efforts. They furnish ample materials for perfectly appreciating the state of colonial affairs before the American war; and as the principles which then influenced the government in its erroneous course are now struggling hard for the mastery, a review of the affairs traced in these writings, and of the mischievous principles which the author resisted, will serve both to recommend what was good in times past, and to justify the call for changes of what is at present notoriously evil. The attentive study of them will serve to promote the success of British colonial enterprise, which is opening a career more brilliant than ever, and it is a worthy task to give to that enterprise its just issue, by correcting the errors of the government, which has too much impeded, and even attempted to stop, what it should have merely guided and duly controlled.

* * *

Of the general character of Franklin it is unnecessary to say much in this place. Our grandsires appreciated him highly, but not one jot beyond his true worth; and it did not require this fine collection of big admirable works to place him in the very first rank among men, for integrity, patriotism, and genius. But we are bound to observe, that Dr. Sparks' additions to the writings of Franklin already before the world, justify its good opinion of this great man, and are even adapted to extend his high reputation. In the new biography, Mr. Sparks triumphantly refutes the old imputation of Franklin's having misused a large sum of public money which passed through hands in Paris during the revolutionary war, and also shews satisfactorily, that in a protracted dispute with one of his colleagues, Mr. Lee, the great patience and prudence of Franklin were a match for the petulance of a disappointed expectant of the vigorous old man's well-filled office. This part of the biography, with the letters upon it, ought to be published in separate form, to be distributed among public functionaries of all ranks, for their comfort and guidance. The ill-judged accusations of Mr. Lee against Franklin are shewn to have been met at home in a manner that does great credit to the good sense and fair dealing of the government whom both were serving.

Franklin's sympathies were not confined to men of his own colour. In 1754, he drew up some general rules for the intercourse of the colonists with the Indians, which are good as far as they go. In 1764, he laboured most zealously, and at the hazard of his life, to defend the Indians of Pennsylvania from the foulest oppression; and his writings abound in appeals in their favour. In 1771, he proposed a plan, and offered to subscribe to execute it, in order to civilize the '*brave and generous*' New Zealanders, then lately visited by Captain Cook. The scheme, which was proposed in London, met with no countenance. On the contrary, Sir Joseph Banks, who should have supported it, suggested instead, that *convicts* should be turned loose in New Zealand, and in a few years Great Britain planted a convict settlement in its neighbourhood, which has done enormous evil to its people.

In regard to the negroes and to the slaves in America, Dr. Franklin was ever among the foremost to improve their condition. His last public act, at the age of eighty-four, was as President of an American Anti-Slavery Society. Nevertheless, it must be confessed that he was not altogether superior to the prejudice of colour. He would be just to the Negro *in his own country*, and would have made great sacrifices to abolish slavery throughout the world, as well as the slave trade, and even to improve the free coloured man; but he would join in measures also tending to inflict enormous injury on these free coloured men, in order to preserve the white race *pure*. This was the vice of his age—to have been superior to which would have made him a greater man; but it is so far from being yet eradicated from the minds of good men, that very few of us are entitled to sneer at the deficiency in him.

As we have intimated, the great value of this edition of Franklin's works lies in the full display it affords of British *Colonial* history during the few years immediately preceding the American revolution, and in the clear exposition of the real causes of that revolution. Both taken in connexion with the result of the struggle, so far as we can yet appreciate that result, are calculated, we repeat, to teach British statesmen, and the British people, the most useful of lessons, which they are far too reluctant to learn.

Prior to 1776, no such thing was, we think, known to the English colonial constitutions as a *crown colony*, in the modern sense of the word,—that is to say, a colony governed by the mere will of the sovereign exercised through a minister—legislation and taxation, *ad libitum* of the Colonial Office, without a local elective assembly, and by crown judges, more or less, without juries. Even the military fortress of Gibraltar, according to the old lawyers, was entitled to the latter degree of popular administration whenever fifty or sixty people could be got together to form the grand and petit inquests; and so early as in D'Avenant's days, a *constitution* was insisted upon for the fishing stations of Newfoundland. Besides this unquestionable practice, another great point of a popular character was clearly settled. Whilst by the law of *Spain*, a royal commission was indispensable to authorize the initiation of a new colon; by English law, on the contrary, a private subject might take the first steps to that end; and if those first steps were suitably taken, the crown usually adopted the countries so acquired by its subjects, allotting to them large tracts of the land, with various privileges, and under various conditions. One of the most remarkable examples of this practice was that of Barbadoes, ultimately settled under judgments of the King in Council, after solemn hearing of all the parties who pretended to titles of any kind in that island; but all sprang from a private subject's acquisition of it, which the crown respected and adopted in sovereignty. In this way also a great country in the western parts of North America, now forming the state of Ohio, was, in Franklin's time, thronged with settlers, of whom many indeed were mere squatters, but whose assumptions of right by possession were respected. Others, setting to work more regularly, and selecting vacant territories for themselves, applied to the crown for grants of the soil. This proceeded long before their applications were agreed to; and Franklin took an active part in the enterprise, prior to 1770. The details of the case fill the greatest part of a large volume of his works. At this period, however, new counsels began to influence our colonial policy. The Earl of Hillsborough was one of the chief patrons of this new policy, which ultimately engaged the country in the unhappy American war. The essential characteristic of this policy was to substitute official despotism for popular government in the colonies. He was at the head of the Board of Trade, which, at that time, extensively administered all colonial subjects; and in that department he actively and perseveringly opposed the projected colony on the Ohio, of which Franklin was the representative in London. The opposition to this Ohio colony, bore a striking resemblance to that which was so unfortunately persevered in, in our own time, in regard to New Zealand and Natal, in South Africa. In a petition to his Majesty in council, a price, in money and in certain quit-rents, was offered for the land which the crown had bought of the Indians, and all just and legal rights to any parts thereof were prayed to be reserved to the persons entitled to them. The country thus sought to be formed into a new colony, amounted to about sixty millions of acres, or two-thirds of New Zealand in extent. Lord Hillsborough had, with much duplicity, urged the parties to ask for this large tract, in the hope that its extent would defeat their object. The Lords of the Treasury, before whom the case came, having required the opinion of the Board of Trade, the report, understood to have been written by his lordship, contained the following objections to the scheme.

The interest of the Indians was first set up against it, on the allegation that the crown had solemnly promised not to make settlements in the country in question; whereas, the colony asked for would ruin them. *It was then said that the only way to save the natives was to stop settlements altogether*. It was added, that the policy of the government was to confine the American colonies to a line not far westward; which would bring them easily within the reach of British trade, and under British authority, which inland colonies would not permit.

It was admitted that the back country abounded in new settlements; but it was argued warmly that they ought to be checked, not encouraged; and they ought be governed, it was said, by an old adjoining colony.

Accordingly, the Board of Trade, under his lordship's influence, advised that the application should be rejected; and to make sure work, that a proclamation should be issued against any new settlement in that quarter for the present.

A memorial drawn up by Dr. Franklin, replied, that the parties asked for a colony on the condition that the Indians should *consent* to alienate their rights; and it shewed, that boundaries between them and the settlers had been solemnly fixed, and that in 1764 *ministers had determined to obtain an Act of Parliament for the regulation of Indian affairs on a proper system*, founded on the purchase of lands a good boundary line on the borders to prevent complaints, on account of encroachments. *The Act of Parliament was not passed*; and from 1765 to 1768 great numbers of people settled over the mountains, which irritated the Indians and led to several murders. Troops were sent to dispossess the settlers, but the expedition failed. Emigration increased, and the Indians continued to demand payments for their lands, which was ultimately arranged, so that the country was legitimately open to settlement; and the memorial insisted that *the establishment of law and good government over the thousands of people scattered beyond the mountains would satisfy all parties*. 'Great numbers of your people,' said the Indian chiefs on the Ohio to General

Gage, 'have settled throughout the country, and we are sorry to tell you, that several quarrels have happened between them and our people, in which lives have been lost on both sides. We now see the nations round us and you, people ready to embroil us in a quarrel, which gives us great concern, as we, on our parts, want to live in friendship with you. *You have always told us you have laws to govern your people by, but we do not see that you have*; therefore, unless you can fall upon some method of governing your people, it will be out of the Indians' power to govern their young men. We assure you the black clouds begin to gather fast in this country, and if something is not soon done these clouds will deprive us of the sun. We desire you to give the greatest attention to what we now tell you; as it comes from our hearts, and from a desire we have to live in peace and friendship with our brethren the English.'

This memorial of Dr. Franklin denied that public policy opposed such colonies as that asked for, and cited reports of the Board of Trade as early as 1748, directly recommending this very settlement. It also proved, by figures, that British trade must be advanced by it.

In conclusion, after shewing that neither proclamations, nor the dread of savages, would stop the thousands of colonists, who were in the interior, the memorial asks, with great force, '*Is it fit to leave such a body of people lawless and ungoverned?*' Will sound policy recommend this manner of colonizing and increasing the wealth, strength, and commerce of the empire: or will it point out that it is the indispensable duty of government to render her *subjects useful subjects*; and for that purpose immediately to establish law and subordination among them, and thereby early confirm their attachment to the law, traffic, and customs of this kingdom?

The result of the struggle was favourable to the adventurers; and Lord Hillsborough, mortified at the failure of his opposition, resigned his office. It was, however, too late; and what our colonial administration of that day delayed so long, was eagerly completed by the revolutionary government at Washington.

The Ohio case was the last that occurred of this character before we lost the old American colonies. It strikingly exemplifies the ancient British way of founding new colonies by private enterprise under the control of the crown— a combination which, *if properly reduced to a system*, and which has been lost sight of, is alone calculated to ensure great and early colonial success. The weakness of the Ohio Company's case was, the want of any suitable provisions to protect and elevate the aborigines; but that want has never been supplied by the crown, during the long period of its having usurped the exclusive command of colonial affairs, by the establishment of the crown colonies since

1782. On the contrary, when the crown has been most absolute in the form of constitutions, and most powerful in fact, as in New South Wales and Van Diemen's Land, the aborigines have suffered most; and it is one of the great merits of the revival of the ancient practice in the New Zealand case, that the private parties have done much to redeem the past in this respect, although much still remains undone.

It is unnecessary to examine those parts of this edition of Franklin's works which present the details of the immediate causes of the revolutionary war, and of the conduct of that war, or rather the *negotiations* in which Franklin, of all the Americans, was the most actively engaged; although to a diplomatist, this portion of the work, and Mr. Sparks similar publication, *the Diplomatic Correspondence of the American Revolution*, furnish materials of surpassing value. Pending the war, however, there occurred an incident which we have the means of describing even more in detail than is done by the able editor of these volumes. Two great changes of opinion took place in England in the few years before and during the contest. Prior to 1776, the British public sympathised with the colonists. Afterwards, for about two years, appeals to our forefathers' pride, and to their cupidity, succeeded in exciting their worst passions *against* their American fellow-countrymen. This bad feeling, however, soon gave way; and, in 1778, they began to perceive that the best British interests were violated by the continuance of hostilities. It was accordingly in this year that the incident alluded to occurred. Plans of reconciliation were proposed by the wisest members of the legislature, and by other good men, and much favoured by the public. Of such plans, one of a very singular character was offered to Dr. Franklin, at that time minister from the United Colonies to the court of France. The whole contest, which was distinguished by as much good logic as good fighting, did not produce a more remarkable document than this letter.

* * *

The chief points of the new plan of government which accompanied this letter, were, that the consent of the colonies should be indispensable to all future constitutional changes—that each colony should choose its own form of government, and appoint its own executive officers—that colonists should be eligible to fill public offices in Great Britain, only by special acts of parliament, but in all other respects should enjoy the rights of British subjects—that a central court of American peers for appeals from all other courts, and to be named by the king, should be created, with a final appeal to the House of Lords—that a congress of delegates from all the colonies should be assembled once in seven years to make general laws and vote money, subject to the approval of parliament—that the army and militia be under the crown, and be governed by the British Mutiny Act—that parliament shall vote men and taxes for the public services of America, as well as of Great Britain, but the amounts to be proportionate to the population of both countries— that the votes of taxes by the colonial legislature should be subject to the direct veto and regulation of parliament—that the customs tariff be settled by the colonial legislature, but subject to parliamentary revision—that British manufactures should have the preference in American ports—*that American trade should otherwise be free with all the world.* Besides all this, Washington, Adams, Hancock, Franklin, and some others, were to have certain offices and great personal rewards. Franklin attached the more importance to the proposals, because he believed them to have been approved by the British ministry. But he rejected the advance without a moment's hesitation.

The scheme of an American House of Peers long attracted attention in high quarters in England; and if that absurd idea of setting up an institution for which materials, analogous to those which support it in England, cannot be created, could by some ingenious contrivance converted into another proposition made twenty years before the American war, and revived more than once in the last ten years,—namely, into a proposition *for electing representatives of the colonies and India in a House of Commons*, many existing grievances would gradually disappear. Franklin was favourably inclined to this plan; which was also advocated by Dr. Adam Smith; but it has never been seriously taken up by any party, either at home or in the colonies.[2]

The reflection which arises strongly from the opposition of Lord Hillsborough to the Ohio colony, and from the formal scheme of colonial misgovernment, which the foregoing letter admits to have existed, is confirmed by an anecdote preserved by Mr. Sparks on the occasion of Lord Chatham's fatuous plan of conciliation, 'which was treated,' says Franklin, 'with as much contempt by the Lords as they could have shown to a ballad offered by a drunken porter;' and at this time, Lord Shelburne furnished the key to all the mis-government of the old colonies, which ended so disgracefully to England. 'In these matters,' said his lordship, 'parliament only obeys the dictates of a ministry, who in nine cases out of ten are governed by their under secretaries'—*Sparks*, vol. x., p. 437.

This imputation has not, unfortunately, been proved by modern experience to be a mere ebullition of spleen, or 'obstructive opposition;' nor has such undue influence had one whit better effect on our colonial affairs since, than before the American war. But its entire discomfiture in the late New Zealand case, permits a hope that a reform of the wretched system is at hand.

The independence of the United States being established in spite of the anticipations of M. de Weissenstein, Dr. Franklin passed many years as American minister in France, and died at a very advanced age in his own country, full of honours. In that great country his example and his opinions have gained a powerful hold upon the minds and conduct of millions of practical men; and this influence is far from being limited to the United States. In Great Britain, and throughout Europe, not to speak of the widely spreading European society scattered over all other quarters of the globe, the name and the works of Franklin are familiar to vast numbers of civilized people in many various departments of science, morals, and politics. It remains, perhaps, for us one day to put a great political principle which he advocated, to the test. Recently, one of the most remarkable productions of the American press, 'The Prize Essays upon a Congress of Nations for the adjustment of international disputes, and for the promotion of universal peace without resort to arms,' properly ranked his authority among the highest in favour of this object. 'We daily make great improvements,' says Franklin, 'in natural—there is one I wish to see in moral—philosophy; the discovery of a plan that would induce and oblige nations to settle their disputes, without first cutting throats. When will human reason be sufficiently improved to see the advantage of this?' The man who succeeded in introducing an article against privateering into a treaty of amity, even with one European state, is an excellent authority in such a matter; and although it may be too sanguine to expect, yet the ultimate attainment of the proposed object cannot be doubted now that the good seed is well sown. Already has that seed of good-will been cherished with admirable results; and the men who have in the United States taken a prominent lead in this sublime cause, may justly join with those who in England share their principles, in rejoicing at the fruits of their labour.

Whilst we are writing, the most immediate occasions for hostility are passing off; and it is impossible not to recognise in the conduct of large bodies of the Americans, and among their leading men, the good disposition towards peace, which Franklin, above all men, fostered so anxiously. Happily, a corresponding good spirit in this country is opposed to violent councils; and among the better signs are to be reckoned the proposal of measures among us, like the two favourite projects of Franklin. A motion has lately been prepared for the House of Commons for abolishing privateering; and our Peace Society has taken much pains to spread abroad the proposal for a congress of civilized nations to remove by negotiations the causes of war.

To promote such measures, few things would more conduce than familiarity with the writings and life of Dr. Franklin; and we are glad to have had means of devoting a portion of our pages to the recommendation of this edition of his works.

Notes

1. New South Wales, Van Diemen's Land, Swan River, South Australia, the Cape of Good Hope, Mauritius, Ceylon, Malta, Guiana, Trinidad, Sierra Leone, and New Zealand, not to add Indian and Chinese settlements.
2. What Romans dreamed about upon this subject may possibly remain to be realised by Englishmen.

Anonymous
"Books of the Month" (1844)

How different this superb octave of six hundred pages, with its clear, eye-rejoicing type, white paper and ample margins, from the dim, dingy, contemptible little tome which we remember reading, more than a quarter of a century ago, as we slowly walked home from school—having doubtless surreptitiously bestowed upon its enticing pages sundry odd minutes and quarters in school, which should have been honestly devoted to the "hard" mysteries of practice, compound division and the rule of three. We remember the very air and aspect of that miserable little "24 mo;" its small, almost illegible print, the type having probably been worn out in New York or Boston before it fell into the hands of the country publisher; its whity-brown, rough, flimsy paper; even its wretched sheepskin binding, mottled with meandering streaks of black, in the old fashion of "English Readers" and "American Preceptors."

But the "Life of Franklin" which we devoured then with such relish was the same autobiography that is so much more nobly lodged in this goodly octavo; with a difference however, for the knowledge of which we are indebted to Mr. Sparks. It seems that what we and thousands of others have read as Franklin's account of himself was in fact a translation from the French. The original autobiography was done into that language from Franklin's original manuscript, while he was minister at the Court of Versailles, by one of his friends, and the translation was published soon after his death. A re-translation was made from this, and published, in England; and it was from this version that the multitudinous American editions were mostly copied. A curious instance of literary transmigration.

But it is not for the restoration of the genuine autobiography alone that American literature is indebted to Mr. Sparks. Franklin carried his memoir only to 1757; Mr. Sparks has furnished a continuation, occupying about the same number of pages as the autobiography, and including, of course, the most important and interesting events in which Franklin bore so large a part—the events immediately preceding and attending the establishment of the colonies as independent states. In this Mr. Sparks has made a very acceptable and valuable addition to our national biography; for, as everybody knows, the agency of Franklin was scarcely less extensive or effectual in the deliberative and diplomatic management of the revolution then was that of Washington in the military.

Francis Bowen "Sparks's Life and Works of Dr. Franklin" (1844)

The writings of Franklin, if not of such preëminent and abiding importance for the history of the country as those of Washington, possess a more varied interest than the latter, and offer a wider theme for inquiry and comment. He was eminent in so many different departments of thought and action, and his works relate to so great a variety of topics, that an edition of them requires a great range of illustration, and leads to numerous branches of collateral research. The task of the editor, also, involved some peculiar difficulties. Franklin had all the generous carelessness of a great mind respecting his own reputation. He wrote and labored for particular and immediate ends, and, if these were attained, he cared comparatively little for what his contemporaries or posterity might think of his own agency in the matter. He published anonymously many pamphlets and brief essays on political topics, always to effect some special object,—to correct an erroneous impression, or to make an important statement of facts; and he showed no anxiety about collecting or claiming them afterwards. If it had not been for the zeal of a few correspondents and friends, like Benjamin Vaughan, Peter Collinson, M. Dubourg, and others, many papers of great interest would either have been lost, or never have been ascribed to him as their author. Disputes whether he was the writer of some curious essays arose in his lifetime, which he cared not to settle; and some questions of this sort remain yet undetermined, though the investigations of Mr. Sparks have put most of them at rest. His epistolary style was remarkable for ease, grace, and humor, and many of his letters are occupied with topics of great interest; but he seldom kept copies of them, he never demanded them back from his correspondents, and the consequence is, that a great number of them are irretrievably lost. There was ample room, therefore, for the labors of an editor, not only in supplying proper elucidations of matter that had been already published, but in retrieving from obscurity and loss many valuable documents.

* * *

This work is one of the most fascinating autobiographies in English literature. There is a singular charm about it, attributable in some measure to the interest of the events and the graces of the style, but in a much higher degree to the frankness, simplicity, and completeness of the exhibition of the writer's character. It is a book both for boys and men,—an admirable picture of the pursuit of knowledge, fame, and fortune, under difficulties, and an instructive manifestation of the workings of character, which the philosopher and the moralist need not be ashamed to study. Many years have passed since we first read it, and returned to its perusal again and again, with an interest not at all inferior to that with which every child hangs over the well thumbed pages of the standard juvenile books. Truth gradually assumes its superiority of interest over fiction, and the man returns with fresh delight to the "Life of Franklin," when he has ceased to care much about "Robinson Crusoe," or "The Pilgrim's Progress." Yet, perhaps, the book owes something of its attractiveness to the fact, that it possesses one of the most common and pleasing attributes of fiction,—that the story is carried out with what is called poetical justice. It shows the gradual, and what we instinctively consider the natural, triumph, in the affairs of this world, of those qualities of character, which we involuntarily love and respect, over those which reason and conscience alike require us to shrink from and condemn. In real life, casual and adverse circumstances interrupt, modify, and pervert what seems to be the course of justice, and we have recourse to fiction in order to find events that harmonize with the conclusions of our reason and the dictates of the moral sense. Sometimes, the reality points the moral quite as impressively as the poet or the novelist would have it; and then fact assumes the interest of fiction, and we dwell upon the incident with a pleasure which shows that it is one of rare occurrence. Usually, because our observation does not take in a range of events of sufficient extent, or because all the rewards of meritorious conduct are not of a definite and outwardly visible character, the incidents of real life seem to run counter to our expectations and our moral judgments.

Franklin wrote his memoirs in the manner of an old man having a number of his grandchildren about his knees, and telling them come pleasant story in order to enforce and illustrate his affectionate inculcation of virtuous and prudent conduct. The language is simple and graphic, the incidents are natural, and the moral is most impressively taught, though never brought obtrusively forward. The burden of the whole narrative is, that industry, temperance, and frugality lead by gradual but sure steps to the attainment of wealth and happiness; while indolence, carelessness, and vice bring their own punishment along with them. The lesson is trite enough, and owes all its impressive character to the skill of the narrator, the minuteness with which the incidents are related, and the conviction of the reader that it is a true story. The writer keeps back nothing; he mentions his past errors and occasional lapses from virtue with the same delightful simplicity and frankness that mark the account of the more honorable portions of his life. And with what admirable distinctness and discrimination are the several characters in the little narrative brought forward, and made to play their several parts! The sketches of the able and lively, but careless and dissolute, Ralph; the idle printer, Keimer; the promise-breaking governor, Keith; and the rattling and imprudent George Webb, who ran away from the University of Oxford in order to become a printer's apprentice in Philadelphia, might all be placed beside the admirable portraits in the "Vicar of Wakefield." Indeed, the homely air of Franklin's narrative, and the total want of reserve in speaking of his own weaknesses and his most private concerns, often remind one strongly of the worthy vicar. The incidents connected with both his courtships and his marriage, though of quite a delicate nature, are told with perfect simplicity and fulness, and without a word of apology or comment. He shows no sensitiveness, no secret pride, no artifice, no morbid reference to self. He writes the private history not only of his actions, but of his thoughts, with as much coolness as if he were describing a merely fictitious personage. In this respect, his autobiography is without a parallel in any language. The frankness of Rousseau's "Confessions" is all assumed; the writer is always acting a part, and is most theatrical when he affects to be most free from artifice. The simplicity of Franklin is that of a child; it wins our love rather than commands our admiration.

Minuteness of narration, whether in fiction or in real life, has a singular charm for all readers. It is the great secret of the most successful novelists, biographers, and historians. The reader often gladly leaves the stately and gloomy pages of Tacitus, wonderful as they are for sententious philosophy and eloquent invective, to take up the homely "long stories" of the simple and garrulous Herodotus. The same quality constitutes the unsurpassed excellence of Boswell in his department. Defoe and Richardson are indebted to it almost exclusively for their brilliant success. Miss Austen,—dear Miss Austen,—who never says a brilliant thing, nor paints a perfect character,—who is neither witty, nor passionate, nor eloquent,—is still minute, homelike, and true; and by these qualities alone, she twines about the inmost fibres of her readers' hearts. It is not easy to say why these qualities are so attractive. One reason, perhaps, may be traced ultimately to the instinctive love of the human mind, especially in all exhibitions of nature, for the truth. Now, the only truth is the *whole* truth. The complete portrait is the only faithful portrait. The only true history or biography is that which tells all. The reality of such a narrative is the only one that is attested by our own experience, which necessarily comprehends the whole of our own thoughts, motives, and actions; the slightest and most trivial, as well as the most important. The piecemeal exhibition of another's life finds no counterpart in our own memories, which embrace every incident in our own career. It is no more a fair portraiture of the other's character, than a few bricks are a fair specimen of a vast edifice. The simplest minds, therefore, when they wish to create an illusion, or to convince another of a fact, heap up as many details and trivial concomitant circumstances as possible, as vouchers of their veracity, though none of them have any logical connection with the main incident. Mrs. Quickly's comic enumeration of all the circumstances under which Jack Falstaff promised to marry her is a fair instance in point. In the case of children, the illusion created in this way is perfect; and even grown persons may confess, that, if the story of Robinson Crusoe is not true, it deserves to be.

Franklin's autobiography interests us, because it tells the whole story of his life,—his good and bad qualities, his failings and errors, and even those small vices which are more humiliating to confess than great sins. He showed the strength of a great mind by keeping nothing in reserve, by writing with a view only to the effect which his memoirs would have on the formation of the lives and characters of others, and without any regard to the opinions of posterity respecting himself. This indifference about his own reputation—one of the most striking traits of his character—is manifested by the point at which he left the personal narrative unfinished. He traces the history of the runaway printer's apprentice down to the time when he had become a respectable mechanic, in moderate circumstances, and had even risen to the dignity of a seat in the provincial legislature. He leaves it for others to write. the memoirs of the distinguished statesman and philosopher, who commanded the attention and respect of the whole civilized world.

* * *

The question respecting Franklin's character as a moralist is more difficult than any which we have yet considered. The individuality of the man, the striking and peculiar traits of his disposition, are most clearly seen under the moral aspect of his life and writings. His "Poor Richard" is the most original and characteristic of all his productions. It supplies the key to his autobiography; its spirit pervades all his publications; it furnishes the explanation of his career as a patriot, a philosopher; and a philanthropist; it was acted out through his whole life. Whatever may be thought of the doctrine it teaches, its merits and originality as a work of genius cannot be denied. Few works have been more widely popular, or have been productive of such extensive and permanent effects. It was eminently calculated for the immense circulation among common readers which it almost immediately obtained. Drawn up chiefly in the form of homely proverbs, unequalled for humor, for pithy and terse expression, and for direct application to the object in view, and professing to teach the way to wealth and happiness, it became the manual of every aspiring tradesman and mechanic, and the indirect means, as the maxims were repeated from mouth to mouth, of shaping the character of many who never saw it in print. The scheme of the wise man for modelling the minds and determining the destiny of a whole people, by writing its ballads rather than its laws, was surpassed by the genius of the Philadelphia printer, who made a collection of proverbs for his countrymen, and formed the national character.

We include under the general name of "Poor Richard" the whole body of prudential maxims that first appeared in the almanac of that name, which was projected, edited, and published by Franklin for many years. Most of them were collected some time afterwards, and published separately, under the title of "The Way to Wealth"; and this was the work which underwent so many translations in Europe, and obtained so great circulation and celebrity there. It has appeared in a version even into Modern Greek. Taken together with the other essays on moral and religious subjects and the economy of life, it presents a full view of what may be called the Franklinian morality. The whole should be viewed in connection with that very homely scheme of moral reformation, mentioned in the autobiography, where the principal virtues and the days of the week appear arranged in the form of a multiplication table, the object being to perfect the character by keeping an exact record of daily transgressions.

There is not much sentiment or enthusiasm in such a scheme. It is plain even to coarseness; it is humble almost to meanness. It is the essence of worldly wisdom, the bible of prudent conduct. The whole is a lesson given by a shrewd and sagacious old man, of benevolent impulses and even a warm heart, wary but upright, prudent but philanthropic, self-seeking but just,—a lesson given to the young mechanics and traders among his countrymen, impressing upon them the importance of integrity, industry, sobriety, and economy, as opening a sure path to success in life. It is the true manual of utilitarianism; Jeremy Bentham only borrowed and marred it. Though we may wish that it were animated with a stronger and loftier feeling, that it set forth nobler aims, that it breathed more of an earnest Christian spirit, we cannot deny its admirable adaptation to the purpose which the author had in view. The motives proposed were by no means the highest, but they were effective for the classes whom they were designed to influence. The homely and good-natured tone, the playful illustrations, the clear and pointed style, and the good sense and obvious earnestness of the writer, make these essays models of popular exhortation. The mind which would pronounce them *vulgar* is vitiated by sickly refinement. There is nothing vulgar in the attempt, however prosecuted, to make large bodies of men more honest and intelligent, more economical, sober, and industrious.

It is proper to try these essays only by an ethical standard. Whatever may have been the religious opinions of Franklin, he was not directly influenced by them, when his only object was to give prudential advice to his countrymen. Certainly there is nothing in these essays, which is offensive to Christianity, or which directly militates with its spirit. They form a practical system of utilitarian ethics. To say that this system is vastly inferior to the morality of the gospel is not at all to the purpose; as much as this must be admitted of every scheme of morals, in which the subject is viewed only by the light of nature and conscience. The ethical doctrines of Franklin must be compared with the speculations of Socrates and Cicero, of Hobbes and Hume, of Paley and Bentham, and not with the teachings of the Saviour. And here it may be as well to remark of his religious belief, that it contained a recognition of all the truths of natural religion, including the doctrines of immortality and a future retribution, and, so far as we can perceive, a faith in the divine mission of the Saviour. It coincided in most respects with the opinions of the Unitarians of the present day; and if religion was not as solemn and earnest a thing with him as with many of that sect, the misfortune must be ascribed in part to the coldness of his temperament.

Utility may be considered both as a test, and as a motive, or cause, in ethics. To say that all virtuous actions are also useful, and, therefore, that utility is often a very convenient criterion whereby to distinguish right from wrong, is quite a different thing from saying, that actions are right because they, are useful, and, consequently, that utility is the very essence of virtue. No one denies the former proposition, or the propriety of adopting it as a guide to conduct, unless he be one of those blind enthusiasts, who repudiate all regard to consequences, and adopt the fanatical maxim, that we must act from moral impulse alone, and leave the results with God. The proper answer to such persons is, that, in morals, the act and its consequences are one, and we have no right to proceed upon a partial view. The deed which will ultimately be injurious to others is as wrong as that which does immediate harm; and reason is given to us that we may take care of the future, as well as of the present. So far, therefore, as Poor Richard shows the intimate connection between virtue and well-being, so far as he proves that to be honest and true is the best mode of becoming wealthy and happy, he is a sound moralist. Nor will any great objection be made to his doctrine, if he holds up this fact as one of the inducements to virtuous conduct. The theory of religion, no less than of pure ethics, sanctions an appeal to man's instinctive desire of future happiness, as a motive and an incitement to an upright and holy life. This is but a preparatory step, it is true; for that virtue is imperfect, is even mean and grovelling, which is not practised for its own sake.

That beautiful law of our mental constitution, which accounts for the formation of what are called "secondary desires," affords a means for the purification of the motive, and for a passage from the selfish to the disinterested stage of moral progress. The process is a simple one, being merely a transference of the affections from the end to the means. By the association of ideas, that which was at first loved or practised only as an instrument, becomes the leading idea and the chief object of pursuit. Thus, in the downward course, money, which is at first desired only as a means of gratifying the appetites, or of answering still higher ends, becomes itself "an appetite and a passion," and the habit and the vice of avarice are formed. And so, in our upward progress, the honesty, which was first practised only because it was "the best policy," the worship of God, which was first paid only as the price of heaven, become at last the unbought and unselfish homage of the soul to uprightness, holiness, and truth. Virtue deserves its name only when, by long practice, it has become a fixed habit; for then only is it freed from the stain of selfishness. The terrors of the law are proclaimed to the sinner only that he may be able to overcome the first shock of the transition from sin to holiness; its promises are reserved for those only who, by patient continuance in well-doing, have become alike indifferent to the debasing fear and the debasing hope.

Only through the process which we have here attempted to explain can we account for the fact, that Franklin, after undergoing a full course of "Poor Richard" morality, became a strictly pure, upright, and benevolent man. The virtues which he cultivated and recommended because they tended to promote success in life, he came at last to love and practise for their own sake. His integrity few will venture to question; and he was a philanthropist in the broadest and most honorable meaning of the term, seeking the good of his fellow-men by methods which did as much honor to his intellect as to his heart. He was the most rational of reformers, the most sensible and judicious in adapting his precepts and plans of improvement to the circumstances and characters of those whom he addressed. It is idle to lament his want of sentiment and enthusiasm, his low and practical views of life, his appeals to humble and even selfish motives. He understood the disposition and temperament of the people for whom he wrote and labored, and aimed to influence their conduct by the means which were most likely to produce an immediate effect. He possessed in an eminent degree that shrewdness and knowledge of human nature, for which the natives of New England are proverbial, and which the great circulation of his writings has unquestionably done much to sharpen and increase. He delighted in the use of simple and innocent artifices, by which to convert men to his purpose, and, as it were, to cheat them into doing good to themselves; and he describes the success of these little stratagems with great humor and delight. The account given in the autobiography, of the manner in which he carried through several plans for the improvement of the city and the welfare of the inhabitants, is an amusing and instructive sketch, and quite as characteristic as any thing in the work. He knew that men, taken in the mass, must often be treated like children, must be coaxed and allured into doing what is for their own good, must be trained by go-carts and leading-strings, before they can tread securely the path to virtue and happiness. The picture of a wise and benignant old man, contributing by such humble but effective means to the welfare of his fellow-men, is one which the zealot and the idealist may not dare to despise.

* * *

The literary merits of Dr. Franklin's publications are universally acknowledged. Though he received no academical instruction, and in early life did not enjoy the society of men of taste and letters, he labored on the formation of his style with great care. Fortunately, he chose Addison as his model, being accustomed to rewrite a paper of "The Spectator" from his general recollection of its contents, and then to compare his version with the original. We are not sure that this practice can be generally recommended for imitation, as it is likely to lead to a too slavish copying of another's manner. But the simplicity of Franklin's taste, the fertility of his mind, and his earnestness of purpose, guarded him against affectations and puerilities, and he did not attempt to transfuse into his own manner all the peculiarities of his model. Notwithstanding this early and diligent study of composition, the style in his productions was always made secondary to the thought. The practical and utilitarian turn of his mind prevented him from writing when he had nothing to say, and made him studious of those qualities which he had observed to be most effective in converting readers to his purpose. His compositions, therefore, do not exhibit extraordinary elegance or polish; but they are easy, pointed, and natural, abounding with happy turns of expression and felicitous illustrations. He had that frankness and *bonhommie*, which render the style a picture of the man, and which never fail to please, though they may not instruct or convince. He was not a wit, but a humorist; and the playfulness of his manner, coupled with his obviously benevolent intentions, leads the reader on by an irresistible charm, and steals away his assent by gaining his affections. The trifles which he wrote in Paris, for the amusement of the gay society there, show all the lightness and spirit that distinguish the people for whom they were composed.

* * *

We have no room for extracts from his letters, which present some of the finest models of epistolary composition in the English language. It is difficult to say which are deserving of most admiration, those written to his intimate friends on the ordinary topics of social intercourse, or his business correspondence with politicians and philosophers. Pleasantry, in the former, is sometimes carried a little too far; but they abound with indications of the good sense and ingenuity of the writer, and show a truly affectionate spirit towards his friends. The ease and simplicity of the language are admirable, and a sunny cheerfulness overspreads them, which keeps the reader in constant good-humor. The same traits appear, to some extent, in his political correspondence; but the earnestness and deep feeling of the writer are here more apparent. His attachment to his native land was so strong, that injuries inflicted upon it drew from him indignant and bitter comments, which were never elicited by wrongs done to himself. His confidential letters to David Hartley, who was for a time an unrecognized medium of communication between him and the English ministry, have some energetic passages, in which the vituperation is carried to the utmost point that is consistent with dignity. His firmness and resolution during the darkest periods of the American war are remarkable. After the Declaration, though he was made the organ of several attempts at a reconciliation, he seems hardly to contemplate the possibility of the struggle terminating on any other terms than an acknowledgment of the entire independence of this country.

* * *

He was now in the full enjoyment of a serene and happy old age, looking forward with pleasure, but without impatience, to the termination of his career. He had the same cheerful activity of mind, the same interest in philosophical subjects, which he had manifested in the whole preceding portion of his long life. He was at ease in his domestic circumstances, and was surrounded by a happy family of grandchildren, and a circle of intimate and admiring friends. His correspondence was still extensive, and some of the most admirable letters that ever came from his pen, showing all his characteristic gayety, benevolence, and inquiring habit of mind, were written at this period. A stranger visited him in the summer of 1787, and found him in the open air, seated under a large mulberry-tree in his garden, with a small party of friends around him. He conversed with his usual cheerfulness and animation, and showed with great interest some curious objects of natural history, and a large work upon botany, which he was then studying with much ardor. The sickness of death came upon him, but did not impair his serenity of mind, or the activity of his moral and intellectual powers. "A few days before he died, he rose from his bed, and begged that it might be made up for him, '*so that he might die in a decent manner.*' His daughter told him, that she hoped he would recover, and live many years longer. He calmly replied, '*I hope not.*'" He died on the 17th of April, 1790, at the age of eighty-four years, leaving a reputation, as a diplomatist, philosopher, and philanthropist, inferior to none which belongs to the history of the eighteenth century, and as a statesman and a patriot, second only to him whose name is always first in the hearts of his American countrymen.

AUTOBIOGRAPHY, LIFE, AND *COMPLETE WORKS* (BIGELOW) AND *WRITINGS* (SMYTH) (1868–1908)

As an American diplomat in Paris, John Bigelow tracked down the original holograph manuscript of Franklin's autobiography, the one that Temple Franklin had so thoughtlessly traded away, the only one containing part four, which had never before been published in English. Consequently, Bigelow decided to prepare an edition of his own. It appeared in 1868 as *The Autobiography of Benjamin Franklin*—the first time the work was published under that title. Bigelow used Sparks's edition of the first three parts as his copytext, emending them with reference to the holograph manuscript. He then printed the fourth part, edited from that manuscript. For the first time, Bigelow also published Franklin's outline for the work, which contains many vital details that never reached the pages of the autobiography.

John Cordy Jeaffreson's notice of Bigelow's edition in the London *Athenaeum* constitutes one of the lengthiest reviews of Bigelow's edition to appear. A small part of it is excerpted as the first document in this subsection. Jeaffreson's general animosity toward the United States prompted him to read Bigelow's edition with belligerence and, therefore, clouded his judgment. Jeaffreson concludes that what Bigelow found in France was not Franklin's authoritative version but a rough draft. He recommends that editors should use William Temple Franklin's version of the autobiography for all future editions. The errors in Jeaffreson's interpretation of the Franklin manuscript apparently went unnoticed. Three years later he was chosen as an inspector for the Royal Commission on Historical Manuscripts.

Bigelow's editorial work on Franklin did not end with the autobiography. Far from it. In 1874, he prepared a three-volume edition titled *The Life of Benjamin Franklin*, which consisted of the autobiography with a continuation formed from extracts of Franklin's letters and other writings. Franklin's autobiography was traditionally published with a biographical continuation. Bigelow's *Life* was the first to attempt a continuation in Franklin's own words. Innovative in terms of biographical technique, Bigelow's *Life* anticipates the twentieth-century developments in documentary biography made by Jay Leyda.

An anonymous reviewer in *The Independent* offered some general thoughts on biography writing. Despite its title, *The Independent* was a Christian magazine, whose editors and contributors ran scared when they encountered anything that deviated from strict orthodoxy. Unsurprisingly, its reviewer finds fault with Franklin's original attitude toward established religion.

The London edition of Bigelow's *Life of Benjamin Franklin*, which appeared in 1879, elicited extensive comments from two British reviewers, Thomas Hughes and William Stebbing. Both authors show a much greater sensitivity to Franklin and the American values he represented that their countryman Jeaffreson. Both were amply qualified for the task. Besides being a social reformer, Hughes was one of the finest literary stylists in Victorian England. His classic, *Tom Brown's School Days* (1857), is one of the finest works of English prose to emerge during the century. Stebbing, a journalist and a scholar, would turn to writing biography late in life.

Hughes's review is partly reprinted as the next document in this subsection. He sums up British attitudes toward Franklin over the course of the nineteenth century, which he sees as a matter of growing distrust. The British essays included in the present volume confirm Hughes's analysis. The intention of his review was to restore British appreciation of Franklin. Hughes stresses Franklin's importance in forming the American national character. American readers appreciated Hughes's review. It was reprinted multiple times in the contemporary American periodical press.

In the great tradition of the British reviews, William Stebbing uses Bigelow's *Life* as a jumping-off point to discuss broader topics. He examines Franklin's theory of colonial rule. Anticipating the rapprochement between Britain and the United States that would occur in the coming years, Stebbing suggests that perhaps the two were doomed to clash because of the incompatibility of their rival great-ness. Furthermore, he provides an excellent survey of events leading to the American Revolution from a British perspective. Getting down to Franklin's writing style, Stebbing calls his anecdotes "as bracing as quinine." He recognizes Franklin's importance to modern psychology, echoing an idea suggested by Henry T. Tuckerman. Stebbing asserts that Franklin's philosophy will never grow old and favorably compares him to Addison, Bunyan, and Voltaire. Stebbing calls Franklin's autobiography one of "mankind's greatest literary possessions."

Bigelow continued his editorial activities with *The Complete Works of Benjamin Franklin* (1887–1889), a ten-volume set that presented more than three hundred new items. As Paul Leicester Ford observed in *Franklin Bibliography* (1889), Bigelow's chronological organization marked a distinct improvement over previous collections, which had been organized thematically. Since the volumes of Bigelow's *Complete*

Works were issued separately and since they were expensive, the edition attracted minimal attention in the press. Most of the reviews discuss Bigelow's editorial method but have little to say about Franklin himself.

Much the same could be said about the next collected edition of Franklin's writings. Prepared by Albert Henry Smyth, *The Writings of Benjamin Franklin* (1905–1907) also appeared in ten volumes and was published over a three-year period. It, too, added many new items to the Franklin canon. A large cache of documents in the possession of the Fox family was given to the University of Pennsylvania in 1903. Smyth's edition was the first to take advantage of this collection. In addition, Smyth was the first to reprint Franklin's "Silence Dogood" essays. The reviews of the Smyth edition, three of which are briefly excerpted here, spent time retelling Franklin's life and discussing Smyth's editorial method, but had little new to say about Franklin for the most part.

William P. Trent, the leading American literary scholar of his generation, read the first volume of Smyth's edition alongside two other books about Franklin. The reviews of the other two books are excluded here. The following excerpt consists largely of Trent's general remarks about Franklin. Trent appreciates him for his various talents, but faults him for his lack of poetry and piety. Because of these faults, he ranks Franklin below Samuel Johnson and George Washington. Despite his personal faults, Franklin's autobiography joins *Robinson Crusoe* as one of the two most important books in the English language.

Paul Elmer More's review reflects his pretentiousness. It is scattered with classical adages and aphorisms; he regrets that Franklin was not steeped in the classics. More also regrets the commercial aspects of Franklin's *Autobiography*, disliking anything involving the world of business. More echoes Matthew Arnold's comment about Franklin's combination of good sense and humanity. B.O. Flower, editor and social reformer, recognizes the general importance of rediscovering lives of the founders of American democracy. In the first decade of the twentieth century, Franklin's life remained a model for young men and women. Can the same be said of today? In the first decade of the twenty-first century, does Franklin's life remain a model for young men and women?

JOHN CORDY JEAFFRESON "THE AUTOBIOGRAPHY OF BENJAMIN FRANKLIN" (1868)

The appetite of the Americans for literary discoveries and original documents concerning spatters of small or no importance is akin to the spirit which inspired the American tourist to exclaim, "No, we have no Herculaneum and Pompeii, but I guess we precious soon shall have." Just as the newness of their political life makes them exaggerate the importance of the third-rate actors in their Revolutionary War, the newness of their literary history must be held accountable for their habit of magnifying documentary molehills into mountains, and manufacturing controversies out of boxes of waste paper. They have no 'Vision of the Ploughman,' or 'Junius's Letters,' concerning whose authorship they can have doubts, theories, disputations, but they precious soon will have; and, in the meantime, they are very clever in making a pother about the linings of old trunks, or any scrap of paper on which one of their notabilities may have penned a few lines of personal gossip.

Their newest achievement in the way of literary exhumation is the discovery of the original manuscript of Benjamin Franklin's repeatedly-published Autobiography; and, in this seventy-ninth year after its author's death, they put the *ipsissima verba* of the sacred document before the awe-stricken world of letters, introduced by a preface, in which Mr. Bigelow states through what channels the manuscript came into his possession, and would fain take away the reader's breath by the astounding announcement that the most widely circulated text of the personal memoir differs from the original autograph in no less than twelve hundred places. "I have availed myself," says the editor, "of my earliest leisure to subject the memoir to a careful collation with the edition which appeared in London in 1817, and which was the first and only edition that ever *purported to have been printed from the manuscript.* The results of this collation revealed the curious fact that more than twelve hundred separate and distinct changes had been made in the text, and, what is more remarkable, that the last eight pages of the manuscript, which are second in value to no other eight pages of the work, were omitted entirely. Many of these changes are mere modernizations of style, such as would measure some of the modifications which English prose had undergone between the days of Goldsmith and Southey. *Some Franklin might have approved of; others he might have tolerated; but it is safe to presume that very many he would have rejected.*" The italics of this quotation are our own; and we employ them to draw attention to certain points on, which we will at once speak our mind. In the first place, the current edition of the Autobiography does not purport to have been printed from the manuscript now published for the first time. Secondly, instead of concurring with Mr. Bigelow's estimate of the alterations; we incline to the opinion that, with the exception of the omission of the last eight pages of manuscript, which can be satisfactorily accounted for, the twelve hundred separate and distinct changes do not contain one that

"Franklin would have rejected without ceremony." On the contrary, it seems to us highly probable, from Mr. Bigelow's own testimony, that the eleven hundred and ninety-nine alterations were Franklin's own work, with the exception of such emendations of orthography and punctuation as may be reasonably assigned to the readers for the press. The manuscript from which the edition of 1817 was printed was the work which Franklin designed to put in print; and, unless Mr. Bigelow can show that that manuscript was a literal transcript of what he is pleased to call the original autograph, we must hold the editor of 1817 innocent of that wholesale tampering with Franklin's work which is now charged against him, by insinuation rather than by express terms. It may be that the editor of 1817 discharged his function with an excess of officious zeal; but, in the total absence of evidence that he so erred, we think it rather more than probable that, instead of being what can fairly be called the autograph of the work, Mr. Bigelow's discovered manuscript is merely the rough copy of the authentic production.

ANONYMOUS
"THE LIFE OF BENJAMIN FRANKLIN" (1875)

The problem, how to describe a life, seems to be less complex and less difficult than the problem, how to live; and yet a good biography is even rarer than a well-spent life. Mr. Bigelow's method of constructing "the Life of Franklin" is new. He has collected from the voluminous writings and correspondence of Franklin himself passages which, together, give a very full account of the man and of his achievements; and, arranging these in the order of events, he has connected and illustrated them by brief comments. Thus the subject of the work is always in the foreground, telling his own story. The reader enters into Franklin's habits of thought, learns to see his aims and circumstances with his own eyes, forms his personal acquaintance as he does that of Socrates or of Johnson, in the pages of Xenophon or Boswell. The editor modestly hides behind his hero, and becomes the most impersonal of biographers. He takes no side in most of the controversies depicted; thrusts neither his name nor his views upon our notice, but assumes the duty of patiently searching for evidence, and of impartially setting forth the facts, when ascertained. True, he cannot conceal the positiveness of his own opinions, nor indeed the strength of some of his prejudices; but these are mostly not formally asserted and sustained by argument; they are often, with more effect, quietly suggested and enforced by the selection and arrangement of the text. We call the method new, although nothing has been more common than to make the substance of a biographical work out of the writings of the subject; because the plan has never been so rigidly carried out before, in framing a complete story of a long and memorable life, in which the framer resolutely restricts himself to the work of a compiler. Mr. Bigelow, in his own name, says no more than is indispensable to make Franklin's words understood; sometimes, we think, not enough for this purpose; but such singular reticence, as a contrast to the tedious garrulity common among biographers, is too precious as an example not to cover some defects. This will be the more readily granted when it is observed how full the book is of marks of honest work; so that any lack of communicativeness on the editor's part can not be ascribed to indolence or haste.

As a whole, the book is a remarkable success. That is to say, there is no other biography which can be compared with this in the acquaintance it gives the reader with Franklin's mind and character. Even as a record of events it is much less defective than might be expected. The "Autobiography" comes down to the fifty-second year of his age; and after that time his activity in public affairs was so great and so unremitting that it has been found possible, from his correspondence, to compile an almost unbroken narrative. The diligence and skill with which this has been done leave little to be desired. It is rather in the earlier part of the work that the reader will lament the excessive self-restraint of the editor. The autobiography itself is by far the most precious and important book in the first century of American literature. Few books have been more widely read by three generations of men, in all civilized nations; yet it remained for Mr. Bigelow to publish it for the first time in a complete and accurate form. His "Historical Sketch of the fortunes and misfortunes" of Franklin's autograph manuscript is of extreme interest; and the critical restoration of Franklin's own text is a service to letters which, if this edition had attempted nothing more, would suffice to give it standard value. Yet there are objects of legitimate curiosity in Franklin's history on which the autobiography, left a fragment, yields no satisfaction; and we turn for information to the biographer. For an instance, the later years of Franklin's life were embittered by his "son," William Franklin, who forgot what was due to his country and to his father, and gave himself to their enemies. As late as 1784, the old man wrote to William: "Nothing has ever hurt me so much, and affected me with such keen sensations, as to find myself deserted in my old age by my only son; and not only deserted, but to find him taking up arms against me in a cause wherein my good fame, fortune, and life, were all at stake."[1] Even in his last will, prepared with the utmost deliberation in 1788, after making a bequest "to my son, William Franklin, late Governor of the Jerseys," he adds: "The part he acted against me in the late war, which is of public notoriety, will account for my leaving him no more of an estate he endeavored to deprive me of."[2] Again, after this estrangement from his son, Franklin attached himself closely to that son's son, William Temple Franklin; made him a constant companion, and strove, with more zeal than he ever exercised in seeking any other personal end of the kind, for his advancement in public life. Though evidently disappointed in the young man's abilities, he confided in him to the last, and left him all his papers and manuscripts, thus constituting him the trustee and guardian of his fame. The grandson betrayed his trust. That he sold it out to the British government—that, for seven thousand pounds in money, he contracted to suppress the truth confided to him, to the injury of his grandfather's fame and of his country's honor, is suspected, not proved;[3] but if acquitted of this crime, it can only be by pleading guilty to incapacity and negligence unparalleled in administering such a charge. The children and the grandchildren of great and good men do not commonly thus imitate the viper; and most students of Franklin's life will think it a significant circumstance, which ought to be known to all who read of the ingratitude of this son and grandson, that neither of them was born in wedlock. It was not necessary that Mr. Bigelow, in order to avoid the appearance of cheap moralizing, should suppress this fact, and leave the reader, until he meets a casual hint in the last volume, to suppose that William was his father's rightful heir, the son of Benjamin and Deborah Franklin. Few, perhaps, will be misled in a matter so notorious as this; but it is surely an imperfection in a biography to omit the most widely known facts concerning its subject; and this omission is but one of several which add emphasis to the modest words of Mr. Bigelow's preface, "These volumes are not intended to displace or replace any other of the many biographies of Franklin with which our literature has been enriched." We do not hesitate to say that these volumes are not only, as they now stand, a far closer approach to the needed and satisfactory "Life of Franklin" than any of the biographies referred to; but that, with a little greater fullness of illustration and comment in the editor's notes, they would be well worthy to "displace" and "replace" them all.

For the test of merit in a biography is the degree of acquaintance it gives us with the man; not with the events of his period. The ambition to write history has been the bane and ruin of biographers, and the most successful among them have been the few who, like Carlyle, are too great to be spoiled by this ambition, or, like Boswell, too little to feel it. Our knowledge of the people with whom we live is one; our knowledge of the great characters of history is another. What would not the scholar give to reach as clear a mental view of Pericles, of Cicero, of Charlemagne, of Bacon, as he has even of the casual associates of his business life? To know their thoughts and motives as well? Yet not of one of these associates, not even of his must intimate and oldest friends, could he probably write a biographical sketch, giving the principal facts of his outer life, as accurately and completely as he could of any one of the great names foremost in history. It is the biographer's art to bring the man into converse with us: to show him in the garb, occupation, and associations of his daily life; to awaken our personal interest in his perils, struggles, sufferings, and triumphs; to stir in us the passions under which he acted, and to lead us to adopt in sympathy the very prejudices, ignorances, and errors which wrought him evil. It is only thus that we can be prepared to enter with him upon those supreme moments of life which reveal the whole man in one deed or word—but only to those who have known him well already; to see Caesar at the Rubicon, Luther at Worms, Washington when told of Burgoyne's surrender, or Chase when required, as Chief-Justice, to try his own "greenbacks" by the constitution. Franklin's life is one of the most attractive subjects for biography that can be found, not because it abounds in stirring incidents, but because of the wonderful richness and variety in his mind and character. He touched the world on many sides; he lived very near his fellow men; he took a conspicuous part in the largest questions which were solved or decided in his time; and through all we know of him, from childhood to extreme age, he was so peculiarly himself that no course of conduct, no page of writing, which is recorded of him, could be mistaken for the work of any other man. Add to this the fact that his character, as a whole, is singularly representative—that nearly all that is noteworthy in the American people as a nation is found in Franklin at its best, and in full development—and we perceive something of the sources of interest which lie in such a life.

The same considerations may suggest to us, also, the extreme difficulty, in this case, of the task which the biographer commonly assumes, of "summing up" the character of his subject. This has been attempted for Franklin by many writers, but never with tolerable success. Many assertions concerning him, indeed, maybe made without dispute. He had great self-reliance, indomitable perseverance; was not precocious, was, indeed, rather slow in his early mental growth, but distinguished from the first by caution in reaching conclusions, by ingenuity in devices, and by a prodigious appetite for knowledge; and he retained the freshness of his youthful intellect even in old age, to a degree hardly equaled, learning to converse in French after he was three-score and ten. He looked further than other men into the likely results of opinions and actions; and carefully disciplined himself in the habit of weighing them by their consequences, and of judging all things by utility to the exclusion of passion. His practical sagacity looked upon every inconvenience, from a smoky chimney to an oppressive government, as a difficulty to be removed, and neither his patience nor his ingenuity in devising remedies was ever exhausted. Easy and familiar in manner, absolute in self-control, always tolerant and courteous when most persistently seeking his ends, he was one of the ablest diplomatists of his age; and the charm of his conversation made him for many years the first idol in the Pantheon of Conversation, the court circles of France. Though almost isolated from the world of scientific activity, he greatly advanced the methods of experimental research, and made the largest single contribution to physical science which it received in his generation. His benevolence was broad and active; his patriotism, as soon as he had a country or "the hope of a country" to love, sprang into full being, and remained till death a master passion. Industrious, temperate, frugal, fond of acquiring, regarding wealth with the eye of a man of the world, rather than of a philosopher, he was yet so far above the capacity for mean motives in great actions, that the tory historian of Europe, in glorifying the reign of George III, enumerates among the characters which adorned it, "the incorruptible integrity of Franklin,"[4] with reason, for had it been less than incorruptible, that reign, on this side of the Atlantic, would have been longer and more disastrous. And in future ages, when the two great curses of the civilization of the last century reach their proper place in the scorn of mankind, the glory of his public character will be greater than now; for it will be understood how great a thing it was to be the first advocate in America of the abolition both of personal and of commercial serfdom—of African slavery and of protective taxation.

All these traits will be admitted, and might be illustrated at length from the volumes before us. But there are other questions concerning Franklin's character, on which rash judgments, on both sides, are daily uttered, but on which every judgment is worthless, unless carefully formed, and upon full knowledge. For instance, to John Adams, who, though nearly thirty years younger than Franklin, was on several occasions closely associated with him, the old statesman was always an object of dislike and suspicion. He regarded Franklin as cunning, malicious, deceitful, and selfish. This view seems to be hereditary; it has certainly survived, in the Adams family, the animosities of a century ago; for Mr. C. F. Adams, in his life of his grandfather,[5] makes an elaborate attack upon Franklin's morals, in more moderate language than old John Adams would have used, but of much the same import. "A defective early education," he tells us, "made his morality superficial even to laxness, and undermined his religious faith. . . . That nice sense which revolts at wrong for its own sake, and that generosity of spirit which shrinks from participating in the advantages of indirection, however naturally obtained, were not his." And this belief in the insincerity of the man will be found to be more than hinted again and again in the voluminous writings of the three great statesmen named Adams. On the other hand, we have such estimates of his character as that given by Mr. Parton in his life of Franklin: "I have ventured to call Franklin the consummate Christian of his time. Indeed, I know not who, of any time, has exhibited more of the spirit of Christ."[6] It is impossible to reconcile such a difference. It is equally impossible to compromise it. But if a reader is confused by finding such inconsistent judgments abroad in the world, he may turn to Mr. Bigelow's work for the best and final evidence on the subject; for it gives him the facts—the deeds and words of Franklin himself, which he may read with a vision unperverted, either by an old hurt to family pride, or by a modern passion for rhetorical paradox.

All questions as to the relation of Franklin's life to Christian morals will be settled at once by reading his scheme of virtues,[7] thirteen in number. The last is, "13. HUMILITY. Imitate Jesus and Socrates." This is the only mention made of the founder of Christianity in his autobiography, with all its detailed discussions of virtue. What Franklin understood by imitating Jesus is made clear by his own words, "My list of virtues contained at first but twelve; but a Quaker friend having kindly informed me that I was generally thought proud; that my pride showed itself frequently in conversation; that I was not content with being in the right when discussing any point, but was overbearing, and rather insolent, of which he convinced me by mentioning several instances; I determined endeavoring to cure myself, if I could, of this vice or folly among the rest, and I added *Humility* to my list. . . .

"I cannot boast of much success in acquiring the *reality* of this virtue, but I had a good deal with regard to the appearance of it. I made it a rule to forbear all direct contradiction to the sentiments of others, and all positive assertion of my own. I even forbid myself . . . the use of every word or expression in the language that imported a fixed opinion, such as *certainly, undoubtedly*, etc., and I adopted instead of them *I conceive, I apprehend*, or *I imagine* a thing to be so or so; or it *so appears to me at present*. . . . And this mode, which I at first put on with some violence to natural inclination, became at length so easy, and so habitual to me, that perhaps for these fifty years past no one has ever heard a dogmatical expression escape me. And to this habit (after my character of integrity) I think it principally owing that I had early so much weight with my fellow-citizens, . . . and so much influence in public councils when I became a member."[8]

It would be unfair to illustrate this passage by the stanza from "The Devil's Thoughts" of Coleridge, upon "pride that apes humility"; but even this would be less absurd than to give to the system of morality, of which it is a fragment, the name of Christian. To Christ, duty means the subjection of the will in love to a superior being, the subordination of every motive to the pleasure of his infinite benevolence. To Franklin, duty is but prudence, made respectable by breadth of view. His scheme of morality is far inferior to that of the modern utilitarian school of Austin, Bain, and Mill, because it is far less complete; but it bears nearly such a relation to theirs as the fragmentary precepts of virtue in the Talmud bear to the Sermon on the Mount. With Christianity it has scarce anything in common. We do not compare their merits; we do not now insist that one is better than the other; but simply that they are different, that between Franklin's moral teachings and those of the New Testament there is a gulf which can not be bridged. While yielding to none in our sense of his great services to our country and to mankind, we must protest that to call Franklin a Christian is as misleading and inaccurate as to call Louis XIV a republican, or Jeremy Bentham a poet.

On the other hand, the impartial student of Franklin's life will be slow to accept the harsh judgment of the Messrs. Adams upon his sincerity. John Adams was a man of blunt and aggressive honesty, always harsh in judging motives, and especially rash to condemn those whom he could not control. Franklin's facile, winning manners were to him proof that the man was hollow and untrue. He never could understand how a mind that was fixed in its convictions and faithful to its aims might still wait long and patiently for the time of loud assertion and of violent struggling. But the ultimate difference between them was of manners rather than of morals; Adams's were direct, impatient, outspoken; Franklin's finished, courteous, diplomatic. In substantial fidelity to every trust, it will be hard, indeed, to find a real difference between them, and a comparison with John Adams in this respect is the severest test that can be applied to any man. It is true that, on a single occasion, if Mr. C. F. Adams's inference is correct, Dr. Franklin confesses that he was a party to "a falsehood," to whose "audacity" it is not easy to find a parallel.[9] On Monday, May 9, 1792, in a conversation between Mr. Thomas Grenville and the Count de Vergennes, the former "remarked that the war had been provoked by the encouragement given by, France to the Americans to revolt. On which the Count de Vergennes grew a little warm, and declared firmly that the breach was made, and our independence declared, long before we received the least encouragement from France; and he defied the world to give the smallest proof of the contrary. 'There sits,' said he, 'Mr. Franklin, who knows the fact, and can contradict me if I do not speak the truth.'"[10] Mr. Adams is surprised that Franklin gives this story "without a word of comment," and remarks that "even his silence was equivalent to an affirmation of the fraud." That the irritable and restless integrity of John Adams would have protested at once, under such circumstances, and in protesting would have violated a most sacred confidence, and possibly imperiled the existence of his country, may be admitted, without blaming Franklin for his wise and honorable silence; never more honorable than when he thus exposed himself even to unjust reproach of the most intolerable character for the sake of the cause he served. Here was an instance in which the perfect standard of truth did not require the silence to be broken; and while the man of sensitive honor would feel an impulse to break it, and did feel the impulse, as the fact that he recorded the incident shows, yet the man of wise self-control would sacrifice it as a personal impulse, and confine his protest, for the time, to his own mind, where it could do no harm.

We earnestly commend this invaluable work to the study of young Americans as one of the best hand-books of practical life within their reach. It is too admirable in plan and in its general execution not to become a standard, upon its subject, in all American libraries. The selection of the matter, indeed, and the manner of the editorial illustration, show the hand of a master, and maybe substantially accepted as final. There are a few defects, which may easily be removed; the chief of which is the want of some pages of narrative "filling," to make the story consecutive. The Index ought to be constructed anew, as the one given is nearly worthless, being filled with typographical errors beyond precedent, and still further marred with errors of gross ignorance, which stamp it as the work of one who has not even read the book with attention. For instance, what could be worse than constantly to confound Thomas Grenville, the unimportant youth who opened negotiations with the American commissioners in 1782, with his father, George Grenville, the author of the Stamp Act, who had then been dead twelve years?

Notes

1. Vol. iii, p. 279.
2. Vol. iii. p. 470.
3. Vol. i. p. 59.
4. Alison chap. lx.

5. Vol. i. p. 450, *sq.*

6. Vol. ii. p. 646.

7. Vol. i. p. 229, *sq.*

8. Vol. i. p. 242, *sq.*

9. Life of John Adams, i. 434.

10. Bigelow, Vol. iii. p. 102.

THOMAS HUGHES "BENJAMIN FRANKLIN" (1879)

The appearance of a new edition of Mr. Bigelow's "Life of Franklin" may be, we trust, the means of calling the attention of the reading public in England to a remarkable book, and of modifying in some respects the popular judgment of a more remarkable man. It has often struck us as strange that Franklin should never, in the last hundred years, have become popular in England—should rather, indeed, have been regarded with distrust, if not with dislike, even up to the present time. There is much in his career, as well as in his personal qualities and character, which appeals to popular instincts, and would have led one to expect a very different appreciation of the great New Englander. He was one of the class of self-made men, so indiscriminately honoured by the British public; and a self-made man in the best sense, who had fought his own way to the front, not only without any advantages of birth or education, but with perfectly clean hands: in the moderate fortune he left behind him there was not a dirty shilling. Of the remarkable group of Revolutionary leaders in the great struggle of the colonies, he was the only one in the first rank not gentle born: all the rest were of the gentry—Washington, Madison, and Jefferson, the sons of Virginian planters; Adams, Hamilton, and Jay, of leading New England and New York families—and all of them brought the highest culture the colonies could give to their great work. But Franklin's father (though of good yeoman stock in the old country, which he had left when quite young) worked still with his own hands at his trade of tallow-chandler in Boston, and took Benjamin, the youngest of his ten children, away from school at the age of nine to help him. One would have expected this fact to tell in his favour in England, where, though birth and privilege enjoy a superstitious reverence and immense advantages in the race of life, the deepest popular instincts are after all decidedly democratic. Then, again, he had all the qualities supposed to be most highly valued by Englishmen: he was an excellent son, husband, and father; moral and temperate from his youth up, but without a tinge of asceticism; scrupulously punctual and exact in money-matters, but open-handed; full of courtesy, sagacity, and humour.

He was probably the most popular, certainty the most prolific author of his day. His paper was the most influential in America, and Poor Richard's sayings were in every one's mouth both there and in England. He published works of mark in natural philosophy, politics, political and social economy, morals and general literature. His discoveries and inventions ranged from the lightning conductor to cures for smoky chimneys—his ingenious speculations, from magnetism and ballooning to cheap cookery; and he gave every invention and speculation freely to the world, having never taken out a patent or claimed protection of any kind. He was a staunch free-trader, and an advocate for the rights of neutrals in war, and of the claim that free ships should make free goods. He was decidedly the most successful man of his day—a quality at least as devoutly worshipped in the nineteenth as in the eighteenth century. His position at Paris in the ten years from 1775 to 1785—first as one of three commissioners, afterwards as minister plenipotentiary for the United States—was quite unique; and the figure, full of interest, of the old shopkeeper and journalist, in his plain suit and spectacles—ingeniously adjusted so that the upper half of the glasses served him in society, and the lower half for reading—wearing his own white hair in the midst of all the befrizzed and bepowdered courtiers of the *ancien régime*; a plain, outspoken Republican, not only holding his own, but the most popular man of the day with the royal family, the aristocracy, the ministers (except Chancellor Necker, who had to find him money for subsidies and warlike supplies); an honoured member not only of the Academy and every Continental learned society of note, but of the Royal Society of England, with whose leading members he was in friendly correspondence in spite of the war; of whom there were more medals, medallions, busts, and pictures than his biographer can count up, so that his face was the best known of any on both sides of the Atlantic—surely it is strange that so singularly attractive a figure should never have fairly found its place of honour in the country of which he was all but born a citizen, where he spent thirteen of his best years, and with whose foremost statesmen and learned men he was on affectionate intimacy up to the day of his death.

So, however, it has been, and though complete editions of Franklin's works and numerous biographies have been published, not only in America, but in France, Italy, and Germany, within the present century, one slight biographical sketch in Chambers's Cheap Library, and one article in the *Edinburgh Review* of 1806, remain the only notices which have issued from the English press of the greatest of American philosophers and diplomatists. To the English reading public, therefore, the stalwart historical figure which, in all its many-sided attractiveness and strength, is so well brought out in these volumes of Mr. Bigelow's, will be almost a stranger, though it is scarcely possible, we should think, that it will continue to be so. The book is not only of deep interest, but is a literary experiment of a novel kind. It consists first of the Autobiography written by Franklin for his son—comprising the first fifty years of his life, and here published for the first time from the original manuscript, of which Mr. Bigelow became possessed during his residence as minister of the United States in France; and secondly, of a history of the remaining thirty-five years, compiled, indeed, and edited by Mr. Bigelow, but really a continuation of the Autobiography, as it consists entirely of extracts from Franklin's diary, correspondence, despatches, and speeches, so that from beginning to end he is telling the story of his own life in his own words. In ordinary cases such an attempt must have ended in failure, but the extraordinary activity of Franklin as a correspondent with private friends, and the conscientious regularity and fulness of his public correspondence, have enabled Mr. Bigelow, with the help of a quite insignificant supplement in the shape of occasional notes, to sustain the interest of the narrative, and to give us a complete picture of Franklin painted by himself, in a book which we have no doubt is destined to remain a classic for all English-speaking people.

We propose here to consider, in such detail as our space will allow, the prejudices, political and religious, which have obscured Franklin's fame in England, and upon which Mr. Bigelow's volumes throw a flood of light. The first are founded on the belief that Franklin, while resident in England and a civil servant of the Crown, was undermining the allegiance of the colonies and fanning their discontent, and that, above all, he was the one American commissioner who desired to humiliate England and to impose unworthy terms on her at the close of the war; the second on the belief that, while professing Christianity, he was in fact a sceptic, who veiled real hostility under a cloak of toleration and friendliness to all Churches and denominations.

* * *

In our endeavour to remove the prejudices which have in great measure hindered the English public from appreciating and enjoying Franklin's life and writings, we have been unable to do more than indicate the charm which runs through the whole of these volumes, and which should win them a very wide popularity. We allude to the genial, sturdy, humorous common sense which, even more than his shrewdness, was the secret of his uniform success in the various and difficult tasks of his long career, from the founding of the first public library and the first fire-brigade in America, to the settlement of the terms of the Peace of 1782 with the ablest European diplomatists. We may conclude, however, with a specimen or two of his characteristic sayings, in the hope that they may lead our readers to the book. When his daughter writes to him for lace and feathers amongst other articles from Paris, he replies by sending everything else, but declines to foster "the great pride with which she would wear anything he sent," showing it as her father's taste, with "If you wear your cambric ruffles as I do, and take care not to mend the holes, they will come in time to be lace; and feathers, my dear girl, may be had in America from every cock's tail." "You are young, and have the world before you; *stoop*, as you go through it, and you will miss many hard thumps." "The eyes of other people are the eyes that ruin us. If all but myself were bland, I should want neither fine clothes, fine houses, nor fine furniture." "A rogue hanged out of a family does it more honour than ten who live in it." "If there be a nation that exports its beef and linen to pay for the importation of claret and porter, while its people live on potatoes, wherein does it differ from the sot who lets his family starve and sells his clothes to buy drink?" His opposition to the creation of the Order of the Cincinnati in the States at the close of the war, and his suggestion that if "the Cincinnati go on with their project the badges should ascend to their fathers and mothers, instead of descending to their children, in obedience to the Fourth Commandment," is a delightful specimen of his method of preaching simplicity of life to his countrymen, but too long for quotation, as are the well-known papers on the "Whistle," and his "Conversation with the Gout," and "The Wreckers."

The ideal American as he has been painted for us of late, is a man who has shaken off the yoke of definite creeds, while retaining their moral essence, and finds the highest sanctions needed for the conduct of human life in experience tempered by common sense. Franklin is generally supposed to have reached this ideal by anticipation, and there is a half-truth in the supposition. But whoever will study this great master of practical life in the picture here painted by himself, will acknowledge that it is only superficially true, and that if he never lifts us above the earth or beyond the domain of experience and common sense, he retained himself a strong hold on the invisible which underlies it, and would have been the first to acknowledge that it was this which enabled him to control the accidents of birth, education, and position, and to earn the eternal gratitude and reverence of the great nation over whose birth he watched so wisely and whose character he did so much to form.

William Stebbing "Bigelow's Life
of Benjamin Franklin" (1880)

If the several causes of the foundation of the Republic of the United States were ranged according to their respective importance, first of all would come the perverse policy of Mr. George Grenville, and the want of moral courage in Lord North to resist the unenlightened obstinacy of George the Third. If not demerits but only merits were classified, an equal rank, and that the highest, must be assigned to George Washington and Benjamin Franklin. So far as any historical events can be appropriated to individuals, those two men were the joint authors of the great Republic. The common English impression of Franklin recognises only two stages in his career. From the struggling printer he is transformed at a bound into the powerful diplomatist who tore asunder Great Britain and her American colonies. The actual Franklin rose gradually to this enormous influence. He had already become independent in fortune before he engaged in public affairs. When he had once taken to public life, he made it his profession, though he sighed after science. Step by step he grew to be the most prominent citizen of Philadelphia. He was appointed Clerk of the General Assembly of Pennsylvania; he became a justice of the peace, an alderman, a burgess of the Assembly. He established the first public library in America. He founded an academy and a hospital. He set on foot a militia force for the defence of the province against the French in Canada. "There was," he writes in his Memoirs, "no such thing as carrying a public-spirited project through without my being concerned in it." If it were so small a matter as clearing away the dust from the roadways or lighting the city, he had to set the example. One question was always asked when subscriptions for an improvement were requested: "Have you consulted Franklin, and what does he think of it?" From Pennsylvania his influence spread throughout the American colonies. He was appointed Postmaster-General for America. That office he kept for over twenty years. His enemies in England often hoped to taunt him into surrendering it. But he lacked, he was in the habit of saying, "the Christian virtue of resignation." It was his rule "never to ask for offices," but also "never to resign them." Franklin had passed his seventieth year before he arrived at the Court of France as the champion of American independence. A long and active life had preceded his greatest exploit, the conclusion of the Peace of 1783.

In view of an impending war with France in 1754, he drew up a plan for "the union of all the colonies under one government, so far as might be necessary for defence, and other important general purposes." The scheme roused jealousy in England, and Franklin attributes to that feeling the despatch of General Braddock from England with two regiments of regulars for the expedition against Fort Duquesne. Though the project of the campaign was not Franklin's, it was only by his help that the army was able to move a step. Horses and carriages could not be procured until Franklin had personally guaranteed payment to the lenders. He accompanied the force, and in vain endeavoured to dissuade the General from marching in a slender line nearly four miles long through a country infested by hostile Indians. The General's answer was: "The savages may indeed be a formidable enemy to your raw American militia; but upon the King's regular and disciplined troops, sir, it is impossible they should make any impression." In the panic which followed Braddock's defeat, Franklin carried a Bill in the Pennsylvania Assembly for the embodiment of a militia force. To concentrate more attention on the movement, he persuaded the Governor to proclaim a fast, that "the blessing of Heaven might be implored on our undertaking." He even obtained subscriptions from Quakers for gunpowder under the euphemism of "bread, flour, wheat, and other grain." He raised and commanded a regiment, Governor Dunbar offered to commission him as general of a force which he was to raise and lead against Fort Duquesne. Franklin had the modesty to decline the service which had proved fatal to Braddock. But he might reasonably have esteemed himself not much inferior in soldierly competence to incapables such as the British Government thought good enough for colonial commands. Of Braddock's successor, Lord Loudoun, he writes: "I wondered much how such a man came to be entrusted with so important a business as the conduct of a great army; but having since seen more of the great world, and the means of obtaining and motives for giving places, my wonder is diminished."

In the years between 1743, when he began to have leisure for public affairs, and 1757 when he came to England as Agent for his province, he was preparing the lesson he applied eighteen years later. He was learning to despise the Home Government's method of managing colonial affairs, and to value aright the internal strength of the colonies for their own defence. He arrived in London on July, 27, 1757, no obscure stranger, but the most prominent citizen of the most important foreign possession of the Empire. The object of his journey had nothing in it of hostility to the Crown. The real sovereigns of Pennsylvania were not the House of Hanover, but the family of William Penn. The heirs of Penn appointed the Governor of the province, and their governor's one care was to see that none of the public burdens touched the vast estates of the Proprietary. Their nominee, the Governor, refused his assent to any tax from which his principals were not expressly exempted. At every step for the protection of the province by the maintenance of an efficient militia, the Assembly found itself checked in its measures for raising the necessary revenue by a veto from the Governor. Franklin was the most energetic enemy of the Proprietary. His future implacability against the American "Loyalists" originated probably in his early resentment against the Penns, who were among the foremost of them. So far the province felt itself drawn to the Crown through their common interest in defensive measures against hostile Indians and Frenchmen. Indeed, at the Privy Council, Lord Mansfield used his authority to break down the Proprietary's obstinacy. Yet even so early as this, Franklin's indignation was stirred by the exorbitant claims of the Crown to authority over the colonies. Within a few mornings after his arrival in London the accomplished and eccentric Lord Granville, better known as Carteret, who was President of the Council, granted him an interview. Lord Granville then surprised him by the statement that "the King's instructions to his governors, being first drawn up by judges, then considered in council, after which they are signed by the King, are, so far as they relate to you Americans, the law of the land, for the King is the legislator of the colonies." "His lordship's conversation," wrote Franklin, "a little alarmed me as to what might be the sentiments of the Court concerning us." For the moment Franklin's aim was to extort liberty from the ungenerous domination of a private family. He registered, however, the pretensions of the royal prerogative as matter of warning.

On his second visit to England he bore originally a commission only from the Pennsylvanian Assembly. To the Agency for Pennsylvania were gradually added the Agencies for Georgia, Massachusetts, and New Jersey, as the colonies found that what had been only a theory of the royal prerogative was in process of conversion into practice. He had come once more in 1763 to intercede against the King Log of the Proprietary Constitution. He found himself confronted with much more formidable claims of the British nation and Parliament. He still is seen, as in old days, appealing to the Sovereign; only formerly it was against the Penns he besought his aid, now it is against the King's own Ministers. The Stamp Act was passed by Parliament on the pretext of reimbursing this country for the cost it had defrayed in expelling the French from Canada and Nova Scotia. Franklin, by conversation, by private letters, and in the public press, was always forward to deny that the colonies owed any debt to the mother-country. The mother-country had engaged in war with France for its own ambitious purposes. The war was not a colonial, but an imperial war. The colonies had, he would have admitted, benefited by the results of the war. He was always forward to express his delight at the subjugation of the French territories. But he rejoiced "not merely as a colonist, but as a Briton." A moral duty lay on the colonists, their Agent confessed, to pay their share of the expenses because they were Britons. The fact, however, he asserted, was that they had already paid their share, and more than their share. "Every year during the war requisitions were made by the Crown on the colonies for raising money and men. They made more extraordinary efforts in proportion to their abilities than Britain did." What was that proportion, he urged, was matter for grave consideration. He complained that it was a favourite device, "in order to render the taxing of America a popular measure, to insist continually on the topics of our wealth and flourishing circumstances, while this country is loaded with debt, great part of it incurred on our account." The truth was, according to him, that, magnificent as he accounted American prospects, the present was discouraging. Colonies, he forcibly argued, are not, like their countrymen at home, heirs to many generations of laborious ancestors. They have to do all for themselves; their expenses press so closely on the heels of their resources that a great part of the charges for the rout of Braddock and the triumphs of Wolfe and Amherst "lies still, in 1766, a load of debt upon them."

Even had Great Britain made them its debtors by relieving them from the perpetual terror of French attack at its own sole cost, the discharge of the moral debt should have been matter of mutual arrangement. But the colonies were being taxed by a Legislature in which they were not represented. When their aid in money had formerly been required, the custom had been to ask it of their Assemblies, as the Crown asked it of Parliament. On all proper occasions they were ready to grant aid as Parliament granted it. "We of the colonies have never insisted that we ought to be exempt from contributing to the common expenses necessary to support the prosperity of the Empire." They did insist that the money of the King's subjects in America could no more be taken from them without their own consent, obtained through their representatives, than from the King's subjects in England. "If the Parliament has a right thus to take from us a penny in the pound, where is the line drawn that bounds that right, and what shall hinder their calling, whenever they please, for the other nineteen shillings and eleven pence?" Franklin's theory of the relation of the colonies to Great Britain was that they were "only connected, as England and Scotland were before the Union, by having one common sovereign, the King." The founders of the colonies expressly went to the New World to escape from the tyranny of English statutes. "They took with them, however, by compact, their allegiance to the King, and a legislative

power for the making a new body of laws with his assent, by which they were
to be governed. Hence they became distinct States, under the same prince,
united as Ireland is to the Crown, but not to the realm, of England, and
governed each by its own laws, though with the same sovereign, and having
each the right of granting its own money to that sovereign."

The weak point in Franklin's theory of colonial rule is that it implies the
King could come to the consideration of colonial questions as if for the time
he were transported bodily, and unattended by any of his Parliamentary
advisers, across the Atlantic. Franklin would have been as unwilling that Lord
Hillsborough should dictate to the colonies under cover of the King's name as
that Parliament should dictate. Probably he would not have been disposed to
deny the difficulty of emancipating the King whenever he had to exercise his
colonial prerogative from an English sovereign's deference to the Ministers
delegated by Parliament. But when Englishmen dwelt upon the "inconvenience"
of a theory which supposed the division of "an empire into many separate
states," he answered that "an inconvenience proves nothing but itself." It was,
however, his consciousness of the difficulty of fastening upon the King double
functions which doubtless suggested to him, as to his friend Lord Kames, a
consolidating union of Great Britain and the American colonies as the way
out of the dilemma. If the colonies sent members to Parliament, Parliament in
taxing them would not have been disjoining taxation from representation. The
King, in exercising his colonial prerogative at the instance of his Parliamentary
advisers, would have been exercising it with the implied assent of his colonial
subjects. Franklin's logical objection to the actual mode in which the King
and the British Parliament claimed to rule the colonies was that colonists
were treated as possessed of inferior liberties to their fellow-subjects here.
They were governed without having a voice in their government. The grant of
proportionate representation in the Imperial Parliament to Pennsylvania and
the rest would have brought their subjection to the supremacy of Parliament at
all events into logical conformity with the theory of the British Constitution.

That any such Parliamentary union with the North American colonies
would have been permanent it is impossible to believe. Franklin affected to
think "it would probably subsist so long as Britain shall continue a nation."
On the contrary, the first occasion on which the colonial representatives
had been overborne by the English and Scotch members would have
dissolved it. Franklin himself would have been the first to denounce a
connection in which British representative heads were counted as against
colonial. Great Britain and the American colonies were doomed to part
by the very incompatibility of their rival greatness. The projects Franklin

and some of his English and Scotch allies devised with a view to averting the catastrophe carried on their face proof of their want of reality. It was, however, a gratuitous addition to the shock of predestined separation that British politics should at the time have been passing through a stage of moral degradation which intensified the violence of the wrench. Almost more grievous still was the coincidence that it was the fate of England to have Franklin, of all men, for witness to the decay.

In the earlier years of the reign of George III the whole body of British politics was sick, it seemed, to death. Franklin's letters home reveal it in all its ghastly infirmities. The few statesmen who were incorrupt were technical fanatics, like Mr. George Grenville, or "inaccessibles," like Lord Chatham. Public men were commonly of a much weaker moral or mental fibre. There was the careless King's Minister, like Lord North, who for the sake of peace with his colleagues, "some of whom could not be brought to agree to the repeal of the whole Stamp Act," suffered his better sense to be overridden, and consented to maintain "the duty on tea, with the obnoxious preamble, to continue the dispute." There was the man of pleasure, like Lord Clare, who, "after we had drunk a bottle and a half of claret each, hugged and kissed me, protesting he never in his life met with a man he was so much in love with." There was the official, incapable of understanding that a colony could have rights, like Lord Hillsborough, "whose character is conceit, wrong-headedness, obstinacy, and passion." There was the Minister with an instinct of equity, but without the moral courage to adhere to it, like Lord Dartmouth, "with dispositions for the best measures, and easily prevailed with to join in the worst." There was the mob of peers, not vouchsafing even to consider, still less to understand, Lord Chatham's plan for pacification: "Hereditary Legislators! There would be more propriety, because less hazard of mischief, in having, as in some University of Germany, hereditary professors of mathematics." There was a House of Commons, costing "no less than four thousand pounds for a member." There was the abandonment of London for days to "a drunken mad mob," which had made a hero of "an outlaw and an exile of bad personal character." "I went last week to Winchester, and observed that for fifteen miles out of town there was scarce a door or window-shutter next the road unmarked with 'Wilkes and Liberty,' and 'No. 45.'" There was, at least in the American's eyes, "in short, a whole venal nation, now at market, to be sold for about two millions, and able to be bought out of the hands of the present bidders, if he would offer half a million more, by the devil himself." This was a population which talked of "our colonies," as if Pennsylvania and Massachusetts and Virginia were private possessions of every ignorant

Englishman. To Englishmen an American's apology for existence was that he made a market for English goods. These people, who thought themselves competent to legislate for America, could scarcely point out its place on the globe. They would not of themselves have seen any incongruity in Franklin's jest that the King of Spain had contracted for the casting of a thousand guns at Quebec, or detected the absurdity of his assurance that "the grand leap of the whale in the chase up the Falls of Niagara is esteemed, by all who have seen it, as one of the finest spectacles in nature." For a time the King was the refuge of Americans enraged and outraged by the pretensions of men they despised to lord it over their superiors in character and public spirit. Franklin records with delight so late as 1772 how "the King has been heard to speak of me with great regard." He loved to contrast the goodness of the King with the stupid selfishness of the nation. But gradually he begins to "suspect, between you and me, that the late measures have been very much the King's own, and that he has in some cases a great share of what his friends call firmness." He hopes still that, "by some painstaking and proper management, the wrong impressions the King has received may be removed." At length the suspicion becomes certainty, the hope fades, and he is forced to the conclusion, which was unhappily only too true, that "the King hates us most cordially" in the aggregate, and "that insidious man," Franklin, in particular.

King George thought all who disagreed with him madmen or rogues. We know from the Shelburne Correspondence how he consoled himself at the end of the American war with the reflection that "knavery seems to be so much the striking feature of the inhabitants, that it may not in the end be an evil that they will become aliens to this Kingdom." At all events, his instinct of aversion from Franklin did not deceive him. Whatever was vicious and out of joint in the relations between England and its colonies showed uglier and more misshapen as reflected through Franklin's eyes. It was not by any design or desire of Franklin that his mission in England irritated every disposition in the two peoples to quarrel. His correspondence shows that, though he could not avoid perceiving the blunders of English dealing with America, he would have been far from disinclined to aid in correcting them. He had shown himself so temperate a mediator between the two countries, that when the Stamp Act was promulgated in America in 1766, his house and family in Philadelphia were threatened by a mob. His complaint in 1768 had probably not been insincere that, as he had rendered himself suspected in England of being "too much an American," in America, on the contrary, he was suspected of being "too much an Englishman." He argued that "between the governed and governing every mistake in Government, every encroachment on right, is not worth a rebellion." To the very eve of the civil war he was ready to discuss ways by which it might have been avoided. Yet an agent of the colonies much less acute, much less of an impassioned enthusiast for peace, with a far inferior title to gain an audience of Ministers and orators, would have had more chance of success in appeasing the feud. As we read the correspondence which Mr. John Bigelow has compiled and condensed in his 'Life of Franklin,' published in 1879, we feel the issue of the controversy to be a foregone conclusion. Franklin taught his countrymen to despise the mother-country. He seemed always to be presenting an ultimatum. In 1766 he writes of the Stamp Act: "As to executing the Act by force, it is madness, and will be ruin to the whole." In 1771 he writes to the Massachusetts Committee of Correspondence about the exaction of customs in America by Parliament, that civil war is the certain result. "The bloody struggle will end in absolute slavery to America, or ruin to Britain by the loss of her colonies; the latter most probable from America's growing strength and magnitude." Another representative of the colonies would probably have begun by assuming the indissolubility of the bond which united Great Britain and its American settlements. Franklin showed himself to his countrymen perpetually in the act of testing the chain, to judge where were the weak links at which it might be expected to break. Instead of a mediator come to negotiate a removal of colonial grievances, he appeared in the character of a judge pronouncing a divorce of the Colonies from Great Britain for British infidelity, cruelty, and general desertion of duties.

Jobbing English politicians felt and resented the tone of scornful superiority in Franklin's remonstrances on behalf of his constituents. They exulted in the opportunity afforded them for a retort by his appearance before the Privy Council to give evidence on the petition of Massachusetts for the removal of Governor Hutchinson and Lieutenant-Governor Andrew Oliver. The ground of the petition was that correspondence which had fallen into Franklin's hands between them and a Mr. Whately, who had been private secretary to Mr. George Grenville, convicted them of having incited the British Government to the measures whence had issued the strife between it and the colonies. The scene in the Council Chamber on the historical 29th of January, 1774, was an explosion of wrath long pent up. The whole, as Franklin wrote to Mr. Cushing, was "in all probability preconcerted." The thirty-five Privy Councillors, forgetting that they were sitting as judges, "frequently laughed outright," as Dr. Priestley narrates, "at the sallies of" Mr. Wedderburn's sarcastic wit." They were charmed to retaliate thus on the Transatlantic moralist who, they well knew, had been for seventeen years cataloguing their follies and corruptions. They were not altogether wrong in condemning the conduct of Franklin in that transaction. It is not necessary to accept Wedderburn's insinuation that Franklin had employed his opportunities as American Postmaster-General to intercept Governor Hutchinson's letters home. Mr. Charles Francis Adams's account is probably true, that the papers were delivered to Franklin by Sir John Temple. Not the less had both Franklin and the Assembly of Massachusetts violated, in the use they made of them, the confidence of private correspondence. Franklin's defence has been commonly accepted by Americans. It was that private letters written by a highly placed official on public questions to a member of the British Parliament could not be described as private letters. That was the conclusion also of the Massachusetts House of Representatives. The fallacy of such a position is apparent. It is at least as extraordinary that Franklin should have thought the misuse of Governor Hutchinson's correspondence balanced by the publication and despatch to the English Government of the letters sent by Franklin as the Agent of the Massachusetts Assembly to the Assembly. Obviously publicity, though within a limited circle, was contemplated by the writer himself as a property of the letters to the Assembly, and privacy as a property of those of Governor Hutchinson to Mr. Whately. Most extraordinary of all was Franklin's profession of amazement in the account he published of the whole transaction that the British Government should not have profited by the occasion and left Governor Hutchinson and his brother officials "like the scapegoats of old to carry away into the wilderness all the offences which have arisen between the two countries." He did not understand, any more than after the war, when Great Britain interceded for the restoration of the Loyalists who had suffered in its cause, that a Government cannot with any self-respect cast the consequences of its blunders on subordinates who have served it. He actually appears to have anticipated gratitude from British Ministers for the part he had played in the miserable business. "A Court clamour," he exclaims in his narrative, "was raised against me as an incendiary! The very action upon which I valued myself as, it appeared to me, a means of lessening our differences, I was unlucky enough to find charged upon me as a wicked attempt to increase them. Strange perversion!"

The 29th of January, 1774, shattered what Franklin was fond of calling that "China vase," that "beautiful porcelain vase," the British Empire, as then constituted. From that day, though Franklin himself was possibly unconscious of the catastrophe, no hope remained of reconciling the claims of Great Britain to sovereignty, and of the colonies to equality. On the day following the baiting at the Council Office, he was informed that "his

Majesty's Postmaster-General had found it necessary to dismiss him from the office of Deputy Postmaster-General in North America." He lingered in England for another year and four months, observing "a cool, sullen silence" to Ministers. He kept, he writes, "a separate account of private injuries, which," he adds, "I may forgive." He certainly never forgave them. But, though henceforth he did not court, neither did he reject, overtures for an arrangement of the difficulty between the two kindred peoples. Interminable negotiations passed between Franklin on one side, and Lord Howe, Lord Hyde, Dr. Fothergill, Mr. David Hartley, and Mr. Barclay, on the other, for a basis of settlement. Franklin visited Lord Chatham at Hayes, to consult on possible means of accommodation. The great man's equipage was seen at Franklin's door in Craven Street, "on the very day twelve months," as Franklin proudly notes, "that the Ministry had taken so much pains to disgrace me before the Privy Council." Franklin by no means repulsed the assistance thus proffered for the reunion of the two countries. He remarked, with pleasure, the sympathy of Dissenters and Irishmen, and other victims of English legislative exclusiveness, with the resistance of the colonies, and their belief that "the salvation of English liberty depended now on the perseverance and virtue of America." The negotiations went on as merrily as if none of the parties to them entertained any suspicion that the subject-matter of their conferences had ceased to exist, that the British Plantations in North America had expanded into a nation. Even at this distance of time, an English student is sensible of a sort of despair, from the consciousness how only the surface was stirred by these elaborate discussions. The deliberations commonly accompanied or followed a game of chess between Franklin and Lord Howe's sister. They had neither less nor more of seriousness about them than the tournament of the chessboard. On points of detail Franklin was ready enough to give way. He offered to pledge his personal security for the repayment to the merchants of their losses on the tea thrown into Boston harbour. When it came to the question of conceding legislative independence to the colonies, neither could he abate, nor the English volunteer pacificators yield, a jot. The utmost to which Franklin's English friends felt they could even offer to pledge the British nation was, that the bare right of Parliament to supremacy should be so guarded in its exercise as to be practically dormant. Chatham himself could not presume to ask of the nation at large anything higher. When, moderate as was Chatham's plan for a settlement, and enormous as was his personal authority, the Peers would not so much consider it as to allow it to lie on their table, it may easily be conceived how utterly insoluble had the crisis become.

Yet of the two sides there was on the English more, it may almost be said, of good faith than on the American. We are far from imputing conscious insincerity to Franklin. He foresaw war as the necessary consequence of a failure to repair the breach; and his common declaration may be believed, that he was almost inclined to think "there was never a good war, nor a bad peace." He was no fanatical admirer of particular forms of Government. But circumstances, he obviously felt, had cut off from England its American Colonies, and there was no possibility of healing the wound. His Quaker, Dissenter, and Chathamite friends could scarcely believe in such a schism in the imperial unity. At the moment of recognising the independence of the United States, seven years later, statesmen looked forward to a possible return of the colonies to their allegiance. No Englishman could comprehend, as could Franklin, the capacity of the colonies for standing alone. In exhorting, when the British Ministers had shown themselves unbending in 1775, the Americans to resist, for that "nothing could secure the privileges of America but a firm, sober adherence to the terms of the association made at the Congress," men like Barclay and Fothergill hardly suspected that the firmness meant final separation. In asserting that "the salvation of English liberty depended on the perseverance and virtue of America," they were thinking of Americans as fellow-subjects, whose voices in favour of liberty would be added to their English voices in right of their common country. We can see more clearly in these days, and so could Franklin in his. An United American Congress was sitting at Philadelphia, and Benjamin Franklin had been scolded and sneered at by the Solicitor-General of England and the King's Councillors as a thief. It would have been wonderful surgery to reincorporate the bleeding limb in the old body. It would have needed nothing less than a miracle when the fragment torn from the mutilated British trunk was itself grown into a breathing being.

Franklin shook the dust of England from his feet as a subject of King George when he set sail for America in 1775. When he returned to Europe it was to watch and to baffle from Passy the clumsy efforts of British Ministers to make a solitude where they had failed to maintain peace. He was so far a diplomatist that he had studied human character for seventy years. Yet in England his diplomacy had only exasperated. In France he accomplished as much against England as Washington with all his victories. His knowledge of French was so indifferent, that on one occasion during the sitting of the Academy he was observed to "applaud the loudest at his own praises." He did the work, he never learned the dialect, of diplomacy. He was that strange creature, a Republican at the Court of a pure monarchy. In Paris his defects were virtues. His scientific fame spoke for itself in purest Parisian French. As a politician, he was to the Court the dire enemy of England; to the jaded society of Paris he was the representative of a new world of feeling and thought. His New England astuteness seemed to Parisian courtiers patriarchal innocence. His naive stories and illustrations, which a thousand admirers were ready to translate and repeat in every circle of the town, were as bracing as quinine. His very costume, "his hair hanging, his spectacles on his nose, his white hose, and white hat under his arm," in the midst of absurd perukes and brocaded suits, came like a revelation of free nature to the slaves of fashion. He became, to his own amusement, the idol of Paris. "Mr. Franklin," writes a contemporary Parisian, "is besieged, followed, admired, adored, wherever he shows himself, with a fury, a fanaticism, capable no doubt of flattering him and doing him honour, but which at the same time proves that we shall never be reasonable." He tells his daughter that incredible numbers had been sold of clay medallions of him, "some to be set in the lids of snuff-boxes, and some so small as to be worn in rings." "Pictures, busts, and prints have made your father's face as well known as that of the moon." A great Parisian lady wrote fifty years later to the respectable Ticknor in language which implied that she thought Bostonians and Patagonians kindred peoples. After the same fashion, Versailles was never perhaps quite certain that the New England philosopher was not of Red Indian descent. But love does not reason. Paris had fallen in love with Franklin, and in homage to him grew enamoured of simplicity.

No Englishman was ever so caressed in Paris, for the very reason that Franklin was, and was not, an Englishman. As the American sage and philosopher, he performed as much for his country as he accomplished by his diplomatic skill. But he was a diplomatist too, and of high rank in the art. Colleagues and rivals, like his detractor Arthur Lee, or even Jay and Adams, who, as Mr. Fitzherbert wrote, in a letter quoted by Lord Edmond Fitzmaurice in his Life of Lord Shelburne, "rather fear than are attached to him," might be pardoned for inability to understand the source of his influence. They did not venture to deny the fact. In the only serious instance in which, with reference to the disputed fishery and boundary rights, he was accused of neglecting the interests of his countrymen, his colleagues certified that he had defended those interests with his counsels and his authority. On another and more important point, he not merely co-operated but took the initiative. Englishmen and Canadians, who mutually cherish the connection of the Dominion with Great Britain, may well shudder at the contemplation of the extreme risk that connection ran from British statesmen's weariness of

the war, and from Franklin's superior diplomatic keenness. A man who had
gone through the campaign with Braddock, who had shared in the alarms
and labours of the period which followed the British defeat, and exulted in
the triumph of Wolfe, was not likely to depreciate the value of Canada. The
moral right of the colonies to the old French possessions in North America
had been a special question in the futile negotiations between himself and
Lord Howe in England. When the war commenced, he sought to induce
France to help the colonies to wrest Canada and Nova Scotia from England.
As soon as the negotiations for peace with England opened, his great efforts
were directed to persuade the English Commissioner, Richard Oswald, to
see the utility of ceding those territories as proofs of a desire for that "sweet"
thing, a "reconciliation," and as a safeguard against future causes of strife.
Oswald, a prosperous Scotch merchant, was, as Franklin says of him, an old
man who had "nothing at heart but the good of mankind, and putting a stop
to mischief." He does not seem to have been fit to cope with a philanthropist
like Franklin. He had happened to let fall an opinion, that "the giving up of
Canada to the English at the last peace had been a politic act in France, for
that it had weakened the ties between England and her colonies, and that he
himself had predicted from it the late revolution." Franklin, who had been
preparing the ground by asserting the title of the United States to reparation
over and above the mere grant of peace for the injuries England had inflicted,
proposed that Canada should be given and accepted as such reparation. He
applied Oswald's own argument to the future: "I spoke of the occasions of
quarrel that might be produced by England continuing to hold Canada,
hinting at the same time, but not expressing too plainly, that such a situation,
to us so dangerous, would necessarily oblige us to cultivate and strengthen
our union with France." Oswald "appeared much struck with my discourse."
Franklin had already developed a scheme on paper which he lent to Oswald
to read and meditate upon. The plan was, that "Britain should voluntarily
offer to give up the province, though on these conditions, that she shall in all
times coming have and enjoy the right of free trade thither, unencumbered
with any duties whatsoever; that so much of the vacant lands shall be sold as
will raise a sum sufficient to pay for the houses burnt by the British troops
and their Indians, and also to indemnify the Royalists for the confiscation of
their estates." Oswald, he says, "told me that nothing in his judgment could be
clearer, more satisfactory, and convincing, than the reasonings in that paper;
that he would do his utmost to impress Lord Shelburne with them." Franklin,
in reporting by letter this conversation to his brother Peace Commissioner,
Adams, describes Oswald's remarks rather more fully than in the semi-

official journal he kept. He tells Adams, on April 20, 1782, his proposal about Canada: "Mr. Oswald liked much the idea, but said they were too much straitened for money to make any pecuniary reparation; but he should endeavour to persuade their doing in this way." Oswald went to England to confer with Lord Shelburne, taking Franklin's paper with him. On his return to Paris, he informed Franklin that "it seemed to have made an impression, and he had reason to believe that it might be settled to our satisfaction towards the end of the treaty; but in his own mind he wished it might not be mentioned at the beginning; that his lordship indeed said he had not imagined reparation would be expected, and he wondered I should not know whether it was intended to demand it." A day or two after, Franklin conversed again on the subject with Oswald. "Oswald repeated to me his opinion, that the affair of Canada would be settled to our satisfaction, and his wish that it might not be mentioned till towards the end of the treaty." Franklin relied on the assistance of French statesmanship in pressing his advantage against British dejection. But the extracts from French despatches printed in M. de Circourt's translation of Mr. Bancroft's history demonstrate that no one was more bitterly opposed than the French Ministers to the annexation of Canada to the United States. Eager as they had been to promote the separation of the British provinces in America from the mother-country, M. de Vergennes was entirely opposed to any extension of the emancipated territory. Perhaps he still cherished a hope that the French provinces in America, which had been conquered by England only twenty years before, might one day be brought back to their allegiance to the Court of Versailles.

Franklin, as a diplomatist, was not peremptory in insisting on abstract rights of his country, still less on his own dignity. But he studied the French men and the French women who ruled France, and he probed to the bottom the instincts of the French governing class, without losing his own. About alliances in general he was not solicitous. Before he started on his own mission to Europe he had in Congress, though in vain, deprecated the sending a "virgin" republic "suitoring" for the friendship of European Powers. "It seems to me," he writes, "that we have in most instances hurt our credit and importance by sending all over Europe begging alliances, and soliciting declarations of our independence. The nations, perhaps, from thence seemed to think that our independence is something they have to sell, and that we do not offer enough for it." Writing to Jay, at Madrid, in April 1782, he exclaims: "Spain has taken four years to consider whether she should treat with us or not. Give her forty, and let us in the meantime mind our own business." Five years before, in 1777, he and his fellow-representatives of the United States in Europe had received instructions that, "in case France and Spain will enter into the war, the United States will assist the former in the conquest of the British sugar islands, and the latter in the conquest of Portugal, America desiring only for her share what Britain holds on the continent." Americans must blush to think that their new-born commonwealth should have condescended to purchase aid towards its emancipation by offers to help in enslaving another free state which had never done it any injury. We are glad, for the credit of Franklin, that he simply recites these instructions in a letter to Arthur Lee, who was at Burgos. He adds not a word implying approval of the dishonourable bribe to Spain.

But, in fact, he cared indeed little for European alliances except the French. To consolidate that he was all complaisance. His tact alone prevented a rupture with the French Ministers through the signature, in December 1782, behind their backs, of the preliminary treaty between Great Britain and the United States. His brother Commissioners, Jay and Adams, suspected that the French Government wished to protract the negotiations for its own objects, however the United States might suffer by the prolongation of the war. Their suspicion was not without foundation; and Franklin, when he understood the facts, concurred with their decision to proceed independently. But he had the wisdom, which his colleagues lacked, to be content with starting peace on its route without breaking down the bridge by which it had crossed before he knew whether it might not be useful for a retreat. To the French Minister's reproaches on the departure from good fellowship, he replied by the soft answer which turns away wrath. He defends himself, and Jay and Adams, against the charge of anything worse than "indiscretion," and "neglect of a point of *bienséance*." To those two offences he pleads guilty. But he warns M. de Vergennes not to forget the effect of a quarrel upon "the English, who, I just now learn, flatter themselves they have already divided us." The friendly relations of France and the United States had seemed in danger of being completely overclouded when Franklin's amiable apologies restored peace. Two days after the French Ministerial remonstrance, the United States actually received from the French Treasury a loan of six million francs, which infused new life into their military operations. Jay and Adams, "who," observes M. de Vergennes, "do not pretend to recognise the rules of courtesy in regard to us," could never have obtained that aid. Franklin's brother Commissioners underrated the gain to the United States from French succour. Without the diversion France created in Europe, and the subsidies she granted, it is almost impossible that the Congress should not have been compelled to conclude a humiliating peace with King George. Franklin understood that the French alliance was vital to his people, and he spared no pains that he might confirm it. As Jefferson said of him, in extolling his diplomatic dexterity, he, by his reasonableness, moderation, and temper, so won the confidence of the French Ministers that "it may truly be said they were more under his influence than he under theirs."

Englishmen were not so criminal, nor was England so near to the close of its greatness, as Franklin supposed. On the other hand, neither was the power of France so deeply rooted as it appeared to his friendly eyes, nor French assistance to the struggling Republic so generous as he habituated himself to represent it. While he was quick to detect the perversion of free institutions to the purposes of selfish corruption in England, he chose to be for the most part utterly blind to the more radical vices of French government and society. He remarks, almost as if it were matter of praise, that "the *noblesse* always govern here," and that "trade is not their admiration." On his journey, in 1785, through France to Havre, where he was to embark for America, he was entertained at the magnificent château of the Archbishop of Rouen, Cardinal Rochefoucauld. He seems not to have felt the Revolution in the air, and goes out of his way to testify that "the Cardinal is much respected and beloved by the people of this country." In England the foundations were sound. Much practical liberty, and even good administration, were compatible with electoral dishonesty and political perversity. But Franklin could perceive no hope of a remedy for the inconsistencies between theory and practice which disgusted him. Not altogether in jest does he advise Englishmen to "dissolve your present old crazy Constitution, and send members to Congress." The entire order of things in France was rotten at the core, yet Franklin was more than half inclined to live and die there. When the tempest had actually begun to rage, he still regarded it as a passing gust. He writes in October, 1788, to his friend M. le Veillard: "When this fermentation is over, and the troubling parts subsided, the wine will be fine and good, and cheer the hearts of those who drink of it." Had his life lasted a little longer, he would have had to lament the deaths on the scaffold of the correspondent to whom he wrote thus confidently, and a multitude of other friends.

Franklin simply did not see the instability of that charming Parisian society to which he discoursed in his shrewdly witty parables. We suspect that he only affected not to perceive the selfish motives at the bottom of the invaluable assistance the French nation and Government afforded his country. Chivalrous Frenchmen like Lafayette, in advocating the American cause, were protesting more against Court absolutism at home than against the imperial tyranny of Great Britain. Frenchmen generally and their rulers,

when they succoured the United States, were merely fighting, as they had
fought a generation earlier, England in America. They longed to recover
Canada. When they had convinced themselves that their American allies
would not consent to their return as sovereigns to any part of the North
American continent, they liked better to leave their old dominions in the
hands of England than struggle for their transfer to the emancipated British
colonies. Whilst Great Britain remained still a neighbour they believed the
Republic would not be able to dispense with the shelter of French protection.
Franklin, who weighed human motives, especially when not altogether
noble, with unerring sagacity, was possibly more desirous to convince
Robert Livingston than himself convinced, when he wrote: "The ideas of
aggrandisement by conquest are out of fashion. The wise here think France
great enough; and its ambition at present seems to be only that of justice and
magnanimity towards other nations, fidelity and utility to its allies." With this
amiable construction which Franklin puts on the motives of French kindness
to the American colonies of England in 1783, it is interesting to contrast
his view of French official civilities sixteen years before. In 1767, after his
examination by the House of Commons on the subject of the Stamp Act, the
French Minister Plenipotentiary in London, M. Durand, called upon him.

> "M. Durand," writes Franklin to his son, "is extremely curious to
> inform himself on the affairs of America; pretends to have a great
> esteem for me; invited me to dine with him, was very inquisitive,
> makes me visits. I fancy that intriguing nation would like very much
> to meddle on occasion, and blow up the coals between Britain and
> her colonies; but I hope we shall give them no opportunity."

The certainty that, had the American connection with Great Britain
survived the Stamp and Tea Duty Acts, it must have collapsed in wider ruin a
little later, produces a feeling of indifference to the personal incidents which
contributed to the actual catastrophe. Otherwise, English readers of these
volumes might be disposed to repine that Franklin should not have bestowed
on the task of reconciling England and the colonies some of the unfailing
bonhomie which kept the peace between the United States and France. As,
when the war was once begun, every feature in the French national and
political character was interpreted by him too kindly, so all in the English
were interpreted too harshly. He made no account of the difficulties inherent
in the relations of the colonies and the mother-country. To him there could
be no fault on the former side, because there was nothing not faulty on the
latter. He hears with delight of the vengeance of which the "No Popery"

mob was the unconscious instrument upon Lord Mansfield and Governor Hutchinson. "Lord Mansfield's house is burnt. Thus he who approved the burning of American houses has had fire brought home to him. He himself was horribly scared, and Governor Hutchinson, it is said, died outright of the fright." He speculates with pleasure on the possible wreck of the whole British Empire: "If the English lose their Indian commerce and one battle at sea, their credit is gone, and their power follows." He foretells that the war "must end in the ruin of Britain, if she does not speedily put an end to it." He believes every tale of the "cruel captivity" to which "our brave countrymen," "martyrs to the cause of liberty," are subjected, "fed scantily on bad provisions, without warm lodging, clothes, or fire." He denounces the war "on the part of England as, of all the wars in my time, the wickedest, having no cause but malice against liberty, and the jealousy of commerce." He despairs of seeing its end because, he writes to an Englishman, "your thirsty nation has not drunk enough of our blood." Every Englishman is held by him guilty of complicity. But he attached especial guilt to politicians. He had written while fresh from England, in 1775, to his old friend, William Strahan, the King's printer: "Mr. Strahan, you are a Member of Parliament, and one of that majority which has doomed my country to destruction. You have begun to burn our homes and murder our people. Look at your hands; they are stained with the blood of your relations. You and I were long friends; you are now my enemy, and I am yours." Guilty above other Members of Parliament were, in his eyes, the King's Ministers. "I never think," he writes to Mr. James Hutton, in 1778, "of your present Ministers and their abettors but with the image strongly painted in my view of their hands, red, wet, and dripping with the blood of my countrymen, friends, and relations." Upon King George himself, once his admired mediator between a despotic Parliament and oppressed colonies, he pours out all the vials of his wrath. He charges upon the King the destruction, "in a continued course of bloody wars, of near one hundred thousand human creatures." To Franklin the King must account for two thousand scalps torn from defenceless farmers, their wives, and children, by the savages he hired. To Franklin the royal wickednesses are the best evidence of immortality. "The more I see the impossibility, from the number and extent of his crimes, of giving equivalent punishment in this life, the more I am convinced of a future state in which all that here appears to be wrong shall be set right."

The disposition in Franklin to misjudge England impresses readers of his correspondence the more that he was by theory and practice generally indulgent to principles and conduct differing from his own. So ostentatiously violent are his outbursts of anger at the English King, Ministers, and nation, and, with this exception, so universally philanthropic and moderate are Franklin's general sentiments and language, that it is sometimes hard to smother a suspicion that the harshness against his former fellow-subjects and Sovereign was a species of affectation. A more probable hypothesis would be that it was nature's revenge for the regular and continued repression to which from early manhood he had subjected his natural disposition. From the training his Autobiography shows him to have undergone, we can infer something of his original temper. In that unique work, now for the first time, through Mr. Bigelow's care, printed as Franklin wrote it, and with the addition of the last few pages which had never before been published, Franklin alludes to his native impetuosity, and to the means he took to correct it. When young, he was, he says, of a "disputatious turn," a very bad habit, he remarks, into which "persons of good sense seldom fall, except lawyers, university men, and men of all sorts that have been bred at Edinburgh." Noticing that "disputing, contradicting, and confuting people are generally unfortunate in their affairs," he exchanged the habit, after reading Xenophon's 'Memorabilia,' for the Socratic method. "I dropt my abrupt contradiction and argumentation, and put on the humble inquirer and doubter." He became so expert a master of dialectics, that a controversial printer with whom he worked at Philadelphia would at last "hardly answer me the most common question without asking first, 'What do you intend to infer from that?'" As that very irritating substitute for dogmatism proved not more likely to make friends than his former practice, he set himself to curtail it. He retained of the Socratic method "only the habit of expressing himself in terms of modest diffidence." "I never use," he writes, "when I advance anything that may possibly be disputed, the words 'certainly,' 'undoubtedly,' or any others that give the air of positiveness to an opinion, but rather say, 'I conceive or apprehend a thing to be so and so,' or 'It is so if I am not mistaken.'" When he set up his "club of mutual improvement," the Junto, the rules drawn up by him were framed on the same principle. "Everything was studied which might prevent our disgusting each other." "To prevent warmth, all expressions of positiveness in opinions, or direct contradiction, were after some time made contraband, and prohibited under small pecuniary penalties." Restraint at the meetings of the Junto may be responsible in part for the freedom with which, when patriotism seemed to license him, the unlucky Lord Hillsborough is characterised as a compound of "conceit, wrong-headedness, obstinacy, passion, and insincerity." If King George once "the very best king in the world, and the most amiable," is condemned to Tophet for not letting the American colonies go free on their own demand, the warmth of the denunciation may only have been compensation for the careful veneer of calmness upon a nature apparently by no means devoid of passion and excitability. Franklin had brought himself to regard varieties of doctrine and opinion as not worth the friction of loss of temper, with the one exception of the question of national liberty and independence. That appeared to him on a different level altogether. On that he esteemed anger lawful and virtuous, and he seems to have found an occasional fit of temper by no means disagreeable.

Franklin could at once bear vituperation with the stoicism of a tortured Indian, and then turn and wither up an assailant with lightning flash and fire. But the extraordinary feature both in his tolerance and in his intolerance is that no one can ever suppose his indignation was not as much under his command as his patience. His Autobiography and Correspondence are of high value as contributing to the history of a great political and historical epoch. They possess as much value of a different sort, as offering together the most marvellous representation of a formed and built-up character to be found in the whole of the records of psychology. There was the raw, original Franklin, who might have developed in this or that direction; and there was a very different creature, the actual Franklin, as Philadelphia, London, and Paris knew him. The rough material had been hewn and carved and polished into the finished moralist, statesman, diplomatist, fabulist, and general worker in human wit, by a third self, a moral censor who was continually surveying and criticising the new fabric as it grew.

Franklin was at an early period dogmatic. As we have seen, he discovered that was an inconvenient character in which to make the pilgrimage of life. He corrected it at first by enquiring into the foundations of the dogmas of others, instead of propounding dogmas himself. People liked no better to be obliged to render an account of their own beliefs than to have another person's forced upon them; so, his inner monitor accommodated matters by engrafting a habit of suggesting an opinion. Whoever chose were left at liberty to suppose they had elaborated it out of their own heads. There was restlessly free blood in the veins of the Franklins. His father, Josiah, had quitted Ecton, in Northamptonshire, for Boston in 1682, for the sake of liberty of worship. He had a library of "books of dispute about religion," and Franklin when a mere boy read them out of a mere natural "bookishness." Later, when he was about fifteen, "some books against Deism fell into my hands; they were said to be the substance of sermons preached at Boyle's Lectures. It happened that they wrought an effect upon me quite contrary to what was intended by them;

for the arguments of the Deists, which were quoted to be refuted, appeared to me much stronger than the refutations; in short, I became a thorough Deist." There worked the natural Franklin. But he argued from his new point of view to such effect as to convert his friends, and several of them ended by defrauding him. Consequently his monitor "began to suspect that the doctrine, though it might be true, was not very useful." Deism was put out at the door, and "trust, sincerity, and integrity," together with an apparently very sincere faith in Providence, were introduced instead. He accepted even Revelation, to such an extent at any rate, as to assume that, though certain actions might not be bad because they were forbidden by it, or good because it commanded them, yet probably those actions might be forbidden because they were bad for us, or commanded because they were beneficial to us." A man's belief is commonly part of himself, the growth of his own nature. Franklin ceased to be a rationalist because his inner monitor had examined the reasons for and against, and arrived at the conclusion that it was for his general advantage, comfort, respectability, and internal satisfaction to be unenthusiastically religious.

His own devotions he performed at home, but he had so good an opinion of the utility of public services that he persuaded the Federal Convention to open its sittings with prayer. Of the advantages of a regular liturgy he was equally convinced. To popularise the Prayer Book he helped the reformed Lord le Despencer, once the friend of Wilkes and "Abbot" of Medmenham, in abridging it. For his share he took the Catechism and the Psalms. This edifying work was published by a bookseller in St. Paul's Churchyard in 1773. Franklin's heart, however, was at all times more susceptible of charitable than of theological emotions. Writing in 1758 to his sister of an acrostic on her name, in which faith was described as occupying the Christian's ground floor, hope the first floor, and charity the garret, he bids her "Get as fast as you can into the garret, for in truth the best room in the house is charity. For my part, I wish the house was turned upside down; it is so difficult, when one is fat, to go upstairs." Religion moved him, not dogmatic theology. Every one knows his remark: "Orthodoxy is my doxy, and heterodoxy is your doxy." He could not understand why some American gentlemen desiring to officiate according to the rites of the Church of England in the United States, whom the Archbishop of Canterbury refused to ordain unless they took the oath of allegiance, should not ordain one another. As they objected, he asked the Papal Nuncio in Paris to direct a Roman Catholic bishop in America to ordain them. He was surprised that the Nuncio insisted they should turn Catholics first. Mr. Whitefield, he mentions in the Autobiography, "used sometimes to pray for my conversion, but never had the satisfaction of believing that his prayers were answered."

Followers of Whitefield could specify the day and even the minute of their conversion. Franklin had his conversion and its date too. But, as with his religious views and practices, so his morality was done to order. The natural Franklin was ordered by his ruling self "to acquire the habitude of all the virtues." In the year 1728, being then twenty-two, "I convinced the bold and arduous project of arriving at moral perfection. I wished to live without committing any fault at any time. As I knew, or thought I knew, what was right and wrong, I did not see why I might not always do the one and avoid the other." He accordingly divided all the virtues into thirteen, temperance, silence, order, resolution, frugality, industry, sincerity, justice, moderation, cleanliness, tranquillity, chastity, and humility. Humility was not in his first draft. He introduced it, "a Quaker friend having kindly informed me that I was generally thought proud, being in conversation overbearing and rather insolent, of which he convinced me by mentioning several instances." He kept a kind of diary, with a page allotted to each of the thirteen, and "determined to give a week's strict attention to each of the virtues successively."

Order he found the hardest of all the virtues to acquire. "In truth, I found myself incorrigible with respect to order; and, now I am grown old, and my memory bad, I feel very sensibly the want of it." Humility was another difficult virtue. But, writes Franklin, "though I cannot boast of much success in acquiring the reality of this virtue, I had a good deal with regard to the appearance of it." "On the whole," he adds, "though I never arrived at the perfection I had been so ambitious of obtaining, but fell far short of it, yet I was, by the endeavour, a better and a happier man than I otherwise should have been if I had not attempted it." Mr. Bigelow found a marginal note appended to the original MS, from which his edition of the Autobiography is printed: "Nothing so likely to make a man's fortune as virtue." The natural Franklin was guilty, as his own censorious self often remarked, of various "errata" in youth. In his Autobiography and in his letters to friends he avows a wish to have his life come over again, that he might enjoy "the advantages authors have in a second edition to correct some faults of the first." But that probably was only a show of tribute to the virtue of humility. His conscience seems to have cleared itself of all uncomfortable twinges for his youthful misdeeds. Of misdeeds in after life, except in the matter of an occasional second bottle and a preference of riding over walking, he shows no consciousness. Even the glass too much and the bodily indolence brought their own sufficient penalty in visitations of gout, which balanced the account.

Franklin's description of himself, both in the Autobiography and in his correspondence, resembles a little too much the portrait of a self-sufficient, self-made, pompous tradesman. Vice is represented as want of practical wisdom, not as something to arouse shame or moral indignation. Such a disposition would have broken up an empire and plunged the world in war in revenge for London not agreeing with a Philadelphian alderman's estimate of his own merits. He has misrepresented himself. The universal testimony of America, and France, and of a large body of the most upright and honest Englishmen, pronounced Franklin the brightest and least egotistical of companions, the warmest of friends, the most devoted and disinterested of patriots. George the Third's condemnation of his "insidiousness" was testimony to the frankness and simplicity which the King believed to conceal continual intrigues. The King was similarly prejudiced against the French envoy, Rayneval, for having "the appearance of an inoffensive man of business," since "cunning—will be more dangerous under so specious a garb." Franklin was simply one of that class of men to whom the capacity has been given of surveying themselves from the outside as well as from the inside. He desired to judge himself as a stranger would have judged him. Some men do that towards the close of their lives, when their careers are become to them mere matter of history. He did it not in his Autobiography alone, but in every incident of his busy life. The quality in one sense is not very rare. But commonly they who are their own critics lose in courage and decision what they gain by appraising themselves at their proper value. They escape the danger of exaggerating their real merits, and they succumb to the evil of frightening themselves with their own shadows. Self-consciousness and timidity dwarf in them all vigour of growth. The happy peculiarity of Franklin's character was that it remained buoyant and independent in spite of the sense that at the end of each day it was sure to be called up to render an account of itself. His original self took advice from his educated self, yet never ceased to be natural. He studied humanity as mirrored in his own disposition. There he traced the varying strength of motives, and the mode in which they operate. What he saw he was ready enough to expose to the view of other men. The world at large was fascinated and charmed by being admitted to the contemplation of the most masculine and capacious of minds, through which its owner himself was always ready to act as guide.

The strength and variety of his friendships are among the most conspicuous features of his career. We know the fact by his correspondence; and also why it should have been so. As a lad he won predominating influence over more brilliant acquaintances, like Osborn, the "eminent lawyer" with whom

Franklin "made a serious agreement, which Osborn never fulfilled," that "the one who happened first to die should, if possible, pay a friendly visit to the other, and acquaint him how he found things in that separate state." Keith the Governor of Pennsylvania, Burnet the Governor of New York, conversed with him, while a journeyman printer, as almost an equal. Whitefield would not resign the hope of converting so illustrious a moralist. Lord Kames, a forgotten Scotch celebrity, whose fame once ranked with that of Hume and Gibbon, was his intimate, with whom at various times he "passed weeks of densest happiness." Though politics, and perhaps the contrast between his measured equability of manner and Johnson's strongly accented temperament, kept them apart, Boswell was proud to be his acquaintance and his host. Cowper treasured the praises of his poems by "one of the first philosophers, one of the most eminent literary characters that the present age can boast of." Chatham sought his friendship. Fox eagerly claimed him still for a countryman. Lafayette haunted him, much to the disgust of the English Peace Commissioners, who thought they could understand Franklin, but not the French knight-errant. Mirabeau was the bearer of letters of introduction from him to America, and encircled his memory when dead with the halo of his meteoric eloquence. His successor at Paris, Jefferson, agreed that "no one could replace Dr. Franklin," for the reason that no one could excite so much interest as a man. Washington was proud to be counted among his friends. He was honoured by all the kings he ever had an opportunity of meeting, except his own. He was loved by the old lodging-house keeper in Craven Street where he lived. None could have been better company. He could play chess, and the next moment be weaving a new web of politics. He could fathom the secrets of nature, and explain them as if he were telling a fairy tale. He could make a real fairy tale the vehicle for a moral lesson, and hide a political sarcasm in a mock proclamation by the great Frederick. If the company loved its wine, he could drink as stoutly as Dr. Johnson. He had no fear of the gout before his eyes when fair ladies filled the glass, and wits were hanging upon his lips.

He enjoyed a large share of happiness in life, and was grateful for it. He himself has written: "The felicity of my life, when I reflected on it, has induced me sometimes to say that, were it offered to my choice, I should have no objection to a repetition of the same life from its beginning." At the age of twenty-one, he nearly died of pleurisy. "I was," he says, "rather disappointed when I found myself recovering, regretting in some degree that I must now, some time or other, have all that disagreeable work to do over again." As life proceeded he found enough of what was agreeable in it to make up for the vexation of its finiteness. At the age of sixty-three, he could say: "Take one thing with another, and the world is a pretty good sort of world." He would have been content to go on enduring its vicissitudes: "Though living on in one's children is a good thing, I cannot but fancy it might be better to continue living ourselves at the same time." In one way old age itself, which otherwise he would not object to have cured in himself along with other diseases, had its advantages. "As I grow old I grow less concerned about censure." As he grew old, he did not grow less willing to continue that exertion of the energies which to him meant happiness. At the age of seventy he accepted the dangerous and delicate mission to France. "I am," he told the Congress, "but a fag-end; you may have me for what you please." At seventy-nine he still found enjoyment in the management of affairs. Two years later, at the age of eighty-one, his legislative inventiveness was of the greatest benefit to the Convention which met in 1787 to frame the definitive Constitution. Though opposed personally to the system of two legislative Houses, he made the project practicable by his device that all the States should be represented equally in the Upper House, and according to population in the Lower House. If he sighed over his toils at seventy-nine, it was a sigh of satisfaction at the prospect of being "harnessed in the country's service for another year" as President of Pennsylvania. My countrymen, he wrote with manifest pleasure to a friend," engrossed the prime of my life. They have eaten my flesh, and seem resolved now to pick my bones." At the age of eighty-three he still composed poetry, not very good, but not worse perhaps than that he was in the habit of writing sixty years before. Attacked simultaneously—by gout, the stone, and old age, he comforted himself that "only three incurable diseases had fallen to his share, and that these had not deprived him at the age of eighty-one of his natural cheerfulness, his delight in books, and enjoyment of social conversation." If obliged by his three assailants to anticipate death, he solaced himself by thoughts of a term of higher activity, and therefore enjoyment, in another stage of existence. He began to doubt whether the building, his body, did not need so many repairs that in a little time the owner would "find it cheaper to pull it down and build a new one." He avowed "a growing curiosity to be acquainted with some other world," and longed, "free from bodily embarrassments, to roam through some of the systems Herschel has explored, conducted by old companions already acquainted with them." His only hesitation at the age of eighty-two about dying is whether it were not a pity to quit this particular universe at a time of extraordinary "improvements in philosophy, morals, politics, and even the conveniences of common living, and the invention and acquisition of new and useful utensils and instruments." He whispers a wish that the final advance had been made in the particular art of physic, that, "we might be able to avoid diseases and live as long as the patriarchs in Genesis; to which I suppose we should have little objection." It was almost as well that, though in 1788 he had heard rumours of John Fitch's "boat moved by a steam engine rowing itself against tide in our river," and though he appeared to think "the construction might be so simplified and improved as to become generally useful," he could not foresee the full application of the principle. It would have been too tantalizing to know he was leaving life on the eve of such a revolution.

The secret of his happiness was his power of doing whatever was his work for the moment with all his might. He could enjoy the pleasures of life as heartily as he performed its toils. Both were pleasures, if only one kind bore the name. Every faculty of his nature was permitted, and even commanded, to seek in its turn occasions for exercise. His bodily senses were encouraged to gratify themselves as well as the mental. For a sage Franklin seems to have liked good eating and drinking, perhaps even a very little too much. As a boy he was trained to be "quite indifferent what kind of food was set before me, and so unobservant of it that to this day if I am asked, I can scarce tell a few hours after dinner what I dined upon." He took a little later on to a vegetable diet, and used the money he saved to buy books. All the world knows how at Watts's printing-house, in Queen Street, Franklin drank water-gruel to his companions' beer, and outworked them all on the diet. As he became prosperous he acquired a decorous taste for less hermit-like fare. He was fond of madeira. He confesses "for one that if I could find in any Italian travels a receipt for making Parmesan cheese, it would give me more satisfaction than a transcript of any inscription from any old stone structure." Parmesan had still some savour of Arcadia. But in another letter from Craven Street he remarks: "Just come home from a venison feast, where I have drunk more than a philosopher ought." Already at the age, for him very juvenile, of sixty-two, he was becoming stout. He observes: "Men of my bulk often fail suddenly." Paris was not likely to teach him plain living; parties accompanied by innumerable glasses of champagne in his honour must have been so many challenges to gout. At seventy-eight he writes to Strahan, whom he had taken back into friendship, a letter of "chit-chat between ourselves over the second bottle." The next letter in these volumes, addressed to Henry Laurens, begins significantly: "I write this in great pain from the gout in both feet."

His talk of the bottle perhaps savours a little of humorous exaggeration. Certainly, in most points he would have contented Plato himself by his "temperance" and "justice" in respecting the independence both of his neighbours and of the various constituents of his own nature. It was this admirable orderliness of his organisation which leaves on those who only read what he wrote an impression of coldness and absence of generous fervour which his contemporaries did not feel. Franklin, as English politicians knew only too well, could be impassioned and fiery. There are signs in abundance that his heart could be touched as readily and more genially by private griefs and joys. If his acquaintances included a cross-grained aunt and her youthful niece, he could appreciate the tediousness of the companionship for the girl, yet compassionate even more the infirmities of body and temper of the poor old woman. "Invent," he writes to his younger friend, "amusements for her; be pleased when she accepts of them, and patient when she perhaps peevishly rejects them." He lifts up his powerful voice in an appeal for mercy to the "numbers of little innocents who suffer and perish" from its being unfashionable in London, and yet more in Paris, for mothers to nurse their children. In the midst of the turmoil over the Stamp Act, he is anxious in London for news of his young grandson in Pennsylvania: "You have so used me," he writes to his wife, "to have something pretty about the boy, that I am a little disappointed in finding nothing more of him. Pray give in your next, as usual, a little more of his history." We are afraid his admirers must admit that he too easily resigned himself to accept his wife's dread of the sea as a sufficient excuse for their separation during many years. But he thought she was happy with her walnut-trees and grandson; and he soothes the pangs of remoteness compelled by "duty to my country," by choosing London novelties for her, "a crimson satin cloak, the newest fashion," and a gown of flowered tissue, sixteen yards, cost nine guineas; I think it a great beauty." While the Stamp Act was still in force he would not violate the colonial self-denying ordinance by sending Mrs. Franklin presents of British goods. The moment it was repealed, in 1766, he despatches "a fine piece of Pompadour satin, fourteen yards, cost eleven shillings a yard." For his wife's comfort, so long as she remained at Philadelphia, he is ready even to sacrifice the completeness of his electrical apparatus. "If the ringing of the bells connected with the iron rod frightens you, tie a piece of wire from one bell to the other." I am, however, bound to say that he adds: "Though I think it best the bells should be at liberty to ring, that you may know when they are electrified; and when you are afraid, you may keep at a distance."

His purse was always open to a tale of distress. He had an ingenious method of circulating alms, by charging it on the honour of the recipient to pass on the gift to another deserving object, if he should have the means of making payment. He sends five louis d'or to an English clergyman, who had been taken by a French privateer, or perhaps by Paul Jones, and was in prison in Paris. "Some time or other," Franklin tells him, "you may have an opportunity of assisting with an equal sum a stranger who has equal need of it. If so, by that means you will discharge any obligation you may suppose yourself under to me. Enjoin him to do the same. Let kind offices go round." To an American in distress he gives ten louis, bidding him follow the same course: "I hope it may thus go through many hands before it meets with a knave that will stop its progress. This is a trick of mine for doing a deal of good with a little money." He adopted the same system with the salary he received, on quitting his French mission, as President of Pennsylvania. He held that "in a democratical State there ought to be no offices of profit." An envoy might receive a salary, he appeared to think; and an American Postmaster-General might for seventeen years receive the salary in London, and perform its duties by deputy in America. But he drew the line short of Presidents of Assemblies and States. Accordingly, he bequeathed his Presidential salary and its accumulations on trust, among other things, for loans to young artisans. These loans, unlike Franklin's louis d'or, were to be repaid with interest; but the principle was the same. A limited sum was to circulate illimitably in charity from hand to hand. The scheme was unsuccessful, partly from the want of proper objects, and partly from the failure of the legacy to realise the amount it should, by Franklin's estimate of the profits of compound interest, have produced. By the end of two hundred years, two thousand pounds, he computed, should yield eight millions one hundred and twenty-two thousand pounds sterling. As in the eighty-two years from 1790 to 1872 the two thousand produced only a little over ten thousand, that magnificent arithmetical vision would seem to have had some flaw in it. However, the intention was equally benevolent, though the trust in compound interest proved as much a broken reed in Franklin's benevolent hands as in the exceedingly selfish ones of Mr. Thellusson.

His pen was as ready as his purse in the service of all human kindliness. And what a pen it was! It could discourse on metaphysics so lucidly as to make the finest subtleties seem plain moralising. It could tear a sophism to pieces by a query. It could make a simple tale read like a philosophical argument. He could be grave and he could be gay in a breath. On a 'Craven Street Gazette,' composed to amuse an old lodging-house keeper away from home, and probably fearful that the world, or the Strand, would be out of joint before her return from Rochester, he could spend as much wit and humour as on a State paper designed to fire America and sting England. In another tone he translates into human language, for the amusement of a Court lady, the reflections, in the garden of her house, of a grey-headed ephemera, full seven hours old, on the vanity of all things. His 'Petition of the Left Hand' might have been composed by Addison. In it the left hand bewails the partiality which educates the right hand exclusively. Some of Franklin's fables and tales have been so absorbed into the thought of the world that their source is absolutely forgotten. In this manner we may account for a plagiarism not long since by an eminent sanitary authority of Franklin's 'Economical Project for Diminishing the Cost of Light.' The economy consists in rising at six o'clock instead of nine or ten. A wakeful Parisian is represented as having discovered to his great astonishment that the sun actually began to shine at that hour. He calculated the saving to Paris in candle-light, should the city take advantage of the fact, at ninety-six million francs. But the philosophers of the town denied the fact. They proved by common notoriety that there could have been no light abroad at six o'clock, and therefore none could have entered from without. Their explanation was that the "windows, being accidentally left open, instead of letting in the light, had only served to let out the darkness." No one who listened to the recent reproduction of this bright little satire appears to have doubted the re-discoverer's originality. That is a tribute to its modern air. But, in truth, ideas such as Franklin's never become superannuated. Few who use the expression, "to pay dear for one's whistle," know that the dear whistle was a purchase made by Franklin, when seven years old, with a pocketful of pence. Franklin's store was too abundant for him to mind, though some of his fame went astray. "You know," he tells his daughter, "everything makes me recollect some story." It was not recollection so much as fancy. His fancy clothed every idea in circumstances. When the illustration had served its turn, he was indifferent what became of it. If he cared at all, it was that, when borrowed by a newspaper or magazine, it should have its proper allowance of long-tailed s's and italics, and capitals to the substantives. With his old printer's prejudices, he could not understand the modern "fondness for an even and uniform appearance of characters in the line." He was less delighted at the complimentary censure by Lord Mansfield of his witty and bitter 'Edict of the King of Prussia' when reprinted in the Chronicle, than indignant that the Chronicle should have "stripped it of all the capitals and italics that intimate the allusions and mark the emphasis of written discourses, to bring them as near as possible to those spoken." He thought such appeals to the eye help to raise a writer to the level of a speaker, who has at his command both accent and gesture to point his periods. Franklin did injustice to himself when he fancied he wanted such poor mechanical aids. His English had been learnt from "The Pilgrim's Progress" and the "Spectator." It had the force of Bunyan without his ruggedness. It had much of the serene light of Addison, with more raciness and tenfold the vigour. It sparkled with sarcasms as cutting as Voltaire's, but all sweetened with humanity.

If a David Hume might condemn here and there a sprinkling of such words as "pejorate," it was not from poverty but from exuberance of diction that Franklin exposed his vocabulary to criticism. Many of his inventions, or adaptations, such as "colonise," have long been stamped as current English. But he did not covet the fame of an inventor, whether in language, in morals, or in politics. In language he was even a declared foe to change. Writing to Noah Webster, the lexicographer, in 1789 he protests against the new verbs, "notice," "advocate," and "progress." He had as little ambition to be a classic as to be an innovator in English. He wrote because he had something at the moment to say, with a view to procuring that something should at the moment be done. In religion he confessed to a certain liking for heretics, all of whom, so far as he had acquaintance with the class, he declared were virtuous men. What, however, he liked was not their heresy so much as the spirit of self-sacrifice which led them to brave persecution. As a moralist he did not aspire to alter the materials with which he had to deal. He was satisfied that men should make something more of their life, as their life was, without expecting to transform them into angels. When he proposed to himself moral perfection, he was aiming at nothing superhuman. He pared his definitions of the virtues he had resolved to practise down to the moderate level to which he felt himself not unequal. If a defect did not appear to be of a nature necessarily to injure a man or his neighbours, he was not prepared to banish it as a vice. Humility had forced its way in among his ostensible virtues. But humility in his sense is not incompatible with a certain intermixture of vanity. "Most people," he writes, "dislike vanity in others, whatever share they have of it themselves; but I give it fair quarter wherever I meet with it, being persuaded that it is often productive of good to the possessor and to others that are within his sphere of action; and therefore in many cases it would not be altogether absurd if a man were to thank God for his vanity among the other comforts of life." His model of life was adapted rigidly to the ordinary circumstances of humanity. If men seemed to be substantially the better off for the ownership of a quality, Franklin inserted that quality among his virtues. He was always more ready to admit a new candidate to his Olympus than to risk rejecting an addition to the sum of human happiness. He himself believed in a Providence, and apparently in "a particular Providence;" he was not disposed to deny to others the right to disbelieve. When, however, Thomas

Paine, whose work on Common Sense he had warmly patronised, submitted to him a manuscript treatise against "a particular Providence," he earnestly dissuaded its publication. He urged not only the odium it would bring upon the author, but the danger of withdrawing from the weak, the ignorant, the inexperienced, and the inconsiderate, the support which religion affords to virtue. His ideas on the origin of evil were probably not very completely developed. But he thought a Devil very useful for the punishment of criminal wretches who cheated starving orphans of the alms entrusted for their relief. Whatever quality could prove by results that it had contributed to render life more harmonious he was glad to enshrine in his Pantheon, as Romans borrowed foreign gods. His ideal, in morals, in religion, and even in politics, was entirely inductive. He examined life and history to see in what circumstances of belief, education, and government men had enjoyed happiness. The same circumstances might not have suited his character; but he was content not to disturb what appeared to suit others.

One province of his nature there was in which, so far as we are permitted to penetrate it, he was not always weighing the dangers of zeal to the evenness of the balance he was constantly engaged in adjusting. In natural science he was an enthusiast; but that was a matter for himself and not for the outside world. He just mentions in his Autobiography the fact of his electrical experiments, and "the rise and progress of my philosophical reputation," between 1746 and 1753, when the Royal Society bestowed its medal. His Autobiography contains nothing more on the subject, and his correspondence very little. When his views were resisted, he was content to leave them to the judgment of posterity. He writes to an admirer in 1777: "I have never entered into any controversy in defence of my philosophical opinions. If they are right, truth and experience will support them; if wrong, they ought to be refuted and rejected." He had been told King George had exchanged the rebel Franklin's favourite pointed conductors for blunt ones. "If I had a wish about it," remarks Franklin, "it would be that he had rejected conductors altogether as ineffectual." Physical science was too grand a thing for him to care to soil it with controversy. He would gaily dispute upon metaphysics, morals, and politics; upon the philosophy of nature never. Though he loved riches reasonably, he would not mix up so sublunary an application of science even as a stove with money. This typical American was so un-American in one respect as to set his face against monopolies in inventions. His love of his science itself he limited by the sense of other duties. He vigorously deprecates a friend's design to try a balloon journey across the Channel in 1785 as a risk unfair to his family.

Except in science, so far as direct personal influence over posterity is concerned, Franklin did not go the way to secure it. "Poor Richard" was a great power in his own time, just because the object of Richard's mission was not very sublime. For the making of a hero and a leader in the ages to come an admixture of divinity is needed. In Franklin's teaching there was nothing but what had been found in human life as it was. The matter of the teaching was after all ignoble. The world tired of it when it had come to perceive that the ideal propounded was nothing but ordinary prosaic humanity with something pruned off it. While the teacher survived there were a strength and freshness about his doctrines which came from himself, and kept them wholesome and pure. Whatever they might be the man was not ignoble. Somewhat earthy he may have been; he was great in himself; he was greater in his power over himself. His fame was common to two continents, and vital to his own. If George Washington more than any one man saved America from being overrun by German mercenaries, and American liberties from being dragged in the mire by the owners of pocket British boroughs, it was Franklin more than any one man who had made Americans too self-respecting to consent to be slaves; it was Franklin who took the new-born Republic by the hand and seated it among the nations.

We have left ourselves space for only a few words on the distinctive characteristics of Mr. Bigelow's picture of Franklin's personal and political career. Mr. Bigelow reminds his readers that seventy-four years ago this journal censured the want of literary enterprise in the United Slates of America, and of literary curiosity in the English public, which allowed the works of the "only" American philosopher to remain dispersed in isolated volumes and the pages of forgotten pamphlets and periodicals. The "Edinburgh Review" of 1800 could pardon the dearth of English and American enlightenment or gratitude in consideration solely of the greater crime it found reason to charge against the natural heir of Franklin's fame and the Tory ministry of 1795. Franklin designated as his literary executor the grandson whom he had educated, and whom he loved the more for estrangement through political differences from his royalist son, who had been Governor of New Jersey under the crown, and finally became a British pensioner. This grandson, William Temple Franklin, was believed by Jefferson and by many Frenchmen, as well as by the "Edinburgh Review," to have abused the trust by accepting a bribe from the British government to keep from the world, at any rate for many years, the precious papers in his possession. He came from America a few months after his grandfather's death in 1790, for the express purpose of arranging with London booksellers for the publication of the Autobiography and other documents; he made continual statements to the effect that he was engaged in the negotiation, yet the work was not given to the world until 1817. The Autobiography of Franklin had indeed become famous throughout the civilized world. But it was known only at second hand. By some means or other, which have never been disclosed, a French naturalist, a Dr. Jacques Gibelin, obtained the use of a copy. This copy, which comprises only 87 pages of the 200 of Franklin's manuscript, Gibelin translated into French in 1791. From Gibelin's French it was translated back again into English. "To this day," writes Mr. Bigelow, this version "continues to be republished by some of the largest houses, not only in Europe, but in America, under the impression that it is both genuine and complete."

Mr. Bigelow thinks he has detected a probable cause of the deferred fulfillment of the commission to publish Franklin's works and of the disappearance of some of them. In a letter now for the first time published to one of Franklin's closest friends, M. le Veillard, William Temple apologizes for not paying a promised visit to Paris on business connected with the promised publication, on the plea that he "could not possibly leave while a business I had undertaken was pending, for which I received a salary, and which, being now completed, affords me a profit of seven thousand pounds sterling." Mr. Bigelow is incredulous of the reality of a business for which this young man, a stranger to London, and an American citizen, could receive a salary so liberal as to secure to him in six months a profit of 7,000*l*. The salary, capitalized in a sum of 7,000*l*, Mr. Bigelow believes to have been a bribe for postponing a publication which, it might be supposed, would reopen the springs of popular indignation against the folly which had cost Great Britain a splendid empire. The great French war was like a flood. It washed away all memories of those old griefs. In 1817 William Temple Franklin could publish his grandfather's most solemn warnings to mole-eyed British statesmen of 1770 and 1780 without exciting remorseful fears in any politician's breast, or risking a claim for the recoupment of a fee of which he had not executed the conditions.

Mr. Bigelow is not able to prove his charge to absolute demonstration. But he has established a very strong presumption that Franklin's faith in this William Temple, this adopted child of his old age, was another of the philosopher's "errata," as he would himself have said. Happily William Temple had not much opportunity to try his editorial dexterity on very valuable material. Most of his grandfather's writings had already become part of the national literature, or rather of the literature of two nations. Any tampering with them would have speedily been exposed. It might have been apprehended that he could have attempted emendations with successful secrecy in the Autobiography. It is even conceivable that, but for a combination of fortunate circumstances, he might have had both the will and the power finally to suppress a work which, in some particulars, would offend family pride. His grandfather had, however, insured its general safety, and he had himself unintentionally guarded the text from corruptions. Franklin, after writing it in his extreme old age, charged another grandson, Benjamin Bache, to execute one facsimile, if not two, by means of a copying press, for the information of his Parisian friend, Le Veillard, and his English friend, Benjamin Vaughan. Whether the copy promised to Vaughan was ever made and sent has never been ascertained. The French version of the autobiography, which was published in Paris in 1791 by M. Jacques Gibelin, it is conjectured, may have been rendered from it. At all events, M. le Veillard received his copy. The original, with many corrections by Franklin himself, and eight additional pages which were not reproduced in Le Veillard's copy, descended to William Temple with the rest of his grandfather's papers. Had the edition of 1817 been printed from the original, it would have been impossible to prove that Franklin had not himself made the changes which distinguish that edition from others. It so happens, however, that William Temple, when he was still intending to publish the work with all dispatch, had persuaded M. le Veillard to give him his copy in exchange for the original. His motive was the facility the printers would have in printing from the fair copy in exchange for the original. Mr. Bigelow, while United States Minister in Paris, was so fortunate as to obtain from the representatives of M. le Veillard. On collating it with William Temple's edition of 1817 he detected more than twelve hundred alterations. William Temple, or some literary man employed by him to correct the press, had obviously been offended by his grandfather's racy diction. We give a few alterations merely as samples. "Sotting with brandy" is rendered into "drinking of brandy." "A very large" library becomes "a considerable" one; "dramming" is paraphrased by "dram-drinking"; "great guzzlers of beer" is politely softened into "great drinkers of beer;" "footed it to London" is turned into "walked to London;" "behaved very oddly" into "behaved himself very extravagantly;" "with the blessing of God" into "thanks to Providence;" and "Keimer stared like a pig poisoned" into the correct and respectable expression, "Keimer stared with astonishment."

Franklin's Autobiography is one of mankind's greatest literary possessions. General gratitude is due to Mr. Bigelow for presenting it at last in the exact shape in which it issued from the author's memory. At least equal thanks are his right for the loyalty with which he has himself shown the reverence for his subject which he convicts William Temple Franklin of having violated. He has effaced himself, and been content simply to reflect Benjamin Franklin; he has been willing to let the man speak in his own person, and not by the mouth of Mr. John Bigelow. In three volumes all the many sides of the diplomatist, philosopher, moralist, cannot be pictured in full. His scientific achievements, which illuminated every act of his life, appear in these pages only as passing interludes in a busy political career. His state papers, models as they are of lucid argument, are not quoted, but only the conclusions at which they aimed. His system of ethics is revealed by a gleam here and a gleam there. But throughout the work we are conscious of the presence of a living man. At the end of it we feel that we have been conversing with one who did more than all others to rend away the great American colonies from the British Empire; yet we part company with no sense of unkindness toward the author of our loss.

W.P. TRENT "NEW EDITIONS OF FRANKLIN" (1906)

It was to be supposed that the approach of the two hundredth anniversary of Franklin's birth would be marked by the appearance of books dealing with his extraordinary life and presenting afresh those unpremeditated writings which for many years have gained him the position of a true classic. And even if there were no interesting anniversary almost upon us to account for the books here to be noticed, the two smaller would be welcome as convenient reprints, while the larger—the first volume of Prof. Smyth's notable edition— would justify itself by the new material it announces.

Besides, in these days of active scholars and publishers, and of an ever enlarging public, we have no right to be surprised, and still less to complain, that the great writers of the past are brought to our attention in a large variety of forms. Franklin, modest as he was, never dreamed that future members of his craft would set up edition after edition of his "Autobiography," or that, in less than sixty years, his miscellaneous writings would be thrice collected, each time into ten large volumes. Neither he nor his editors nor his publishers should be held responsible for the fact that the shelves and card catalogues of our libraries are being year by year more and more taxed to accommodate books by and about this most many-sided of all Americans. He could not help being interesting, and for nearly two centuries the world has not been able to help being interested in him.

* * *

From bibliographical details Prof. Smyth passes to a cursory discussion of Franklin's works considered as a whole, after which he proceeds to comment upon the philosophical, political, and economic writings, the satires and bagatelles, and the correspondence. There is, of course, little that is new to say about Franklin in his capacity as writer or man of letters; but the obvious things are well put at the beginning of the critical discussion, and then, under the categories named above, the editor, from his large stores of information, gives proofs of Franklin's astonishing acumen, prescience, versatility, practicality, humor, and general range of efficiency which will, I think, surprise by their interest and, in many cases, by their unhackneyed character, even those readers who have thought themselves quite familiar with the attainments of the most variously gifted and thoroughly representative son of the delightful eighteenth century.

The longest and most important section of the introduction is that devoted to the "Philosophical Works." Doubtless many persons have quite a clear conception of Franklin as statesman, sage, creator of "Poor Richard," writer of a classic autobiography, humorist, inventor, and general utility man on a cosmopolitan rather than a parochial scale; but when they come to think of him in his capacity as scientist or natural philosopher, their imaginations get tangled up with his kite, and they can give no very clear account of his scientific acquirements and achievements. Such persons may never find time to read in their entirety Franklin's contributions to "subjects of electricity, seismology, geology, meteorology, physics, chemistry, astronomy, mathematics, hydrography, horology, aeronautics, navigation, agriculture, ethnology, paleontology, medicine, hygiene, and pedagogy"; but they will do well to read what Prof. Smyth has to say about this extraordinary mass of writing done, as it were, all in the day's work, with practically no thought of fame, but with every desire to be useful to the world. Only in connection with an early paper on the causes of earthquakes does the editor, who has evidently taken pains to inform himself on the present state of knowledge in fields of inquiry remote from his own specialties, find himself obliged to characterize Franklin's views as crude and worthless to-day. His anticipation of the wave theory of light, his observation of storms and whirlwinds, his experiments in the production of cold by evaporation, his ingenuity in constructing "magic squares," his interest in nautical matters, in scientific agriculture, and in paleontology, his contributions to the study of medicine and hygiene, would alone suffice to prove him to have been one of the most wide-awake mortals that ever lived; and his pioneer discoveries in electricity afford that solid basis of knowledge and achievement in at least one department of inquiry which seems the necessary foundation of abiding greatness.

It is hard to read Prof. Smyth's pages without coming to the conclusion that the utilitarian printer and citizen of Philadelphia was probably the most many-sided and acute scientist of his remarkable age, and a similar conclusion is forced upon us when we pass to a consideration of what he accomplished in other spheres of usefulness. He does not stand apart in lofty isolation as does Washington, his personality is not so overpowering as that of Johnson, or so dazzling as that of Voltaire; but his nearness to the men of his own day and to us—in a word, the homeliness of his character and his interests, should not be allowed to obscure his essential greatness. A broad plateau is no less wonderful a work of nature than a towering peak.

It would be unfair to Prof. Smyth, upon whom I have already drawn with great freedom, to extract from his introduction many of his choice illustrations of Franklin's phenomenal activity of mind and spirit. I cannot forbear, however, to call attention to the fact that Franklin did not altogether escape the tendency of his age to discover providential purposes in nature, though he fell far short of Bernardin St. Pierre in this exemplary exercise of the imagination. Like Lord Bacon he suffered physical ills from his ardor for making experiments, but fortunately only to the extent of catching an intermittent fever from bending over stagnant water. As he seems to have come in contact with almost every notable figure of his time, we are not surprised to find that Marat and Robespierre wrote him letters. The communication of the latter, who was employed to defend a client who had dared to protect his property with what many regarded as a dangerous nuisance, to wit, a lightning rod, is one of the most interesting of Prof. Smyth's discoveries. Very interesting also are the pages devoted to Franklin's little known services to medical science, which, by the way, brought him in contact with another Frenchman of sinister reputation, however little deserved—Joseph Ignace Guillotin.

Other topics of importance are the indebtedness of Malthus to Franklin, the latter's firm belief in free trade—remember that he was the first citizen of Philadelphia!—Matthew Arnold's failure to perceive the satirical purpose underlying the modernization of six verses in the first chapter of Job, the light thrown on Franklin's comparative inability to write in French, and upon the history of Turgot's famous epigram, the begging letters received by Franklin—one of them from a Benedictine who would pray for the success of the American cause provided his gambling debts were paid—but there is no use in trying to exhaust the list.

Everywhere we touch him he is the human and therefore the fascinating Franklin. This statement is, to be sure, an exaggeration—one of the sort at which he would have smiled with deprecating modesty or else, with a malicious twinkle of the eye, would have told an unsavory anecdote with disenchanting results. There were sides of Franklin's character—well remembered, it would seem, in Philadelphia—that were not at all attractive. Prof. Smyth calls attention in a paragraph to the "smudgy trail" the facetious printer left behind him in the "Pennsylvania Gazette," to the grossness of some of his letters, to the effect of his strong animal instincts upon his conduct.

It is this, combined with his comparative insensibility to poetry and to spiritual religion—which Prof. Smyth does not emphasize—that puts Franklin, in the final analysis, below such men as Johnson and Washington, to whom he was vastly superior in many intellectual respects and who may themselves be justly taxed with aesthetic deficiencies. But when his limitations have been duly considered, it remains true that Franklin, like Defoe, and for much the same reasons; is one of the most fascinating of mortals, at least to students who examine minutely every phase of his character by means of his self-revealing writings. Both men had in its fullest development what may be called the genius for the prose of life. In both this genius is fused with a sort of plebeian spirit, with the result that they do not greatly appeal to over-sensitive souls. Other souls less squeamish, more robust, more catholic, if you will, take a special delight in watching the effects of this combination of democratic and aristocratic elements upon the lives and writings of these two great sons of the people, whose masterpieces will not cease to be read until the precious style affected by numerous moderns becomes an eternal possession of the English-speaking masses. When that delectable day comes, "Robinson Crusoe" and Franklin's "Autobiography" may be banished from whatever substitute the aesthetic world shall have devised for homely bookshelves. Pending this consummation, it is to be hoped that each of the three books here noticed will obtain a broad circulation.

PAUL ELMER MORE
"FRANKLIN IN LITERATURE" (1906)

Franklin was not precisely a man of letters, yet his life is almost literature, and out of it might be made one of the great books. Not only do the salient events of his career take on a dramatic form that is already a kind of literary expression, but he goes further than that and meets the biographer half way, using language as one of his chief instruments of activity. How carefully he trained himself to this end every reader of the Autobiography knows. From childhood he was an eager and critical reader, and few pages of his memoirs are written with more warmth of recollection than those which tell of the books he contrived to buy, Bunyan's works first of all. He seems to think that the "Spectator" had the predominating influence on his style, and apparently he was still under sixteen when an odd volume of that work set him to studying seriously. His method was to read one of the essays and then after a number of days to rewrite it from a few written hints, striving to make his own language as correct and elegant as the original; or, again, he turned an essay into verse and back again into prose from memory. "I also," he adds, "sometimes jumbled my collection of hints into confusion, and after some weeks endeavored to reduce them into the best order before I began to form the full sentences and complete the paper. This was to teach me method in the arrangement of thoughts. By comparing my work afterward with the original I discovered many faults and amended them; but I sometimes had the pleasure of fancying that; in certain particulars of small import, I had been lucky enough to improve the method or the language, and this encouraged me to think I might possibly in time come to be a tolerable English writer, of which I was extremely ambitious." His method—on the whole one of the best of disciplines, better, I think, than the system of themes now employed in our colleges—could scarcely have been anything for Franklin save a precocious discovery, altho it had, of course, been used long before his day. Cicero tells how the orator Crassus had begun to form himself on a plan not essentially different, but turned from this to the more approved exercise of converting the Greek writers into equivalent Latin. *Vertere Graeca in Latinum verteres nostri oratores optimum judicabant*, said Quintilian; and Franklin's language would have gained in richness if he, too, had proceeded a step further and undergone the discipline of comparing his English with the classics.

As it is, he made himself one of the masters of that special style of the eighteenth century which concealed a good deal of art under apparent, even obtrusive, negligences. He professed to model himself on Addison, but his real affinity is more with Swift; or, rather, he lies between the two, with something harsher than the suave impertinence of Addison, yet without the terrible savagery of the Dean. In particular he affected Swift's two weapons of irony and the hoax, and, if he did not quite make literature with them, he at least made history, which his predecessor could not do. Sometimes he was content to borrow an invention bodily—"convey the wise it call"—as when he badgered a rival almanac maker by foretelling the date of his death and then calmly proving the truth of the prophecy out of the poor fellow's angry protestations. And entirely in the vein of Swift, if not so palpably stolen, are a number of his political pamphlets, notably, in the way of irony, the "Rules for Reducing a Great Empire to a Small One." As for his hoaxes they were innumerable and astonishingly effective.

* * *

So it is that speech and action blend together inextricably to form this fascinating literary figure. He moves thru the whole length of the eighteenth century, serene and self-possessed, a philosopher and statesman yet a fellow of infinite jest, a shrewd economist yet capable of the tenderest generosities. There was a large admixture of earth in the image, no doubt. His wit was often coarse, if not obscene, and, as his latest editor observes, leaves a long "smudgy trail" behind it. Not a little that he wrote and that still exists in manuscript is too rank to be printed. One might wish all this away; and yet I do not know; somehow the thought of that big animal body completes our impression of the overflowing bountifulness of his nature. If wishing were effective I would choose rather that he had not made of his Autobiography so singular a document in petty prudence and economy. Nothing in that record is more typical than the remark on his habit of bringing home the paper he purchased thru the streets on a wheelbarrow—"to show," he adds, "that I was not above my business." And for economy, one remembers his visit to the old lady in London who lived as a religious recluse, and his comment: "She looked pale, but was never sick; and I give it as another instance on how small an income life and health may be supported." Possibly the character of his memoirs would have changed if he had continued them into his later years; but I am inclined rather to think that the discrepancy between the breadth of his interests and the narrowness of his professed ideals would have become still more evident by such an extension. The truth is they only exaggerate a real deficiency in his character; there was, after all, a stretch of humanity beyond Franklin's victorious good sense.

B.O. FLOWER "THE LIFE AND WRITINGS OF BENJAMIN FRANKLIN: A BOOK STUDY" (1908)

Perhaps the most important literary labor connected with the work of American men of letters which has been undertaken and admirably performed in recent years, is *The Writings of Benjamin Franklin*, edited by Albert Henry Smyth. We can conceive of few things in the way of books more important to our people, and especially to our young men, than the presentation in an engaging manner of the lives and thought of such great statesmen and way-showers of democracy as Franklin, Jefferson and Washington. These men, who were preeminently master builders of the American state and who in a very substantial manner gave direction and color to the democratic era that was inaugurated by our Revolution, have a message of special value for the sons of democracy to-day, when multitudinous reactionary class-interests and anti-republican forces are subtly at work poisoning the fountains of free government and debauching the ideals of the people. The influences against which Franklin, Jefferson, Washington and their great co-workers so ably contended, throwing with superb self-forgetfulness their lives and fortunes into the hazard for the principles of democracy, are as active and in some respects more insidiously dangerous to-day than in the elder period, because they are chiefly within the State, whereas in the Revolutionary days they were principally far beyond our borders.

The writings and labors of Franklin and Jefferson are especially valuable in that they show so clearly the root principles that must differentiate popular government from class-rule.

Franklin moved slowly and cautiously. He was naturally a man of peace and compromise, but he would not counsel peace when it meant servitude or the sacrifice of fundamental and vital principles; and so all the bribes and seductive inducements indirectly offered him by the wealth and might of England failed signally of their purpose.

* * *

The life and thought of this simple, unostentatious and truly great man, and his lofty patriotism and fidelity to the trust imposed upon him, should be an inspiration to our young men and women of today. The nation he served so whole-heartedly and nobly now calls as perhaps at no other period for consecrated service to the fundamental principles of a democratic republic,—to the ideal of justice, freedom and fraternity. Forces inimical to a democratic republic are actively at work to-day corrupting public servants and the political ideals of the nation and seeking by special privilege and monopoly rights to undermine and destroy a government of the people, by the people and for the people. It is of paramount importance that the young men and women of America shall yield their splendid power and devotion to the same moral idealism that guided Franklin, Jefferson and Washington, and beat back these sinister forces of materialism and reaction. In the presence of the life of Franklin let each lover of free government resolve to consecrate life's best efforts to the cause of genuine democracy, remembering Victor Hugo's injunction:

"Let us consecrate ourselves. Let us devote ourselves to the good, to the true, to the just. . . . Great is he who consecrates himself! Even when overcome, he remains serene, and his misfortune is happiness."

Chronology

⁓⋙⁓ ⁓⋙⁓ ⁓⋙⁓

1706 Benjamin Franklin is born in Boston, January 17, the youngest son of Josiah Franklin, a tallow chandler, and Abiah Folger Franklin.

1714–20 Attends Boston Grammar School first and then George Brownell's English school. Works with his father making candles and soap. Apprenticed to his brother James in the printing business.

1722–23 "Silence Dogood" essays published in James Franklin's paper, *New-England Courant*. Twice takes charge of the paper when James is imprisoned. Leaves Boston September 25, 1723, breaking his indenture. Reaches Philadelphia October 6 and finds work with Samuel Keimer, a local printer.

1724 Sails for London November 5. Obtains works at Samuel Palmer's printing office.

1725 Writes *A Dissertation on Liberty and Necessity, Pleasure and Pain*. Meets several members of London's scientific community. Leaves Palmer's to work for John Watts, another printer.

1726–28 Sails for Philadelphia July 21 with Quaker merchant Thomas Denham, for whom he works upon returning to Philadelphia. After Denham's death, returns to Keimer's shop. Forms Junto with several intelligent and ambitious Philadelphia friends. In 1728, quits Keimer and forms printing partnership with Hugh Meredith.

1729 Begins 'Busy-Body' essays series in February. Writes *A Modest Enquiry into the Nature and Necessity of a Paper Currency*. Buys *Pennsylvania Gazette* from Keimer and transforms it into the finest newspaper in colonial America. His son William is born out of wedlock to an unknown mother.

1730   Forms common-law union with Deborah Read, September 1. William taken into household.

1731   Forms the Library Company of Philadelphia. Forms a business partnership with Thomas Whitemarsh to establish a printshop in South Carolina, the first of several such financial partnerships he would establish.

1732–37   First publishes *Poor Richard's Almanack* in 1732. Proposes many public improvement projects in Philadelphia. Is appointed clerk of Pennsylvania Assembly, October 15, 1736. Begins serving as postmaster of Philadelphia, October 5, 1737.

1743–44   Publishes *A Proposal for Promoting Useful Knowledge* (1743). Daughter Sarah is born August 31, 1743. Publishes *An Account of the New Invented Pennsylvania Fire-Places*.

1745–47   Begins electrical experiments. In 1747 sends first account of electrical experiments to Peter Collinson, who presents it to Royal Society of London.

1748   Retires as printer to devote himself to scientific and civic affairs.

1749   Writes *Proposals Relating to the Education of Youth in Pensilvania*, which establishes the Philadelphia Academy (University of Pennsylvania).

1751   Founds Pennsylvania Hospital. Publishes *Experiments and Observations on Electricity*.

1752   Conducts kite experiment, proving that lightning is electrical in nature. Designs lightning rods to protect homes.

1753   Publishes *Supplemental Experiments and Observations*, his second set of electrical experiments. In September-October negotiates treaty with Ohio Indians at Carlisle, Pennsylvania.

1754   Attends Albany Congress, during which representatives from seven colonies arrange to defend the frontier against French. Publishes his third set of experiments, *New Experiments and Observations on Electricity* in September.

1755–56   Writes biblical hoaxes, "A Parable against Persecution" and "A Parable on Brotherly Love." Travels to frontier to build forts and organize defenses. In 1756, is elected to the Royal Society of London.

1757   Nominated by Pennsylvania Assembly to serve as agent to England. Travels with his son to England. Writes "Father

Abraham's Speech" (*The Way to Wealth*). Reaches London July 26.

1758 Receives honorary doctorate from the University of St. Andrews in Scotland and becomes known as Dr. Franklin. Tours England and Scotland.

1760–62 Publishes *The Interest of Great Britain Considered* (1760). Travels through the Netherlands in 1761. Receives honorary degree of Civil Law from Oxford, April 30, 1762. Returns to Philadelphia November 1, 1762.

1764 Publishes *A Narrative of the Late Massacres*. Is elected Speaker of Pennsylvania Assembly. Leaves Philadelphia November 7 to represent the Pennsylvania Assembly as its agent. Reaches London December 10.

1765–66 Works toward the repeal of the Stamp Act, speaking before the House of Commons on February 13, 1766. His eloquent defense prompts the act's repeal and establishes Franklin as the leading spokesman of the American colonies.

1768–69 Publishes *Causes of the American Discontents before 1768*. Supervises publication of expanded edition of *Experiments and Observations on Electricity* (1769). Is elected president of American Philosophical Society, a position he holds until his death.

1771 Writes the first part of his autobiography. Tours Ireland and Scotland.

1773 Publishes "Rules by Which a Great Empire May Be Reduced to a Small One" and "Edict by the King of Prussia."

1774 Denounced by Solicitor General Alexander Wedderburn before the Privy Council. Attempts negotiations to settle differences between Great Britain and America.

1775 Leaves London, reaching Philadelphia May 5. Is chosen delegate to the Continental Congress by the Pennsylvania assembly. Drafts Articles of Confederation in July.

1776 Appointed by Congress to the Committee of Five to draft the Declaration of Independence. Congress elects him commissioner to France. Leaves Philadelphia in October, taking two grandsons with him, William Temple Franklin and Benjamin Franklin Bache.

1778 Embraces Voltaire at a meeting of the French Academy of Sciences.

1779   Benjamin Vaughan publishes Franklin's *Political, Miscellaneous, and Philosophical Pieces.*

1783–84   Signs definitive treaty of peace between Great Britain and the United States in September 1783. Writes second part of autobiography in 1784.

1785   Leaves France for the last time, reaching Philadelphia September 14. Is elected to the presidency of the Supreme Executive Council of Pennsylvania in October.

1786   Builds addition to his Philadelphia home to house his large personal library.

1787–90   Is named president of the Pennsylvania Society for Promoting the Abolition of Slavery and devotes much effort to abolition. Dies April 17, 1790.

Index